The Ultimate Cheat Sheet for College Math
By
WeSolveThem Team

Book notations

Note: Some symbols may have different meanings in different courses i.e. never assume.

And $\wedge$
Or $\vee$
In $\in$
Manipulation or row reduction occurred $\sim$
Implies $\Rightarrow$
Becomes $\Leftarrow$
If and only if $\Leftrightarrow$
Therefore $\therefore$
Because $\because$
Equivalent/defined as $\equiv$
Euler's number e

$$e = \sum_{n=0}^{\infty} \frac{1}{n!} = \lim_{n \to \infty} \left(1 + \frac{1}{n}\right)^n$$

Any other vector (scalar not bold/hat/vec) $\vec{v} \equiv \mathbf{v}$

Table of Contents

ALGEBRA

General Symbols and Notations

Symbol	Meaning	Example
$=$	Equal	$0 = 0$
$\neq$	Not equal	$1 \neq 0$
$\pm$	Plus or Minus	$x = \pm a \Rightarrow x = a \ \ or \ \ x = -a$
$\mp$	Minus or Plus	$x = \mp a \Rightarrow x = -a \ \ or \ \ x = a$
$iff, \Leftrightarrow$	If and only if	$p \Rightarrow q$ and $q \Rightarrow p$ then $p \Leftrightarrow q$
$\Rightarrow$	Implies	$p \Rightarrow q$
$<$	Less than	$x - a < 0 \Rightarrow x < a$
$\leq$	Less than equal	$x - a \leq 0 \Rightarrow x \leq a$
$\geq$	Greater than equal	$x - a \geq 0 \Rightarrow x \geq a$
$>$	Greater than	$x - a > 0 \Rightarrow x > a$
$\times$	Times	$2 \times 3 = 6$
$*$ or $\cdot$	Multiplication	$2 * 3 = 6$ or $2 \cdot 3 = 6$
$(\ldots)(\ldots)$	Multiplication	$(2)(3) = 6$
$[\ldots](\ldots)$	Multiplication	$[2](3) = 6$
$[\ldots][\ldots]$	Multiplication	$[2][3] = 6$
$[(\ldots)(\ldots)]^{(\ldots)}(\ldots)$	Exponential Multiplication	$[(2)(3)]^{3-2}(3 - 2) = (6)^1(1)$ $= 6$
∞	Infinity	Never ends
Δ	Displacement or change of	$\Delta x = x - x_0$
Σ	Summation	$\displaystyle\sum_{n=1}^{3} a_n x^n = a_1 x^1 + a_2 x^2 + a_3 x^3$
θ	Theta – reserved for angles	$\theta = \dfrac{\pi}{4} = 45°$
$f(x)$	Function of x	$f(x) = x^n + \cdots$
$f(x, y)$	Function of x and y	$f(x, y) = (xy)^n + \cdots$
$\in$	In or element of	$x \in [a, b)$ means $a \leq x < b$
$\forall$	For all	$\forall_x \ (for \ all \ x)$
$\therefore$	Therefore	$x - a = 0 \Leftrightarrow x = a \therefore x = a$
$\because$	Because	$\because x - a = 0, \quad x = a$
$\equiv$	Equivalent	$(-2, 3) \equiv -2 < x < 3$
$(,)$	Open interval	$(-2, 3) \equiv -2 < x < 3$
$[,]$	Closed interval	$[2, 3] \equiv 2 \leq x \leq 3$
$\subset$	Proper Subset	$A \subset B \Rightarrow B \not\subset A$
$\subseteq$	Subset (equal)	$A \subseteq B \Rightarrow A = B$
$[,)$	Half open/closed	$[1, 4) \equiv 1 \leq x < 4$
$\{\ldots, \ldots\}$	Set of numbers	$\{1, 3, 5, 7\}$
$\cup$	Union	$D = (-\infty, 0) \cup (0, \infty)$ $\{1,2,3\} \cup \{3,4,5\} = \{1, 2, 3, 4, 5\}$
$\cap$	Intersection	$\{1,2,3\} \cap \{3,4,5\} = \{3\}$
$\mathbb{R}$	Real numbers	$D = (-\infty, \infty)$
$P(x_0, y_0)$	Point	$(1, f(1))$

Types of numbers

Integers	Rational	Irrational	Complex
$\{\dots, -3, -2, -1, 0, 1, 2, 3, \dots\}$	$\frac{a}{b}, b \neq 0$ and a, b are integers	A number that cannot be expressed as a fraction e.g. π	$x = a + bi$ where a and b are any number

Properties

Reflexive	Symmetric	Transitive	Substitution
$a = a$	$a = b$ then $b = a$	$a = b$ and $b = c$ then $a = c$	$a = b$ then **b** can replace a

Meanings

Both A and B have the same elements $\qquad A = B$

Subset: If every element of a set A is in B $\qquad A \subseteq B \Rightarrow A \subseteq B \wedge B \subseteq A \Leftrightarrow A = B$

Proper Subset: If every element in A is also in B but $A \neq B$: $\qquad A \subset B$

Intersection: The elements that are both in A and in B $\qquad A \cap B = \{x | x \in A \wedge x \in B\}$

Union: All elements from A and B are in A union B $\qquad A \cup B = \{x | x \in A \vee x \in B \vee x \in A \cap B\}$

Compliment: If $A \subset U$, and U is the universal set $\qquad \bar{A} = A^c = \{x | x \in U \wedge x \notin A\}$

Complementation of sets

a. $U^c = \emptyset$ b. $\emptyset^c = U$ c. $(A^c)^c = A$ d. $A \cup A^c = U$ e. $A \cap A^c = \emptyset$

Set Laws

$A \cup B = B \cup A$	Commutative law for union
$A \cap B = B \cap A$	Commutative law for intersection
$A \cup (B \cup C) = (A \cup B) \cup C$	Associative law for union
$A \cap (B \cap C) = (A \cap B) \cap C$	Associative law for intersection
$A \cup (B \cap C) = (A \cup B) \cap (A \cup C)$	Distributive law for union
$A \cap (B \cup C) = (A \cap B) \cup (A \cap C)$	Distributive law for intersection

De Morgan's Laws

i. $(A \cup B)^c = A^c \cap B^c$ ii. $(A \cap B)^c = A^c \cup B^c$

Number of Elements in a Set

Note: $A \wedge B$ are finite sets

$n(A \cup B) = n(A) + n(B) - n(A \cap B)$

$n(A \cap B) = n(A) + n(B) - n(A \cup B)$

$n(A \cup B \cup C) = n(A) + n(B) + n(C) - n(A \cap B) - n(A \cap C) - n(B \cap C) + n(A \cap B \cap C)$

Axioms

Substitution Principle	If $a = b$, then a can be substituted for b
Commutative – Addition	$a + b = b + a$
Commutative – Multiplication	$ab = ba$
Associativity – Addition	$a + (b + c) = (a + b) + c$
Associativity – Multiplication	$a(bc) = (ab)c$
Reflexive	$a = a$
Symmetric	If $a = b$ then $b = a$
Transitive	If $a = b$ and $b = c$ then $a = c$
Distribution Property	$a(b + c) = ab + ac$ and $(a + b)c = ac + bc$
Cancellation Property	$-(-a) = a$
Identity – Addition	$a + 0 = a$ and $0 + a = a$
Additive Inverse	$a + (-a) = 0$ and $-a + a = 0$
Identity – Multiplication	$a(1) = a$ and $(1)a = a$
Multiplicative Property – Zero	$a(0) = 0$ and $(0)a = 0$
Multiplicative Property for -1	$a(-1) = -a$ and $(-1)a = -a$
Multiplicative Inverse	$a(a^{-1}) = 1$ and $(a^{-1})a = 1$

Arithmetic

$$ab \pm ac = a(b \pm c) = (b \pm c)a$$

$$\frac{\left(\frac{a}{b}\right)}{c} = \frac{a}{bc}$$

$$\frac{a}{b} \pm \frac{c}{d} = \frac{ad \pm bc}{bd}$$

$$\frac{a-b}{c-d} = \frac{b-a}{d-c}$$

$$\frac{ab+ac}{a} = b+c, a \neq 0$$

$$a\left(\frac{b}{c}\right) = \frac{ab}{c}$$

$$\frac{a}{\left(\frac{b}{c}\right)} = \left(\frac{a}{1}\right) \cdot \left(\frac{c}{b}\right) = \frac{ac}{b}$$

$$\frac{a \pm b}{c} = \frac{a}{c} \pm \frac{b}{c}$$

$$\frac{\left(\frac{a}{b}\right)}{\left(\frac{c}{d}\right)} = \frac{a}{b} \cdot \frac{d}{c} = \frac{ad}{bc}$$

$$if \ a \pm b = 0 \ then \ a = \mp b$$

Exponents

$$a^1 = a$$

$$a^0 = 1$$

$$a^{-n} = \frac{1}{a^n}$$

$$\frac{1}{a^{-n}} = a^n$$

$$a^n a^m = a^{n+m}$$

$$\frac{a^n}{a^m} = a^{n-m}$$

$$\left(\frac{a}{b}\right)^n = \frac{a^n}{b^n}$$

$$\left(\frac{a}{b}\right)^{-n} = \frac{a^{-n}}{b^{-n}} = \frac{b^n}{a^n}$$

$$(a^n)^{\frac{1}{m}} = a^{\frac{n}{m}} = \left(a^{\frac{1}{m}}\right)^n$$

$$(a^n)^m = a^{nm} = a^{mn} = (a^m)^n$$

Radicals

$$\sqrt{a} = \sqrt[2]{a} = \sqrt[2]{a^1} = a^{\frac{1}{2}}$$

$$\sqrt[m]{\sqrt[n]{a}} = \sqrt[mn]{a} = a^{\frac{1}{mn}}$$

$$\sqrt[n]{a^n} = a, n \ is \ odd$$

$$\sqrt[n]{\frac{a}{b}} = \frac{\sqrt[n]{a}}{\sqrt[n]{b}} = \frac{a^{\frac{1}{n}}}{b^{\frac{1}{n}}} = \left(\frac{a}{b}\right)^{\frac{1}{n}}$$

$$\sqrt[n]{a^m} = a^{\frac{m}{n}}$$

$$\sqrt[n]{a^n} = |a|, n \ is \ even$$

$$\sqrt{x^2} = |x|, \quad -\infty < x < \infty$$

$$\left(\sqrt{x}\right)^2 = x, \quad x \geq 0$$

Complex Numbers

$$x = a \pm ib$$ **Conjugate** $$\bar{x} = a \mp bi$$

$$(a+bi)(c+di) = (ac-bd) + (ad+bc)i$$

$$i = \sqrt{-1}$$

$$i^2 = -1$$

$$\sqrt{-a} = i\sqrt{a}, \ a \geq 0$$

$$x\bar{x} = a^2 + b^2$$

Adding and Subtracting Fractions

$$\frac{a}{b} \pm \frac{c}{d} = \frac{ad \pm bc}{bd} \qquad\qquad \frac{g(x)}{f(x)} \pm \frac{h(x)}{r(x)} = \frac{[g(x)r(x)] \pm [f(x)h(x)]}{f(x)r(x)}$$

Logarithmic

Log "Base" Notation

Note: $\log x = \log_{10} x$ or it may be $\log x = \ln x = \log_e x$; $\log x$ is the general notation for $\ln x$ but in some books or calculators $\log x = \log_{10} x$ and vice-versa.

$$\frac{\ln(b)}{\ln(a)} = \log_a b \qquad\qquad y = \log_b x \;\Rightarrow\; x = b^y \qquad\qquad e = 2.718281828\ldots$$

$$\log_a a = 1 \qquad\qquad \log_a 1 = 0 \qquad\qquad \log_a a^x = x$$

$$\log_e x = \ln x \qquad\qquad \log_a x^b = b \log_a x \qquad\qquad \log_a xy = \log_a x + \log_a y$$

$$\log_a \frac{x}{y} = \log_a x - \log_a y \qquad e = \sum_{n=0}^{\infty} \frac{1}{n!} \qquad\qquad e^{at} = \sum_{n=0}^{\infty} \frac{a^n t^n}{n!}$$

Log "Natural" Notation

*It is unlikely that the notation involving "log" will be used throughout the course; you may see it in the beginning of the course, as a review of some sort but that should be about all you'll see. The "$\ln u$" notation will be the standard as it is easier to manipulate.

$$\log_a b = \frac{\ln(b)}{\ln(a)} \qquad\qquad y = \ln x \;\Rightarrow\; x = e^y \qquad\qquad y = e^x \;\Rightarrow\; x = \ln y$$

$$e = \sum_{n=0}^{\infty} \frac{1}{n!} \qquad\qquad \ln a = \text{undefined}, a \le 0 \qquad\qquad \ln 1 = 0$$

$$\ln e^x = x \;\Rightarrow\; e^{\ln x} = x \qquad \ln e^1 = 1 \;\Rightarrow\; e^{\ln(1)} = 1 \qquad \ln x^b = b \ln x$$

$$\ln xy = \ln x + \ln y \qquad\qquad \ln \frac{x}{y} = \ln x - \ln y \qquad\qquad \ln(x^{-1}) = \ln\left(\frac{1}{x}\right) = -\ln(x)$$

Domains: $\qquad\qquad\qquad \ln x, \quad D = (0, \infty) \qquad\qquad \ln|x|, D = \{x | x > 0, x < 0\}$

*Factoring

$$x^n + x^m = x^n(1 + x^{m-n}) = x^m(x^{n-m} + 1) \qquad x^2 - a^2 = (x + a)(x - a)$$

$$x^2 + 2ax + a^2 = (x + a)^2 \qquad\qquad x^2 + (a + b)x + ab = (x + a)(x + b)$$

$$x^3 + 3ax^2 + 3a^2x + a^3 = (x + a)^3 \qquad x^3 - 3ax^2 + 3a^2x - a^3 = (x - a)^3$$

$$x^3 + a^3 = (x + a)(x^2 - ax + a^2) \qquad x^3 - a^3 = (x - a)(a^2 + ax + x^2)$$

$$(x + a)^3 = x^3 + 3ax^2 + 3a^2x + a^3 \qquad (x - a)^3 = x^3 - 3ax^2 + 3a^2x - a^3$$

Note:

*Common mistake students make when solving for x:

The solution of $x = 0$ was lost, thus:

$$x^2 - x = 0 \quad\Rightarrow\quad x^2 = x \quad\Rightarrow\quad x = 1$$

$$x^2 - x = 0$$

$$\Rightarrow\quad x(x - 1) = 0 \quad\Leftrightarrow\quad x = 0 \ \text{ or } \ x = 1$$

Long Division

(quotient)(divisor)+(remainder)=dividend

$\dfrac{R}{P)\overline{Q}}$	P=Divisor	Q=Dividend	R=Quotient

Complete The Square

$$y = ax^2 + bx + c$$

$$= a\left(x^2 + \frac{b}{a}x\right) + c = a\left(x^2 + \frac{b}{a}x + \left(\frac{b}{2a}\right)^2 - \left(\frac{b}{2a}\right)^2\right) + c$$

$$= a\left(x^2 + \frac{b}{a}x + \left(\frac{b}{2a}\right)^2\right) - a\left(\frac{b}{2a}\right)^2 + c = a\left(x + \frac{b}{2a}\right)^2 - a\left(\frac{b^2}{4a^2}\right) + c$$

$$= a\left(x + \frac{b}{2a}\right)^2 - \frac{b^2}{4a} + c$$

$$\therefore \quad y = a\left(x + \frac{b}{2a}\right)^2 + c - \frac{b^2}{4a}$$

Example 1: Solving for x (Formula 1)

$$ax^2 + bx = 0$$

$$\Rightarrow \quad x^2 + \frac{b}{a}x = \frac{0}{a} \quad \Rightarrow \quad x^2 + \frac{b}{a}x + 0 = 0$$

$$\Rightarrow \quad x^2 + \frac{b}{a}x + \left[\left(\frac{b}{2a}\right)^2 - \left(\frac{b}{2a}\right)^2\right] = 0 \quad \Rightarrow \quad \left[x^2 + \frac{b}{a}x + \left(\frac{b}{2a}\right)^2\right] = \left(\frac{b}{2a}\right)^2$$

$$\Rightarrow \quad \left(x + \frac{b}{2a}\right)^2 = \frac{b^2}{4a^2} \quad \Rightarrow \quad x + \frac{b}{2a} = \pm\sqrt{\frac{b^2}{4a^2}} \quad \Rightarrow \quad x = -\frac{b}{2a} \pm \frac{b}{2a}$$

$$\therefore \quad x = 0 \quad \text{or} \quad x = -\frac{b}{a}$$

Example 2: Solving for x (Formula 2)

$$ax^2 + bx + c = 0$$

$$\Rightarrow \quad x^2 + \frac{b}{a}x + \frac{c}{a} = \frac{0}{a} \quad \Rightarrow \quad x^2 + \frac{b}{a}x + \frac{c}{a} + \left(\frac{b}{2a}\right)^2 - \left(\frac{b}{2a}\right)^2 = 0$$

$$\Rightarrow \quad \left[x^2 + \frac{b}{a}x + \left(\frac{b}{2a}\right)^2\right] = \frac{b^2}{2^2 a^2} - \frac{c}{a} \quad \Rightarrow \quad \left(x + \frac{b}{2a}\right)^2 = \frac{b^2 - 4ac}{4a^2}$$

$$\Rightarrow \quad x + \frac{b}{2a} = \pm\frac{\sqrt{b^2 - 4ac}}{2a} \quad \Rightarrow \quad x = -\frac{b}{2a} \pm \frac{\sqrt{b^2 - 4ac}}{2a}$$

$$\therefore \quad x = \frac{-b \pm \sqrt{b^2 - 4ac}}{2a}$$

Compositions

$$[f \circ g](x) = f(g(x)) \qquad\qquad [f \pm g](x) = f(x) \pm g(x)$$

$$[f \cdot g](x) = f(x)g(x) \qquad\qquad \left[\frac{f}{g}\right](x) = \frac{f(x)}{g(x)}, \qquad g(x) \neq 0$$

Functions

Vertical Line Test

$f(x)$ is a function if it passes the vertical line test i.e. if you draw a vertical line anywhere on the graph, and the graph of f only crosses it once.

Even/Odd Function

Even: $f(-x) = f(x)$ **Odd:** $f(-x) = -f(x)$
      (symmetric with respect to y-axis)   (symmetric with respect to origin)

Average Rate of Change

$$\frac{\Delta y}{\Delta x} = \frac{f(x) - f(x_0)}{x - x_0}, \qquad x \neq x_0$$

Secant Line

The slope of the secant line is the same as the average rate of change i.e. $m = \frac{f(x) - f(x_0)}{x - x_0}$ you then take one of the two points and plug the it into $y - y_0 = \frac{f(x) - f(x_0)}{x - x_0}(x - x_0)$ and simplify.

Difference Quotient

$$m = \frac{f(x + \Delta x) - f(x)}{\Delta x} = \frac{f(x + h) - f(x)}{h}$$

Distance Formula

Distance between two points on a number line

$P(x_0) = P(x_1) = P(a), \qquad Q = Q(x) = Q(x_2) = Q(b)$

$d(P, Q) = \sqrt{(x - x_0)^2} = |x - x_0|$

$\qquad = \sqrt{(b - a)^2} = |b - a|$

$\qquad = \sqrt{(x_2 - x_1)^2} = |x_2 - x_1|$

Distance between two points in a Cartesian coordinate system i.e. x vs. y graph

$P(x_0, y_0), \qquad Q\ (x, y)$

$d(P, Q) = \sqrt{(x - x_0)^2 + (y - y_0)^2}$

Midpoint Formula

$P(x_1, y_1)$ & $Q(x_2, y_2)$

$$m(P,Q) = \left(\frac{x_2 + x_1}{2}, \frac{y_2 + y_1}{2} \right)$$

Quadratic Formula

$$ax^2 + bx + c = 0 \quad \Leftrightarrow \quad x = \frac{-b \pm \sqrt{b^2 - 4ac}}{2a}$$

Proof:

$$ax^2 + bx + c = 0$$

$$\Rightarrow \quad x^2 + \frac{b}{a}x + \frac{c}{a} = \frac{0}{a} \quad \Rightarrow \quad x^2 + \frac{b}{a}x + \frac{c}{a} + \left(\frac{b}{2a}\right)^2 - \left(\frac{b}{2a}\right)^2 = 0$$

$$\Rightarrow \quad \left[x^2 + \frac{b}{a}x + \left(\frac{b}{2a}\right)^2 \right] = \frac{b^2}{2^2 a^2} - \frac{c}{a} \quad \Rightarrow \quad \left(x + \frac{b}{2a} \right)^2 = \frac{b^2 - 4ac}{4a^2}$$

$$\Rightarrow \quad x + \frac{b}{2a} = \pm \frac{\sqrt{b^2 - 4ac}}{2a} \quad \Rightarrow \quad x = -\frac{b}{2a} \pm \frac{\sqrt{b^2 - 4ac}}{2a}$$

$$\therefore \quad x = \frac{-b \pm \sqrt{b^2 - 4ac}}{2a}$$

Discriminant:

      i) Two real solutions if $b^2 - 4ac > 0$

      ii) Repeated solutions if $b^2 - 4ac = 0$

      iii) Two complex solutions $if\, b^2 - 4ac < 0$

Graphing a Line

From the form $y = mx + b$ you can easily graph a line by identifying two points and then connecting them.

The equation will more generally appear as $y = \frac{c}{\pm d}x + b$ where $m = \frac{c}{\pm d}$, c is the rise and $\pm d$ is the run (c always goes up and d goes either left or right.)

The first point is $P_1(0, b)$

The second point is $P_2(\pm d, b + c)$

Plot these two points and connect a line through them.

Point Slope Form:

$$y - y_0 = m(x - x_0)$$

$$m = slope = \frac{\Delta y}{\Delta x}$$

$$\Rightarrow \quad m = \frac{\Delta y}{\Delta x} = \frac{y - y_0}{x - x_0}$$

$$\Rightarrow \quad m = \frac{y - y_0}{x - x_0}$$

$$\Rightarrow \quad (x - x_0)m = (y - y_0)$$

$$\therefore \quad y - y_0 = m(x - x_0)$$

Slope Intercept Form:

$$y = mx + b$$

$$m = slope = \frac{\Delta y}{\Delta x} \quad \Rightarrow \quad m = \frac{\Delta y}{\Delta x} = \frac{y - y_0}{x - x_0}$$

$$\Rightarrow \quad m = \frac{y - y_0}{x - x_0}$$

$$\Rightarrow \quad (x - x_0)m = (y - y_0)$$

$$\Rightarrow \quad mx - mx_0 = y - y_0$$

$$\Rightarrow \quad y = mx - mx_0 + y_0$$

$$\Rightarrow \quad y = mx + y_0 - mx_0$$

$$\Rightarrow \quad y = mx + (y_0 - mx_0), \quad \text{setting } b = (y_0 - mx_0)$$

$$\therefore \quad y = mx + b$$

Standard or General Form

$$Ax + By = C$$

Parallel Line (equal slopes)

$$y_1 = mx + b_1 \parallel y_2 = mx + b_2$$

Perpendicular Line (product of slopes are -1)

$$y_1 = mx + b_1 \perp y_2 = -\frac{1}{m}x + b_2$$

*Domain Restrictions

For the following, $f(x), g(x), h(x)$ are assumed to be continuous for all real numbers.

Polynomial	$(x) = a_0 x^n \pm a_1 x^{n-1} \pm a_2 x^{n-2} \pm \cdots \pm a_n x^{n-n}$	No Restrictions
Fraction	$h(x) = \dfrac{f(x)}{g(x)}$	$g(x) \neq 0$
Radical, if n is even	$f(x) = \sqrt[n]{g(x)}$	$g(x) \geq 0$
Radical, if n is odd	$f(x) = \sqrt[n]{g(x)}$	No Restrictions
Fraction with Radical in denominator	$h(x) = \dfrac{f(x)}{\sqrt[n]{g(x)}}$	If n is even $g(x) > 0$ if n is odd $g(x) \neq 0$
Natural Log	$f(x) = \ln[g(x)]$	$g(x) > 0$
Exponential	$h(x) = f(x)^{g(x)}$	No Restrictions

Inverse Functions

$$y = f(x) \quad \Rightarrow \quad x = f(y^{-1}) = f\big(f^{-1}(x)\big)$$

If $f(x)$ is one-to-one it has an inverse

The domain of $f(x)$ is the range of $f^{-1}(x)$

The range of $f(x)$ is the domain of $f^{-1}(x)$

$$y = f(x) \quad \Rightarrow \quad x = f(y) \quad \Rightarrow \quad y = f^{-1}(x)$$

Asymptotes, Holes and Graphs

An asymptote occurs where the function is getting infinitely close to a line on the graph but never touches the line. *Horizontal asymptotes may cross the line from time-to-time; it is the end behavior we are concerned with.*

There are three types of asymptotes: Horizontal, Vertical and Oblique.

Oblique asymptotes, will most likely, not be used in your calculus course but vertical and horizontal will be used frequently in order to graph functions.

Hole in a Graph	$f(x) = \dfrac{x^2 - 4}{x - 2} \quad \Rightarrow \quad x \neq 2$	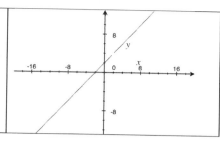

Three General Cases for Horizontal Asymptotes

Since there are so many conditions and situations for asymptotes and the methods learned in algebra are so minimal to what is used in calculus, we will come back to this later.

Case 1

$$f(x) = \frac{x^m + x^{m-1} + \cdots}{x^n + x^{n-1} + \cdots} \qquad n > m \quad \Rightarrow \quad HA: \quad y = 0$$

Case 2

$$f(x) = \frac{x^m + x^{m-1} + \cdots}{x^n + x^{n-1} + \cdots} \qquad n < m \quad \Rightarrow \quad HA: \quad none$$

Case 3

$$f(x) = \frac{ax^m + x^{m-1} + \cdots}{bx^n + x^{n-1} + \cdots} \qquad n = m \quad \Rightarrow \quad HA: \quad y = \frac{a}{b}$$

Ex. 1 Horizontal and Vertical

$$f(x) = \frac{x^2 + x + 1}{x^3 + x^2 + x + 1}$$

$$HA: \quad y = 0, \qquad VA: \quad x = -2$$

Ex. 2 Oblique

$$f(x) = \frac{x^3 + x^2 + x + 1}{x^2 + x + 1}$$

$$No\ HA, \qquad OA: \quad y = x$$

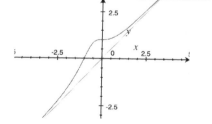

Ex. 3 Horizontal and Vertical

$$f(x) = \frac{3x^3 + x}{2x^3 + 1}$$

$$HA: \quad y = \frac{3}{2}, \qquad VA: \quad x = -\frac{1}{\sqrt[3]{2}}$$

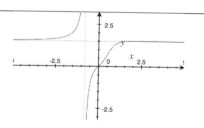

Inequalities

$\lvert f(x) \rvert < a \;\Rightarrow\; -a < f(x) < a$	or $\quad f(x) < a$ and $f(x) > -a$
$\lvert f(x) \rvert \le a \;\Rightarrow\; -a \le f(x) \le a$	or $\quad f(x) \le a$ and $f(x) \ge -a$

Interest Formulas

$$A = A_0 e^{rt}$$

$P = P_0 \left[\dfrac{\frac{r}{12}}{1 - \left(1 + \frac{r}{12}\right)^{-1}} \right]$	L=Loan $P =$ Monthly Payment $r =$ Interest rate for annual $t =$ Loan length in months

Physics Formulas

(rate)(time)=distance $rt = d$

Symmetry

By Point

x-axis	For every point (x, y) there is a $(x, -y)$
y-axis	For every point (x, y) there is a $(-x, y)$
origin	For every point (x, y) there is a $(-x, -y)$

Testing

x-axis: Replace each y with a $-y$, if the same equation results, it is symmetric.
y-axis: Replace each x with a $-x$, if the same equation results, it is symmetric.
Origin: Replace each x, y with a $-x, -y$, if the same equation results, it is symmetric.

Variations (Proportionality)

k is the constant of proportionality	y is proportional to x: y= kx	y is inversely proportional to x: $y = \dfrac{k}{x}$

Common Graphs and Formulas

$$y = x^2$$

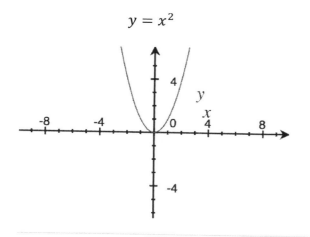

$$y = x^3$$

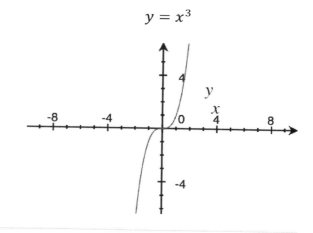

$$y = \sqrt{x}$$

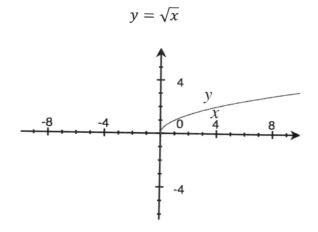

$$y = \frac{1}{x}$$

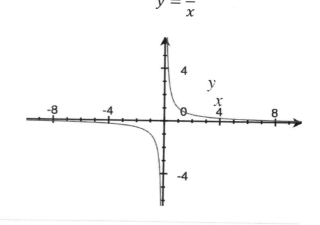

$$y = e^x$$

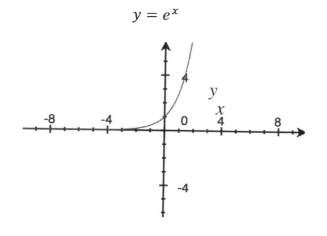

$$y = \ln x$$

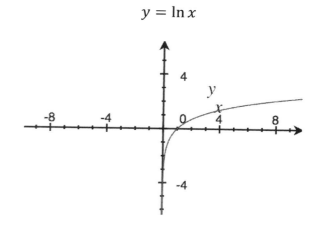

$$x^2 + y^2 = 1$$

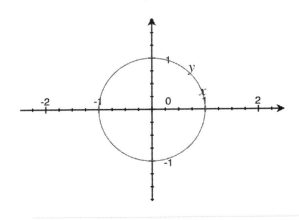

$$x^2 - y^2 = 1$$

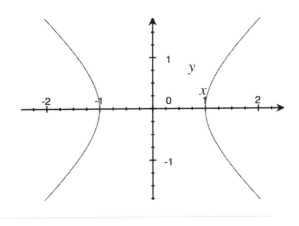

$$y^2 - x^2 = 1$$

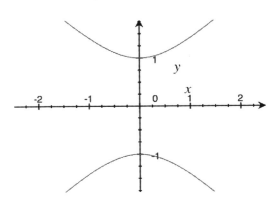

$$y = \sqrt{x^2 - 1}$$

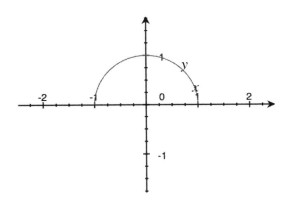

Equation of a Line

$$y = mx + b$$

$$slope = m = \frac{y_2 - y_1}{x_2 - x_1}$$

$$(y_2 - y_1) = m(x_2 - x_1)$$

$$Ax + By = C$$

Equation of Parabola

$$y = ax^2 + bx + c$$

Vertex: $(h, k) = \left(-\frac{b}{2a}, f\left(-\frac{b}{2a}\right)\right)$

$$y = a(x - h)^2 + k$$

Equation of Circle

$$x^2 + y^2 + ax + by + c = 0 \Rightarrow$$

Center: (h, k)
Radius: r

$$(x - h)^2 + (y - k)^2 = r^2$$

Equation of Ellipse

$$\frac{(x - h)^2}{a^2} + \frac{(y - k)^2}{b^2} = 1$$

Right Point: $(h + a, k)$

Left Point: $(h - a, k)$

Top Point: $(h, k + b)$

Bottom Point: $(h, k - b)$

Equation of Hyperbola (1)

$$\frac{(x - h)^2}{a^2} - \frac{(y - k)^2}{b^2} = 1$$

Center: (h, k)
Slope: $\pm\frac{b}{a}$
Asymptotes: $y = \pm\frac{b}{a}(x - h) + k$
Vertices: $(h + a, k), (h - a, k)$

Equation of Hyperbola (2)

$$\frac{(y - k)^2}{a^2} - \frac{(x - h)^2}{b^2} = 1$$

Center: (h, k)
Slope: $\pm\frac{b}{a}$
Asymptotes: $y = \pm\frac{b}{a}(x - h) + k$
Vertices: $(h, k + b), (h, k - b)$

Areas

Square: $A = L^2 = W^2$ Rectangle: $A = L \cdot W$ Circle: $A = \pi \cdot r^2$

Ellipse: $A = \pi \cdot ab$ Triangle: $A = \frac{1}{2}b \cdot h$ Trapezoid: $A = \frac{1}{2}(a + b) \cdot h$

Parallelogram: $b \cdot h$ Rhombus: $A = \frac{pq}{2}$, p and q are the diagonals

Surface Areas

Cube: $A_s = 6L^2 = 6W^2$ Box: $A_s = 2(LW + WH + HL)$ Sphere: $A_s = 4\pi r^2$

Cone: $A_s = \pi r(r + \sqrt{h^2 + r^2})$ Cylinder: $2\pi rh + 2\pi r^2$

Volumes

Cube: $V = L^3 = W^3$ Box: $V = L \cdot W \cdot H$ Sphere: $V = \frac{4}{3}\pi \cdot r^3$

Cone: $V = \frac{1}{3}\pi \cdot r^2 h$ Ellipsoid: $V = \frac{4}{3}\pi \cdot abc$, a, b, c are the radii

Business Functions

Cost Function $C(x)$ Revenue Function $R(x)$

Profit Function $P(x) = R(x) - C(x)$ Marginal Cost Function $C'(x)$

Marginal Revenue Function $R'(x)$ Marginal Profit Function $P'(x) = R'(x) = C'(x)$

Average Cost Function $\bar{C}(x) = \dfrac{C(x)}{x}$

Average Revenue Function $\bar{R}(x) = \frac{R(x)}{x}$ Average Profit Function $\bar{P}(x) = \frac{P(x)}{x} = \frac{R(x) - C(x)}{x}$

Average Rate of Change of f and Slope of Secant Line

$$\frac{\Delta y}{\Delta x} = \frac{f(b)-f(a)}{b-a} = m_{secant} \text{ from } P_1(a, f(a)) \text{ and } P_2(b, f(b))$$

Difference Quotient

$$m_{secant} = \frac{f(\Delta x + x_0) - f(x_0)}{\Delta x}, \Delta x = h \Rightarrow m_{secant} = \frac{f(a+h)-f(a)}{h}, h \neq 0$$

Functions

Constant Function	$y = c$
Identity Function	$y = x$
Square Function	$y = x^2$
Cube Function	$y = x^3$
Square Root Function	$y = \sqrt{x}$
Cube Root Function	$y = \sqrt[3]{x}$
Reciprocal Function	$y = \dfrac{1}{x}$
Absolute Value Function	$y = |x|$
Greatest Integer Function	$y = \text{int}(x)^*$
Piecewise Function	$f(x) = \begin{cases} g(x), & x \in D_1 \\ h(x), & x \in D_2 \end{cases}$
Power Function	$y = ax^n$
Ration Function	$f(x) = \dfrac{g(x)}{h(x)}, h(x) \neq 0$

Graph Shifts and Compressions

Vertically up for $f(x)$	$f(x) + k$
Vertically down for $f(x)$	$f(x) - k$
Horizontally left for $f(x)$	$f(x + h)$
Horizontally right for $f(x)$	$f(x - h)$
$af(x)$ multiply each y-coordinate by a Vertically Compressed: $0 < a < 1$ Vertically Stretched: $a > 1$	(x, ay)
$f(ax)$ Multiply each x-coordinate by $\frac{1}{a}$ Horizontal Compression: $a > 1$ Horizontal Stretch: $0 < a < 1$	$\left(\frac{1}{a}x, y\right)$
Reflection about x-axis	$-f(x)$
Reflection about y-axis	$f(-x)$

Systems of equations

$$\begin{array}{l} ax + by = e \\ cx + dy = f \end{array} \Rightarrow \begin{bmatrix} a & b \\ c & d \end{bmatrix}\begin{bmatrix} x \\ y \end{bmatrix} = \begin{bmatrix} e \\ f \end{bmatrix} \Rightarrow \left[\begin{array}{cc|c} a & b & e \\ c & d & f \end{array}\right]$$

$$\begin{array}{l} ax + by + cz = d \\ ex + fy + gy = h \\ ix + jy + kz = l \end{array} \Rightarrow \begin{bmatrix} a & b & c \\ e & f & g \\ i & j & k \end{bmatrix}\begin{bmatrix} x \\ y \\ z \end{bmatrix} = \begin{bmatrix} d \\ h \\ l \end{bmatrix} \Rightarrow \left[\begin{array}{ccc|c} a & b & c & d \\ e & f & g & h \\ i & j & k & l \end{array}\right]$$

$$\text{The Coefficient Matrix} = \begin{bmatrix} a & b & c \\ e & f & g \\ i & j & k \end{bmatrix}$$

Rank of matrix and pivots

$[1 \quad 1], \quad rank(A_1) = 1$

$\begin{bmatrix} 1 \\ 1 \end{bmatrix}, \quad rank(A_2) = 1$

$[1 \quad 1 \quad 1], \quad rank(A_3) = 1$

$\begin{bmatrix} 1 \\ 1 \\ 1 \end{bmatrix}, \quad rank(A_4) = 1$

$\begin{bmatrix} 1 & 0 \\ 0 & 1 \end{bmatrix}, \quad rank(A_5) = 2$

$\begin{bmatrix} 1 & 0 & 0 \\ 0 & 1 & 1 \end{bmatrix}, \quad rank(A_6) = 2$

$\begin{bmatrix} 1 & 0 \\ 0 & 0 \\ 0 & 1 \end{bmatrix}, \quad rank(A_7) = 2$

$[1 \quad 1], \quad rank(A_8) = 1$

$\begin{bmatrix} 1 \\ 0 \end{bmatrix}, \quad rank(A_9) = 1$

$[1 \quad 1 \quad 1], \quad rank(A_{10}) = 1$

$\begin{bmatrix} 1 \\ 0 \\ 0 \end{bmatrix}, \quad rank(A_{11}) = 1$

$\begin{bmatrix} 1 & 1 & 1 \\ 1 & 1 & 1 \\ 1 & 1 & 1 \end{bmatrix}, \quad rank(A_{12}) = 1$

$\begin{bmatrix} 1 & 1 & 1 \\ 1 & 1 & -1 \\ 1 & 1 & 1 \end{bmatrix}, \quad rank(A_{13}) = 2$

$\begin{bmatrix} 1 & 1 & 1 \\ 0 & 1 & 1 \\ 0 & 0 & 1 \end{bmatrix}, \quad rank(A_{14}) = 3$

Determinate's of a (2x2) matrix

Various ways to check determinant

(2x2):

$$A = \begin{bmatrix} a & b \\ c & d \end{bmatrix} \quad \Rightarrow \quad \det(A) = |A| = \begin{vmatrix} a & b \\ c & d \end{vmatrix} = (a)(d) - (b)(c)$$

$$A = \begin{bmatrix} a & b \\ 0 & c \end{bmatrix} \quad \Rightarrow \quad \det(A) = |A| = \begin{vmatrix} a & b \\ 0 & c \end{vmatrix} = (a)(c)$$

$$A = \begin{bmatrix} a & 0 \\ 0 & b \end{bmatrix} \quad \Rightarrow \quad \det(A) = |A| = \begin{vmatrix} a & 0 \\ 0 & b \end{vmatrix} = (a)(b)$$

Determinate of a (3x3) and higher matrices

Cofactor Expansion

Note:

$$\begin{vmatrix} a & b \\ c & d \end{vmatrix} = (a)(d) - (b)(c)$$

$$\begin{vmatrix} a & b & c \\ d & e & f \\ g & h & i \end{vmatrix} = +a \begin{vmatrix} e & f \\ h & i \end{vmatrix} - b \begin{vmatrix} d & f \\ g & i \end{vmatrix} + c \begin{vmatrix} d & e \\ g & h \end{vmatrix}$$

$$\begin{vmatrix} a & b & c & d \\ e & f & g & h \\ i & j & k & l \\ m & n & o & p \end{vmatrix} = +a \begin{vmatrix} f & g & h \\ j & k & l \\ n & o & p \end{vmatrix} - b \begin{vmatrix} e & g & h \\ i & k & l \\ m & 0 & p \end{vmatrix} + c \begin{vmatrix} e & f & h \\ i & j & l \\ m & n & p \end{vmatrix} - d \begin{vmatrix} e & f & g \\ i & j & k \\ m & n & o \end{vmatrix}$$

TRIGONOMETRY

In trigonometry, much is learned, but to be effective in Calculus, there is only a small portion of trigonometry that must be mastered and memorized in order to solve problems. Mainly: how to evaluate the unit circle, right triangles, perform trigonometric substitutions and a few others. For this portion of the book we will focus on these topics.

*Note:

$$\cos^{-1}\theta = \arccos\theta \neq \frac{1}{\cos\theta}, \qquad [\cos\theta]^{-1} = \frac{1}{\cos\theta} = \sec\theta \neq \cos^{-1}\theta$$

This is a common reason why $\arccos\theta$ (pronounced arc cosine) is used in place of $\cos^{-1}\theta$ (pronounced cosine inverse)

This is true for all functions and operators i.e. $f^{-1}(x)$ is the inverse of f where $[f(x)]^{-1}$ is the reciprocal of f i.e. $[f(x)]^{-1} = \frac{1}{f(x)}$

Radian and Degree Conversion

$$\theta_{\text{degree}} = \theta_{\text{radian}}\left(\frac{180°}{\pi}\right) \qquad\qquad \theta_{\text{radian}} = \theta_{\text{degree}}\left(\frac{\pi}{180°}\right)$$

i.e.

$$\theta_{\text{degree}} = 45° \quad \Rightarrow \quad \theta_{\text{radian}} = 45°\left(\frac{\pi}{180°}\right) = \left(\frac{45}{180}\right)(1^{°-°})\pi = \frac{1}{4}(1^0)\pi = \frac{\pi}{4}$$

Notice that the degree cancels out just like a variable and that the absence of the degree symbols implies radians.

$$\theta_{\text{radian}} = \frac{\pi}{4} \quad \Rightarrow \quad \theta_{\text{degree}} = \frac{\pi}{4}\left(\frac{180°}{\pi}\right) = \left(\frac{180}{4}\right)°\left(\frac{\pi}{\pi}\right) = 45°(1) = 45°$$

Basic Graphs

$$y = \sin x$$

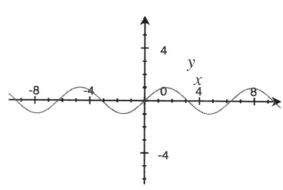

$$y = \cos x$$

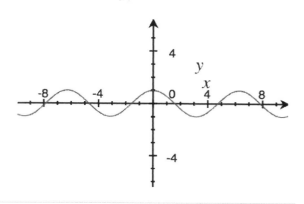

$$y = \csc x$$

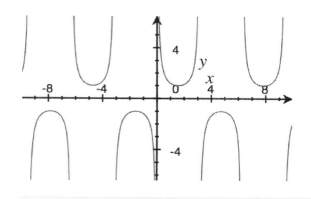

$$y = \sec x$$

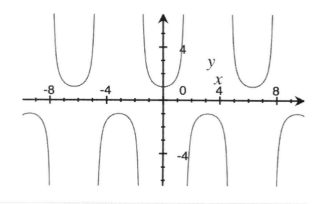

$$y = \tan x$$

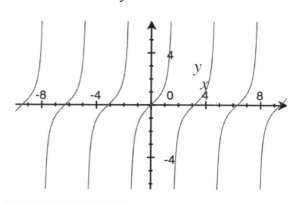

$$y = \cot x$$

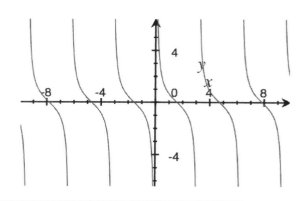

$$y = \arcsin x = \sin^{-1} x$$

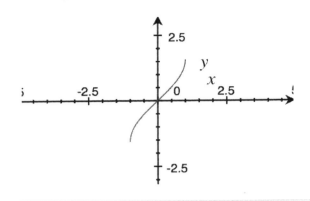

$$y = \arccos x = \cos^{-1} x$$

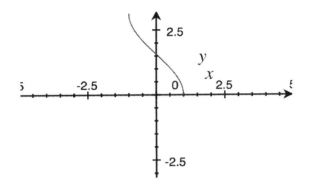

$$y = \arctan x = \tan^{-1} x$$

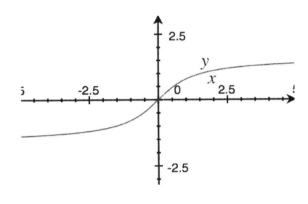

Using Pythagorean's Theorem

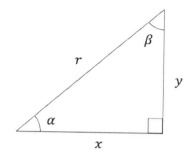

$$x^2 + y^2 = r^2 \quad \Leftrightarrow \quad r = \sqrt{x^2 + y^2}$$

Angle From The Horizontal	Angle From The Vertical
$\cos \alpha = \dfrac{x}{r}$	$\cos \beta = \dfrac{y}{r}$
$\tan \alpha = \dfrac{y}{x}$	$\tan \beta = \dfrac{x}{y}$
$\sin \alpha = \dfrac{y}{r}$	$\sin \beta = \dfrac{x}{r}$
$x = r \cos \alpha$	$y = r \cos \beta$
$y = r \sin \alpha$	$x = r \sin \beta$
$\alpha = \arctan\left(\dfrac{y}{x}\right) = \tan^{-1}\left(\dfrac{y}{x}\right)$	$\beta = \arctan\left(\dfrac{x}{y}\right) = \tan^{-1}\left(\dfrac{x}{y}\right)$

Please note that the previous and following evaluation of a right triangle using functions is not a formal definition or a theorem – it is simply a technique that can be used for simplifying a problem and it should be known that when finding angles, the domain must be considered as well.

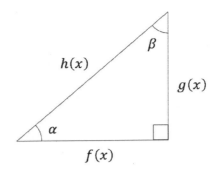

$$[f(x)]^2 + [g(x)]^2 = [h(x)]^2$$

Angle From The Horizontal	Angle From The Vertical
$\cos \alpha = \dfrac{f(x)}{h(x)}$	$\cos \beta = \dfrac{g(x)}{h(x)}$
$\sin \alpha = \dfrac{g(x)}{h(x)}$	$\sin \beta = \dfrac{f(x)}{h(x)}$
$\tan \alpha = \dfrac{g(x)}{f(x)}$	$\tan \beta \, \dfrac{f(x)}{g(x)}$
$\alpha = \arctan \dfrac{g(x)}{f(x)}$	$\beta = \arctan \dfrac{f(x)}{g(x)}$
$f(x) = h(x) \cos \alpha$	$g(x) = h(x) \cos \beta$
$g(x) = h(x) \sin \alpha$	$f(x) = h(x) \sin \beta$

*IMPORTANT: Make sure everything about evaluating right triangles, the unit circle and trigonometric identities is fully understood as this will be used in detail throughout Calculus and Physics.

Trigonometric Formulas and Identities

Because there are quite a few trigonometric formulas and identities and it is quite difficult to memorize all of them, it is extremely important to understand how to derive these formulas and identities from known formulas and identities.

When working in calculus one will frequently replace a trigonometric statement with another trigonometric statement. This is one of the most difficult parts of calculus for people to grasp, it is not because it is hard, it is because students fly through trigonometry and never really understand what they were doing and do not have enough practice with symbol recognition for replacement.

Reciprocal Identities

$$\sin\theta = \frac{1}{\csc\theta} \qquad\qquad \csc\theta = \frac{1}{\sin\theta} \qquad\qquad \tan\theta = \frac{1}{\cot\theta}$$

$$\csc\theta = \frac{1}{\sec\theta} \qquad\qquad \sec\theta = \frac{1}{\cos\theta} \qquad\qquad \cot\theta = \frac{1}{\tan\theta}$$

$$\tan\theta = \frac{\sin\theta}{\cos\theta} \qquad\qquad \cot\theta = \frac{\cos\theta}{\sin\theta}$$

Important: This is a good place to start getting acquainted with how to use trig-substitution, as this will appear frequently throughout calculus.

$$\tan\theta = \frac{\sin\theta}{\cos\theta} = \sin\theta\left(\frac{1}{\cos\theta}\right) \quad\Rightarrow\quad \sin\theta\left(\frac{1}{\cos\theta}\right) = \sin\theta\sec\theta$$

$$\Rightarrow\quad \sin\theta\sec\theta = \left(\frac{1}{\csc\theta}\right)\sec\theta \quad\Rightarrow\quad \left(\frac{1}{\csc\theta}\right)\sec\theta = \frac{\sec\theta}{\csc\theta}$$

$$\tan\theta = \frac{\sec\theta}{\csc\theta} \quad\Rightarrow\quad [\tan\theta]^2 = \left[\frac{\sec\theta}{\csc\theta}\right]^2 \quad\Rightarrow\quad \tan^2\theta = \frac{\sec^2\theta}{\csc^2\theta} = \frac{\tan^2\theta + 1}{1 + \cot^2\theta}$$

As seen in the previous examples, the possibilities for trig-substitution are endless. Often, in calculus, one just has to keep trying different forms until a form that works is found.

Pythagorean Identities

Often students cannot remember all the identities but with $\sin^2\theta + \cos^2\theta = 1$ and a few simple concepts, all the identities can easily be found.

Derivation $\sin^2\theta + \cos^2\theta = 1$:

$$x = r\cos\theta, \qquad y = r\sin\theta, \qquad x^2 + y^2 = r^2$$

$$x^2 + y^2 = (r\cos\theta)^2 + (r\sin\theta)^2 = r^2\cos^2\theta + r^2\sin^2\theta$$

$$= r^2(\cos^2\theta + \sin^2\theta) = r^2(1) = r^2$$

$$\therefore x^2 + y^2 = r^2$$

Derivation for $\tan^2\theta + 1 = \sec^2\theta$:

$$\frac{1}{\cos^2\theta}[\sin^2\theta + \cos^2\theta = 1] \quad\Rightarrow\quad \frac{\sin^2\theta}{\cos^2\theta} + \frac{\cos^2\theta}{\cos^2\theta} = \frac{1}{\cos^2\theta} \quad\Rightarrow\quad \left(\frac{\sin\theta}{\cos\theta}\right)^2 + 1 = \left(\frac{1}{\cos\theta}\right)^2$$

$$\therefore \tan^2\theta + 1 = \sec^2\theta$$

Derivation for $1 + \cot^2\theta = \csc^2\theta$:

$$\frac{1}{\sin^2\theta}[\sin^2\theta + \cos^2\theta = 1] \quad\Rightarrow\quad \frac{\sin^2\theta}{\sin^2\theta} + \frac{\cos^2\theta}{\sin^2\theta} = \frac{1}{\sin^2\theta} \quad\Rightarrow\quad 1 + \left(\frac{\cos\theta}{\sin\theta}\right)^2 = \left(\frac{1}{\sin\theta}\right)^2$$

$$\therefore 1 + \cot^2\theta = \csc^2\theta$$

Even and Odd Functions

$$\text{Even} \quad\Leftrightarrow\quad f(-x) = f(x)$$

$$\text{Odd} \quad\Leftrightarrow\quad f(-x) = -f(x)$$

$$\text{Odd} \qquad \sin(-\theta) = -\sin(\theta)$$

$$\text{Even} \qquad \cos(-\theta) = \cos(\theta)$$

Odd	$\tan(-\theta) = -\tan(\theta)$
Odd	$\csc(-\theta) = -\csc(\theta)$
Even	$\sec(-\theta) = \sec(\theta)$
Odd	$\cot(\theta) = -\cot(\theta)$

Example

There may be a time in Calculus i.e. Integral Calculus or towards the end of the first semester of Calculus or during the second semester, depending... You will need to be able to easily identify an odd function. Here is an example when this may be necessary:

$$\int_{-2}^{2} \frac{\sin(x)\cos(x)}{\ln|x| - \sin^2 e^x} dx$$

This is called a 'Definite Integral,' try not be scared of it, it is actually quite simple to evaluate in this case because $\int_{-a}^{a} f(x)\,dx = 0$ if $f(x)$ is an odd function. We must now show $f(x)$ is an odd function.

$$f(x) = \frac{\sin(x)\cos(x)}{\ln|x| - \sin^2 e^x} \quad \Rightarrow \quad f(-x) = \frac{\sin(-x)\cos(-x)}{\ln|-x| - \sin^2 e^{(-x)^2}}$$

$$\sin(-x) = -\sin(x) \qquad odd$$

$$\cos(-x) = \cos(x) \qquad even$$

$$\ln|-x| = \ln|x| \qquad even$$

$$\sin^2 e^{(-x)^2} = \sin^2 e^{x^2} \qquad even$$

Plug everything back in

$$\therefore \quad f(-x) = -\frac{\sin(x)\cos(x)}{\ln|x| - \sin^2 e^x} = -f(x)$$

In other words, in order to show a function is odd, simply plug a negative sign in with every x and then evaluate each individual function and see if you have an even or odd number of negative signs.

Double Angle Formulas

*Important

The half angle and double angle formulas along with the Pythagorean identities are used frequently throughout calculus. **It is a must** that you memorize the understanding and derivations is fully comprehended.

For a detailed list of all identities, see the reference sheets in the back of the book.

Derivation for $\sin(2\theta) = 2\sin\theta\cos\theta$:

$$\sin(2\theta) = \sin(\theta + \theta) = \sin\theta\cos\theta + \sin\theta\cos\theta = 2\sin\theta\cos\theta$$

Derivation for $\cos(2\theta) = 1 - 2\sin^2\theta$:

$$\cos(2\theta) = \cos^2\theta - \sin^2\theta = 2\cos^2\theta - 1 = 1 - 2\sin^2\theta$$

As one can see, these formulas are all derived from the Pythagorean identities and there are many ways to find them. If this can be understood properly then memorizing them is not entirely necessary.

Other Derivations:

$$\cos 2\theta = \cos(\theta + \theta) = \cos\theta\cos\theta - \sin\theta\sin\theta = \cos^2\theta - \sin^2\theta$$

$$\cos 2\theta = \cos(\theta + \theta) = \cos\theta\cos\theta - \sin\theta\sin\theta = \cos^2\theta - \sin^2\theta = \cos^2\theta - (1 - \cos^2\theta)$$

$$= \cos^2 - 1 + \cos^2\theta = 2\cos^2\theta - 1$$

$$\cos 2\theta = \cos(\theta + \theta) = \cos\theta\cos\theta - \sin\theta\sin\theta = \cos^2\theta - \sin^2\theta$$

$$= (1 - \sin^2\theta) - \sin^2\theta = 1 - 2\sin^2\theta$$

$$\tan 2\theta = \tan(\theta + \theta) = \frac{\tan\theta + \tan\theta}{1 - \tan\theta\tan\theta} = \frac{2\tan\theta}{1 - \tan^2\theta}$$

Half Angle Formulas

$$\sin^2\theta = \frac{1}{2}[1 - \cos(2\theta)]$$

Derivation:

$$\sin^2\theta = 1 - \cos^2\theta = 1 - \cos\theta\cos\theta = 1 - \frac{1}{2}[\cos(\theta - \theta) + \cos(\theta + \theta)]$$

$$= 1 - \frac{1}{2}[\cos(0) + \cos(2\theta)] = 1 - \frac{1}{2}[(1) + \cos 2\theta] = 1 - \frac{1}{2} - \frac{1}{2}\cos 2\theta$$

$$= \frac{1}{2} - \frac{1}{2}\cos 2\theta = \frac{1}{2}[1 - \cos(2\theta)]$$

$$\cos^2\theta = \frac{1}{2}[1 + \cos(2\theta)]$$

Derivation:

$$\cos^2\theta = 1 - \sin^2\theta = 1 - \sin\theta\sin\theta = 1 - \frac{1}{2}[\cos(\theta - \theta) - \cos(\theta + \theta)]$$

$$= 1 - \frac{1}{2}[\cos 0 - \cos 2\theta] = 1 - \frac{1}{2}[(1) - \cos 2\theta] = 1 - \frac{1}{2} + \frac{1}{2}\cos 2\theta$$

$$= \frac{1}{2} + \frac{1}{2}\cos 2\theta = \frac{1}{2}[1 + \cos(2\theta)]$$

$$\tan^2\theta = \frac{1 - \cos(2\theta)}{1 + \cos(2\theta)}$$

Derivation:

$$\tan^2\theta = \sec^2\theta - 1 = \left(\frac{1}{\cos\theta}\right)^2 - 1 = \frac{1}{\cos\theta\cos\theta} - 1 = \frac{1}{\frac{1}{2}[\cos(\theta - \theta) + \cos(\theta + \theta)]} - 1$$

$$= \frac{2}{1 + \cos 2\theta} - 1 = \frac{2}{1 + \cos 2\theta} - \frac{1 + \cos 2\theta}{1 + \cos 2\theta} = \frac{[2 - (1 + \cos 2\theta)]}{1 + \cos 2\theta} = \frac{1 - \cos 2\theta}{1 + \cos 2\theta}$$

Sum and Difference Formulas

$$\sin(\alpha \pm \beta) = \sin \alpha \cos \beta \pm \cos \alpha \sin \beta$$

$$\cos(\alpha \pm \beta) = \cos \alpha \cos \beta \mp \sin \alpha \cos \beta$$

$$\tan(\alpha \pm \beta) = \frac{\tan \alpha \pm \tan \beta}{1 \mp \tan \alpha \, tan\beta}$$

The derivations of the sum & difference, product to sum and sum to product formulas are a bit more complicated. Try to show they are true without referencing anything. This will prove to be an excellent practice. Remember, getting it correct is not always the point of practice. One must sometimes go in the wrong direction to learn that they are not on the right path.

Product to Sum Formulas

$$\sin \alpha \sin \beta = \frac{1}{2}[\cos(\alpha - \beta) - \cos(\alpha + \beta)]$$

$$\cos \alpha \cos \beta = \frac{1}{2}[\cos(\alpha - \beta) + \cos(\alpha + \beta)]$$

$$\sin \alpha \cos \beta = \frac{1}{2}[\sin(\alpha + \beta) + \sin(\alpha - \beta)]$$

$$\cos \alpha \sin \beta = \frac{1}{2}[\sin(\alpha + \beta) - \sin(\alpha - \beta)]$$

Sum to Product Formulas

$$\sin \alpha + \sin \beta = 2 \sin \left[\frac{\alpha + \beta}{2}\right] \cos \left[\frac{\alpha - \beta}{2}\right]$$

$$\sin \alpha - \sin \beta = 2 \cos \left[\frac{\alpha + \beta}{2}\right] \sin \left[\frac{\alpha - \beta}{2}\right]$$

$$\cos \alpha + \cos \beta = 2 \cos \left[\frac{\alpha + \beta}{2}\right] \cos \left[\frac{\alpha - \beta}{2}\right]$$

$$\cos \alpha - \cos \beta = -2 \sin \left[\frac{\alpha + \beta}{2}\right] \sin \left[\frac{\alpha - \beta}{2}\right]$$

Hyperbolic Functions

I rarely see hyperbolic functions in the average calculus course but every once in awhile the topic pops up and it seems like the teacher is obsessed with them when it does. It is good to know how to use them. Not too different from working with trigonometric operations, just a little more involved.

Notation

$$\sinh x = \frac{e^x - e^{-x}}{2}$$

$$\operatorname{csch} x = \frac{2}{e^x + e^{-x}}$$

$$\cosh x = \frac{e^x + e^{-x}}{2}$$

$$\operatorname{sech} x = \frac{2}{e^x + e^{-x}}$$

$$\tanh x = \frac{e^x - e^{-x}}{e^x + e^{-x}}$$

$$\coth x = \frac{e^x + e^{-x}}{e^x - e^{-x}}$$

Graphs

$$\sinh x = \frac{e^x - e^{-x}}{2}$$

$$\operatorname{csch} x = \frac{2}{e^x + e^{-x}}$$

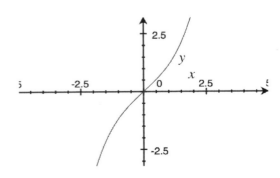

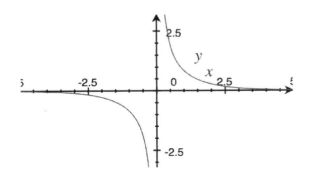

$$\cosh x = \frac{e^x + e^{-x}}{2}$$

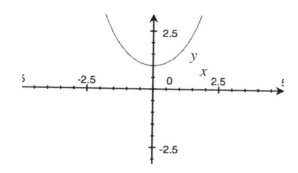

$$\operatorname{sech} x = \frac{2}{e^x + e^{-x}}$$

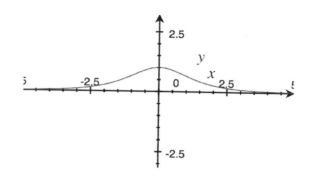

$$\tanh x = \frac{e^x - e^{-x}}{e^x + e^{-x}}$$

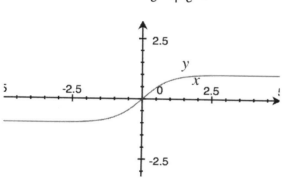

$$\coth x = \frac{e^x + e^{-x}}{e^x - e^{-x}}$$

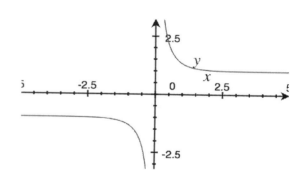

Identities

$$\sinh(-x) = -\sinh x \qquad \cosh(-x) = \cosh x$$

$$\cosh^2 x - \sinh^2 x = 1 \qquad 1 - \tanh^2 x = \operatorname{sech}^2 x$$

$$\sinh(x + y) = \sinh x \cosh y + \cosh x \sinh y$$

$$\cosh(x + y) = \cosh x \cosh y + \sinh x \sinh y$$

$$\sinh^{-1} x = \ln\left[x + \sqrt{x^2 + 1}\right], \qquad -\infty \le x \le \infty$$

$$\cosh^{-1} x = \ln\left[x + \sqrt{x^2 - 1}\right], \qquad x \ge 1$$

$$\tanh^{-1} x = \frac{1}{2}\ln\left[\frac{1 + x}{1 - x}\right], \qquad -1 < x < 1$$

DIFFERENTIAL CALCULUS (CALC I)

Translation-

The limit of f of x as x goes to a	$\lim\limits_{x \to a} f(x)$
f of x approaches the limit as x approaches a	$f(x) \to L \quad \text{as} \quad x \to a$

Notations for Limits

The actual limit	$\lim\limits_{x \to a} f(x) = L \quad \Leftrightarrow \quad L^- = L^+$
Left hand limit	$\lim\limits_{x \to a^-} f(x) = L^-$
Right hand limit	$\lim\limits_{x \to a^+} f(x) = L^+$
Limit exists	$\lim\limits_{x \to a^-} f(x) = \lim\limits_{x \to a^+} f(x)$
Limit does not exists (DNE)	$\lim\limits_{x \to a^-} f(x) \neq \lim\limits_{x \to a^+} f(x)$
Continuous function	$f(a) = L = L^{\pm}$
Left Continuous function	$f(a) = L^-$
Right Continuous function	$f(a) = L^+$
Non-continuous function	$f(a) = Undefined \neq L$

Types of Discontinuity

Jump

Occurs with piecewise functions i.e.

$$f(x) = \begin{cases} -x, & x < 1 \\ x + 1, & x \geq 1 \end{cases}$$

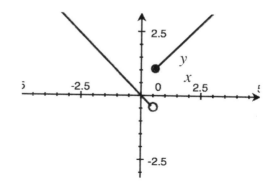

Removable

$$f(x) = \frac{x^2 - 4}{x - 2} = \frac{(x - 2)(x + 2)}{(x - 2)} \quad \Rightarrow$$

$$g(x) = x + 2 \quad \Rightarrow \quad x \neq 2 \quad \therefore \quad f(2) = \frac{0}{0}$$

Occurs at holes in the graph

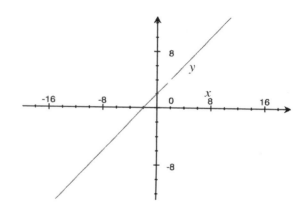

Infinite

$$f(x) = \frac{x^2 + x + 1}{x^3 + x^2 + x + 1}$$

$$\therefore \quad HA: \quad y = 0, \quad VA: \quad x = -2$$

Occurs at asymptotes

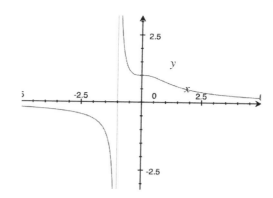

Limit Laws and Properties

Limit of a Constant	$\lim\limits_{x \to a} c = c$
Limit of Single Variable	$\lim\limits_{x \to a} x = a$
If The Function is Continuous	$\lim\limits_{x \to a} f(x) = f(a)$
The Constant Multiple Law	$\lim\limits_{x \to a} [cf(x)] = c \lim\limits_{x \to a} f(x)$
The Sum and Difference Law	$\lim\limits_{x \to a} [f(x) \pm g(x)] = \lim\limits_{x \to a} f(x) \pm \lim\limits_{x \to a} g(x)$
The Product Law	$\lim\limits_{x \to a} [f(x)g(x)] = \lim\limits_{x \to a} f(x) \cdot \lim\limits_{x \to a} g(x)$
The Quotient Law	$\lim\limits_{x \to a} \left[\dfrac{f(x)}{g(x)} \right] = \dfrac{\lim\limits_{x \to a} f(x)}{\lim\limits_{x \to a} g(x)}, \qquad \lim\limits_{x \to a} g(x) \neq 0$
The Power Law	$\lim\limits_{x \to a} [f(x)]^n = \left[\lim\limits_{x \to a} f(x) \right]^n, \qquad n \in \mathbb{N}$
The Root Law	$\lim\limits_{x \to a} \sqrt[n]{f(x)} = \sqrt[n]{\lim\limits_{x \to a} f(x)}, \qquad n \in \mathbb{N}$
Exponential Law	$\lim\limits_{x \to a} a^{f(x)} = a^{\lim\limits_{x \to a} f(x)}$

Infinite Limits

There are three basic cases for evaluating non-trig/log functions at infinity. This is where the horizontal asymptote formulas arise -- used in Algebra.

Case 1:	$\lim\limits_{x \to \infty} \dfrac{x^m + x^{m-1} + \cdots}{x^n + x^{n-1} + \cdots} = 0$	$n > m, \qquad \textit{Multiply by } \dfrac{x^{-n}}{x^{-n}}$ Ratio of polynomials of degree m & n
Case 2:	$\lim\limits_{x \to \infty} \dfrac{x^m + x^{m-1} + \cdots}{x^n + x^{n-1} + \cdots} = \infty$	$n < m, \qquad \textit{Multiply by } \dfrac{x^{-n}}{x^{-n}}$ Ratio of polynomials of degree m & n
Case 3:	$\lim\limits_{x \to \infty} \dfrac{ax^m + x^{m-1} + \cdots}{bx^n + x^{n-1} + \cdots} = \dfrac{a}{b}$	$n = m, \qquad \textit{Multiply by } \dfrac{x^{-n}}{x^{-n}}$ Ratio of polynomials of degree m & n

Precise Definition of a Limit ε, δ

The limit of f of x as x goes to a	$\lim\limits_{x \to a} f(x)$
f of x approaches the limit as x approaches a	$f(x) \to L$ as $x \to a$

Limit

For every $\epsilon > 0$, there is a $\delta > 0$ such that $0 < |x - a| < \delta$ and $|f(x) - L| < \epsilon$

Left Hand Limit

For every $\epsilon > 0$, there is a $\delta > 0$ such that $a - \delta < x < a$ and $|f(x) - L| < \epsilon$

Right Hand Limit

For every $\epsilon > 0$, there is a $\delta > 0$ such that $a < x < a + \delta$ and $|f(x) - L| < \epsilon$

Derivation of "The Difference Quotient"

$$m = \frac{\Delta y}{\Delta x} \quad \Rightarrow \quad \frac{\Delta y}{\Delta x} = \frac{y - y_0}{x - x_0}, \qquad y = f(x)$$

$$\Rightarrow \quad \frac{y - y_0}{x - x_0} = \frac{f(x) - f(x_0)}{x - x_0}, \qquad \Delta x = x - x_0 \quad \Leftrightarrow \quad x = \Delta x + x_0$$

$$\Rightarrow \quad \frac{f(x) - f(x_0)}{x - x_0} = \frac{f(\Delta x + x_0) - f(x_0)}{\Delta x} \equiv \frac{f(x + h) - f(x)}{h}$$

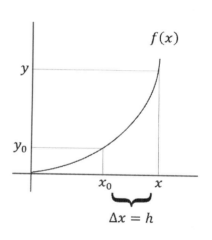

Slope of Secant Line or Difference Quotient

$$m = \frac{f(x + h) - f(x)}{h} \equiv \frac{f(x + \Delta x) - f(x)}{\Delta x} \quad \Leftrightarrow \quad h = \Delta x$$

Intermediate Value Theorem

If f is continuous on $[a, b]$, $f(a) < N < f(b)$ and $f(a) \neq f(b)$, then there is a $c \in (a, b) \ni f(c) = N$. ($\ni$ means "such that")

Common Limits

Infinite Limits

$$\lim_{x \to \infty} x^n = \infty, n > 0$$

$$\lim_{x \to \infty} \frac{1}{x^n} = \infty, n < 0$$

$$\lim_{x \to \infty} e^{-x} = 0$$

$$\lim_{x \to \infty} \frac{1}{\ln x} = 0$$

$$\lim_{x \to \infty} \frac{1}{x^n} = 0, n > 0$$

$$\lim_{x \to \infty} e^x = \infty$$

$$\lim_{x \to \infty} \frac{1}{e^{-x}} = \infty$$

$$\lim_{x \to \infty} \ln[x^{-1}] = -\infty$$

$$\lim_{x \to \infty} x^n = 0, n < 0$$

$$\lim_{x \to \infty} \frac{1}{e^x} = 0$$

$$\lim_{x \to \infty} \ln x = \infty$$

$$\lim_{x \to \infty} \frac{1}{\ln[x^{-1}]} = 0$$

$$\lim_{x \to \infty} \sin x = -1 \text{ to } 1, DNE$$

$$\lim_{x \to \infty} \tan x = -\infty \text{ to } \infty, DNE$$

$$\lim_{x \to \infty} \tan \left(\frac{1}{x}\right) = 0$$

$$\lim_{x \to \infty} \sec \left(\frac{1}{x}\right) = 1$$

$$\lim_{x \to \infty} \sin \left(\frac{1}{x}\right) = 0$$

$$\lim_{x \to \infty} \cos \left(\frac{1}{x}\right) = 1$$

$$\lim_{x \to \infty} \csc \left(\frac{1}{x}\right) = \infty$$

$$\lim_{x \to \infty} \cot x = -\infty \text{ to } \infty$$

$$\lim_{x \to \infty} \cos x = -1 \text{ to } 1$$

$$\lim_{x \to \infty} \csc x$$
$$= -\infty \text{ to} -1 \& 1 \text{ to } \infty, DNE$$

$$\lim_{x \to \infty} \sec x$$
$$= -\infty \text{ to} -1 \& 1 \text{ to } \infty, DNE$$

$$\lim_{x \to \infty} \cot \frac{1}{x} = \infty$$

Derivatives

The Limit Definition of a Derivative

$$f'(x) = \lim_{h \to 0} \frac{f(x+h) - f(x)}{h} \equiv \lim_{x \to x_0} \frac{f(x + \Delta x) - f(x)}{\Delta x} \quad \Leftrightarrow \quad h = \Delta x$$

The apostrophe in $f'(x)$ or y' denotes derivative.

Notations

0th Derivative	$y = f(x) = \dfrac{dF}{dx} = \dfrac{dY}{dx}$
1st Derivative	$y' = f'(x) = \dfrac{dy}{dx}$
2nd Derivative	$y'' = f''(x) = \dfrac{d^2 y}{dy^2}$
3rd Derivative	$y''' = f'''(x) = \dfrac{d^3 y}{dy^3}$
4th Derivative	$y^{(4)} = f^{(4)}(x) = \dfrac{d^4 y}{dy^4}$
nth Derivative	$y^{(n)} = f^{(n)}(x) = \dfrac{d^n y}{dy^n}$

Note:

1. Any derivative after the 3rd is written as $f^{(n)}(x)$ or $y^{(n)}$ *not to be confused with a power* $y^{(4)} = $ 4th derivative $\neq y^4 = y \cdot y \cdot y \cdot y$

2. $\dfrac{d}{d[\ldots]}$ is called "The Derivative Operator" it simply means to take the derivative of whatever follows with respect to whatever is in $[\ldots]$.

Time Derivatives

$\dfrac{d}{dt} y = y'(t) = \dot{y}$, 1st derivative with respect to time

$\dfrac{d^2}{dt^2} x = x''(t) = \ddot{x}$, 2nd derivative with respect to time

The Slope Notation for Calculus

$$m = \lim_{x \to a} \frac{f(x) - f(a)}{x - a} \equiv \lim_{h \to 0} \frac{f(a + h) - f(a)}{h} = m$$

Slope of function aka derivative:

$$f'(x) = \lim_{h \to 0} \frac{f(x + h) - f(x)}{h}$$

$$y = f(x) \quad \Rightarrow \quad y_0 = f(x_0)$$

$$\therefore \quad f(x) - f(x_0) = f'(x)(x - x_0)$$

Tangent Line

$$f(x), \quad x = a \qquad | \qquad y_T = f'(a)(x - a) + f(a)$$

Physics Notation

$$s = s(t), \quad \text{Distance}$$

$$v = v(t) = s' = s'(t) = \frac{ds}{dt} = \dot{s}, \quad 1^{\text{st}} \text{ Derivative Velocity}$$

$$a = a(t) = \frac{dv}{dt} = v'(t) = v' = \dot{v} = \frac{d^2s}{dt^2} = s''(t) = s'' = \ddot{s}, \quad \text{2nd Derivative Acceleration}$$

Derivative Rules (operator notations)

Derivative of a Constant	$\dfrac{d}{dx}c = 0$
Sum and Difference	$\dfrac{d}{dx}[f(x) + g(x)] = \dfrac{d}{dx}f(x) + \dfrac{d}{dx}g(x)$
Power Rule	$\dfrac{d}{dx}x^n = nx^{n-1}$
Constant Multiple Rule	$\dfrac{d}{dx}cf(x) = c\dfrac{d}{dx}f(x)$
Product Rule	$\dfrac{d}{dx}[f(x)g(x)] = f(x)\dfrac{d}{dx}g(x) + g(x)\dfrac{d}{dx}f(x)$
Quotient Rule	$\dfrac{d}{dx}\left[\dfrac{f(x)}{g(x)}\right] = \dfrac{g(x)\dfrac{d}{dx}f(x) - f(x)\dfrac{d}{dx}g(x)}{[g(x)]^2}$
Chain Rule	$\dfrac{d}{dx}[f \circ g](x) = \dfrac{d}{dx}[f(g(x))] = \dfrac{df}{dg} \cdot \dfrac{dg}{dx} = f'(g(x)) \cdot g'(x)$

Derivative Rules (prime notations)

Derivative of a Constant	$(c)' = 0$
Power Rule	$(x^n)' = nx^{n-1}$
Constant Multiple Rule	$(cu)' = cu'$
Product Rule	$[uv]' = uv' + vu'$
Quotient Rule	$\left[\dfrac{u}{v}\right]' = \dfrac{vu' - uv'}{v^2}$
Chain Rule	$[u(v)]' = u'(v) \cdot v'$

Exponential and Logarithmic

	Operator	Prime
exp{u}	$\dfrac{d}{dx}e^{f(x)} = e^{f(x)} \cdot f'(x)$	$(e^u)' = e^u \cdot u'$
Natural Log	$\dfrac{d}{dx}\ln f(x) = \dfrac{f'(x)}{f(x)}$	$[\ln(u)]' = \dfrac{u'}{u}$
Base Log Note: $\log_b a \equiv \frac{\ln a}{\ln b}$	$\dfrac{d}{dx}\log_b f(x) = \dfrac{1}{\ln b} \cdot \dfrac{f'(x)}{f(x)}$	$[\log_b u]' = \dfrac{1}{\ln b} \cdot \dfrac{u'}{u}$
Exponential	$\dfrac{d}{dx}a^{f(x)} = a^{f(x)}f'(x)\ln a$	$(a^u)' = a^u u' \ln a$

Inverse Function Derivative

$$\frac{d}{dx}f^{-1}(x)\bigg|_a = \frac{1}{f'(f^{-1}(a))}, \qquad f^{-1}(a) = b \Leftrightarrow f(b) = a$$

Trig Derivatives

Standard

$(\sin u)' = \cos u \cdot u'$	$(\cos u)' = -\sin u \cdot u'$	$(\tan u)' = \sec^2 u \cdot u'$
$(\csc u)' = -\csc u \cot u \cdot u'$	$(\sec u)' = \sec u \tan u \cdot u'$	$(\cot u)' = -\csc^2 u \cdot u'$

Inverse

$(\sin^{-1} u)' = \dfrac{u'}{\sqrt{1-u^2}}$	$(\cos^{-1} u)' = -\dfrac{u'}{\sqrt{1-u^2}}$	$(\tan^{-1} u)' = \dfrac{u'}{1+u^2}$
$(\csc^{-1} u)' = -\dfrac{u'}{|u|\sqrt{u^2-1}}$	$(\sec^{-1} u)' = \dfrac{u'}{|u|\sqrt{u^2-1}}$	$(\cot^{-1} u)' = -\dfrac{u'}{1+u^2}$

Common Derivatives

Operator

$\dfrac{d}{dx} y = \dfrac{dy}{dx}$	$\dfrac{d}{dx} x^n = n x^{n-1}$	$\dfrac{d}{dx} y^n = n y^{n-1} \dfrac{dy}{dx}$
$\dfrac{d}{dx} e^x = e^x$	$\dfrac{d}{dx} e^{f(x)} = e^{f(x)} f'(x)$	$\dfrac{d}{dx} \ln x = \dfrac{1}{x}$
$\dfrac{d}{dx} \ln f(x) = \dfrac{f'(x)}{f(x)}$	$\dfrac{d}{dx} a^x = a^x \ln a$	$\dfrac{d}{dx} a^{f(x)} = a^{f(x)} f'(x) \ln a$
$\dfrac{d}{dx} (\sin x) = \cos x$	$\dfrac{d}{dx} (\csc x) = -\csc x \cot x$	$\dfrac{d}{dx} (\cos x) = -\sin x$
$\dfrac{d}{dx} (\sec x) = \sec x \tan x$	$\dfrac{d}{dx} (\tan x) = \sec^2 x$	$\dfrac{d}{dx} (\cot x) = -\csc^2 x$
$\dfrac{d}{dx} \sin^{-1} x = \dfrac{1}{\sqrt{1-x^2}}$	$\dfrac{d}{dx} \csc^{-1} x = \dfrac{-1}{|x|\sqrt{x^2-1}}$	$\dfrac{d}{dx} \cos^{-1} x = \dfrac{-1}{\sqrt{1-x^2}}$
$\dfrac{d}{dx} \sec^{-1} x = \dfrac{1}{|x|\sqrt{x^2-1}}$	$\dfrac{d}{dx} \tan^{-1} x = \dfrac{1}{1+x^2}$	$\dfrac{d}{dx} \cot^{-1} x = \dfrac{-1}{1+x^2}$
$\dfrac{d}{dx} \sinh x = \cosh x$	$\dfrac{d}{dx} \csch x = -\csch x \coth x$	$\dfrac{d}{dx} \cosh x = \sinh x$
$\dfrac{d}{dx} \sech x = -\sech x \tanh x$	$\dfrac{d}{dx} \tanh x = \sech^2 x$	$\dfrac{d}{dx} \coth x = -\csch^2 x$

Prime

$$[e^u]' = u'e^u$$

$$[\ln u]' = \frac{u'}{u}$$

$$[a^u]' = u'a^u \ln a$$

$$[\sin u]' = u' \cos u$$

$$[\cos u]' = -u' \sin u$$

$$[\tan u]' = u' \sec^2 u$$

$$[\csc u]' = -u' \csc u \cot u$$

$$[\sec u]' = u' \sec u \tan u$$

$$[\cot u]' = -u' \csc^2 u$$

$$[\arcsin u]' = \frac{u'}{\sqrt{1-u^2}}$$

$$[\arccos u]' = \frac{-u'}{\sqrt{1-u^2}}$$

$$[\arctan u]' = \frac{u'}{1+u^2}$$

$$[\text{arccsc}\, u]' = \frac{-u'}{|u|\sqrt{u^2-1}}$$

$$[\text{arcsec}\, u]' = \frac{u'}{|u|\sqrt{u^2-1}}$$

$$[\text{arccot}\, u]' = \frac{-u'}{1+u^2}$$

Implicit Differentiation

$\dfrac{d}{d[x]}[y]$ *Always pay attention to the variables*	$\dfrac{dy}{dx} = y'$
$\dfrac{d}{dx} y^2$	$2(y)^{2-1} \dfrac{d}{dx} y = 2yy'$
Chain/Power Rule	$\dfrac{d}{dx} y^n = ny^{n-1} \dfrac{dy}{dx} \equiv ny^{n-1}y'$
Chain/Product	$\dfrac{d}{dx}(xy) = x\dfrac{dy}{dx} + y\dfrac{dx}{dx} \equiv xy' + y$
Chain/Quotient	$\dfrac{d}{dx}\left(\dfrac{x}{y}\right) = \dfrac{y\frac{dx}{dx} - x\frac{dy}{dx}}{y^2} \equiv \dfrac{y - xy'}{y^2}$
Logarithmic	$\dfrac{d}{dx} \ln y = \dfrac{y'}{y}$
Exponential	$\dfrac{d}{dx} a^y = y'a^y \ln a$
Euler's Number	$\dfrac{d}{dx} e^y = y'e^y$
Trigonometric	$\dfrac{d}{dx} \sin y = \cos y \cdot \dfrac{dy}{dx} = \cos y \cdot y'$

Tangent Line

$$f(x, y) = 0, \qquad P(a, b) \quad \Rightarrow \quad y_T = f'(a, b)(x - a) + b$$

Related Rates

The idea for related rates, in general, is to find the equation that relates geometrically to the question, implicitly differentiate it, and then plug in the given variables and solve for the unknown. Here are a few examples i.e. just use the equation/formula that mimics the object in question.

Right triangle	$a^2 + b^2 = c^2 \;\Rightarrow\; aa'(t) + bb'(t) = cc'(t)$
Circle	$A = \pi r^2 \;\Rightarrow\; \dfrac{dA}{dt} = 2\pi r r'(t)$
Sphere	$V = \dfrac{4}{3}\pi r^3 \;\Rightarrow\; V'(t) = 4\pi r^2 \dfrac{dr}{dt}$

Hyperbolic Functions

Notation

$$\sinh x = \frac{e^x - e^{-x}}{2}$$

$$\operatorname{sech} x = \frac{2}{e^x + e^{-x}}$$

$$\operatorname{csch} x = \frac{2}{e^x + e^{-x}}$$

$$\cosh x = \frac{e^x + e^{-x}}{2}$$

$$\tanh x = \frac{e^x - e^{-x}}{e^x + e^{-x}}$$

$$\coth x = \frac{e^x + e^{-x}}{e^x - e^{-x}}$$

Graphs

$$\sinh x = \frac{e^x - e^{-x}}{2}$$

$$\cosh x = \frac{e^x + e^{-x}}{2}$$

$$\tanh x = \frac{e^x - e^{-x}}{e^x + e^{-x}}$$

$$\operatorname{csch} x = \frac{2}{e^x + e^{-x}}$$

$$\operatorname{sech} x = \frac{2}{e^x + e^{-x}}$$

$$\coth x = \frac{e^x + e^{-x}}{e^x - e^{-x}}$$

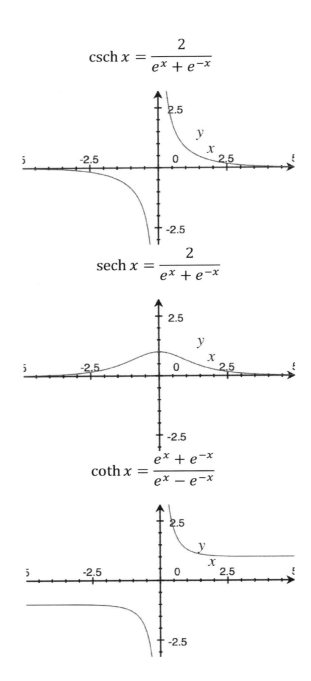

Identities

$$\sinh(-x) = -\sinh x \qquad\qquad \cosh(-x) = \cosh x$$

$$\cosh^2 x - \sinh^2 x = 1 \qquad\qquad 1 - \tanh^2 x = \operatorname{sech}^2 x$$

$$\sinh(x + y) = \sinh x \cosh y + \cosh x \sinh y$$

$$\cosh(x + y) = \cosh x \cosh y + \sinh x \sinh y$$

$$\sinh^{-1} x = \ln\left[x + \sqrt{x^2 + 1}\right], \qquad -\infty \leq x \leq \infty$$

$$\cosh^{-1} x = \ln\left[x + \sqrt{x^2 - 1}\right], \qquad x \geq 1$$

$$\tanh^{-1} x = \frac{1}{2}\ln\left[\frac{1 + x}{1 - x}\right], \qquad -1 < x < 1$$

Derivatives

Standard

$[\sinh u]' = u' \cosh u$	$[\cosh u]' = u' \sinh u$	$[\tanh u]' = u' \operatorname{sech}^2 u$
$[\operatorname{csch} u]' = -u' \operatorname{csch} u \coth u$	$[\operatorname{sech} u]' = -u' \operatorname{sech} u \tanh u$	$[\coth u]' = -u' \operatorname{csch}^2 u$

Inverse

$[\sinh^{-1} u]' = \dfrac{u'}{\sqrt{1 + u^2}}$	$[\cosh^{-1} u]' = \dfrac{u'}{\sqrt{u^2 - 1}}$	$[\tanh^{-1} u]' = \dfrac{u'}{1 - u^2}$
$[\operatorname{csch}^{-1} u]' = -\dfrac{u'}{\|u\|\sqrt{1 + u^2}}$	$[\operatorname{sech}^{-1} u]' = -\dfrac{u'}{u\sqrt{1 - u^2}}$	$[\coth^{-1} u]' = \dfrac{u'}{1 - u^2}$

Extrema

Graphing Process

i)   Identify the domain of the function, asymptotes, and intercepts.

ii)   Compute the first derivative, set it equal to zero and solve for $y' = 0, y' =$ undefined (critical numbers).

iii)   Identify whether the first derivative is positive or negative to the left and right of each critical number. If it is positive, it is increasing. If it is negative, it is decreasing.

iv)   Compute the second derivative, set it equal to zero and solve $y'' = 0, y'' =$ undefined (critical numbers).

v)   Identify whether the second derivative is positive or negative to the left and right of each critical number. If it is positive, it is concave up. If it is negative, it is concave down.

vi)   Verify that the intervals of increasing, decreasing and concavity line up with the domain and then identify whether the critical numbers are maximums, minimums or points of inflection.

vii)   Use this information to graph the function.

Critical Numbers

Critical numbers occur where the derivative(s) is equal to zero and or undefined.

Max/Min

Absolute Maximum	Absolute Minimum	Local Max	Local Min
$f(c) \geq f(x) \, \forall_x \in D$	$f(c) \leq f(x) \, \forall_x \in D$	$f(c) \geq f(x) \, \forall_x \, x \to c$	$f(c) \geq f(x) \, \forall_x \, x \to c$

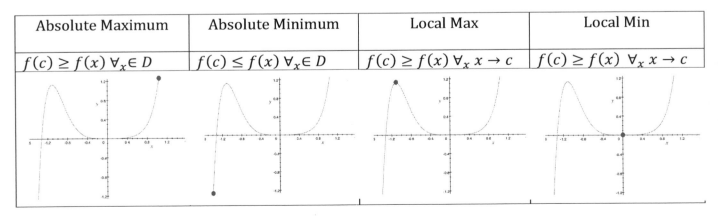

Note: Absolute max/min can occur at locals i.e. if the local is the highest/lowest point on the graph, it is also absolute.

The max/min occur only if $f(c)$ is defined i.e. the function must be continuous at the critical number or end of intervals.

Increasing and decreasing

Wherever the first derivative is positive, the function is increasing. Wherever the first derivative is negative, the function is decreasing.

Concavity

Wherever the second derivative is positive, the function is concave up. Wherever the second derivative is negative, the function is concave down.

Points of inflection

A point of inflection occurs when to the left/right of the critical number have opposite concavity, and $f(c)$ is defined.

Theorems

Rolle's Theorem

If the following three conditions hold, there is a value in the interval (a, b) such that $f'(value) = 0$

1) f is continuous on $[a, b]$
2) f is differentiable on (a, b)
3) $f(a) = f(b)$

Mean Value Theorem

If the following two conditions hold true, then there is a value in (a, b) such that

$$f'(c) = \frac{f(b) - f(a)}{b - a}$$

1) f is continuous on $[a, b]$
2) f is differentiable on (a, b)
3) Simply verify the first two conditions, and the solve for c in the above equations, and then verify c is in (a, b)

First & Second Derivative Test

1st: The first test is too simply test the left and right side of the critical number(s) to see if the function is increasing/decreasing and then if f is defined at that critical number it is a max/min.

2nd: For the second derivative test, there is a maximum or a minimum if the following are true.

Minimum	Maximum	Test Fails
$f'(c) = 0 \ \wedge \ f''(c) > 0$	$f'(c) = 0 \ \wedge \ f''(c) < 0$	$f'(c) = 0 \ \wedge \ f''(c) = 0$

L'Hospital's Rule

Indeterminate Forms

$\lim\limits_{x \to a} f(x) = \dfrac{0}{0}$	$\lim\limits_{x \to a} f(x) = \dfrac{\pm\infty}{\pm\infty}$	$\lim\limits_{x \to a} f(x) = \pm\dfrac{\infty}{\infty}$	$\lim\limits_{x \to a} f(x) = 0 \cdot \infty$
$\lim\limits_{x \to a} f(x) = \infty - \infty$	$\lim\limits_{x \to a} f(x) = 0^0$	$\lim\limits_{x \to a} f(x) = 1^\infty$	$\lim\limits_{x \to a} f(x) = \infty^0$

Rule

If the limit is one of the following forms:

$$\lim_{x \to a} f(x) = \{0 \cdot \infty, \ \infty - \infty, 0^0, 1^\infty, \infty^0\}$$

and can the be manipulated into on of the following forms:

$$\lim_{x \to a} f(x) \sim \lim_{x \to a} \frac{g(x)}{h(x)} = \left\{\frac{0}{0}, \frac{\pm\infty}{\pm\infty}, \pm\frac{\infty}{\infty}\right\}$$

Then

$$\lim_{x \to a} \frac{g(x)}{h(x)} = \lim_{x \to a} \frac{g'(x)}{h'(x)} = \lim_{x \to a} \frac{g''(x)}{h''(x)} = \cdots \lim_{x \to a} \frac{g^{(n)}(x)}{h^{(n)}(x)}$$

Process

You will need to perform manipulations to the functions in order to use this rule (in general).

The most common scenario is applying a logarithmic rule when you have a exponential function

Let $u = f(x)$, and $v = g(x)$

$$\lim_{x \to a} g(x)^{f(x)} = \lim_{x \to a} v^u = \lim_{x \to a} e^{\ln v^u} = \lim_{x \to a} e^{u \ln v} = \lim_{x \to a} e^{\left(\frac{\ln v}{\frac{1}{u}}\right)} = e^{\lim\limits_{x \to a}\left(\frac{\ln v}{\frac{1}{u}}\right)}$$

$$= e^{\frac{0}{0}} = e^{\frac{\infty}{\infty}} =^{\mathcal{H}} e^{\lim\limits_{x \to a} \frac{\frac{d}{dx} \ln v}{\frac{d}{dx} \frac{1}{u}}}$$

Now you may get the exponent into the appropriate indeterminate form, and take the ratio of derivatives.

Note: The previous problems, is a common problem in school. There are many different manipulations for different functions. To list them all would be impossible, and it would take away from the purpose of learning problem solving skills. You will need to use the entire algebraic, limit, and derivative rules together in order to successfully solve the problems.

Optimization

(In general) Optimization is to simply find two functions that fit a geometric shape i.e. one that represents the geometry, and the other to fit the number given in the problem e.g. area of rectangle with perimeter P. Rearrange to plug one function in the other and then use derivative tests to find the max/min(s).

General Idea:

Max are of rectangle with perimeter P

$$A(x, y) = xy, \qquad 2x + 2y = P$$

$$\therefore A(x) = x \left(\frac{P - 2x}{2} \right)$$

Once you find the function that you are trying to optimize, in this case "max area" use the derivative tests to find the values in question.

Business Formulas

Cost Function

$$C(x)$$

Marginal Cost Function

$$C'(x) = \frac{d}{dx} C(x)$$

Demand/Price function (price per unit)

$$p(x)$$

Revenue

$$R(x) = p(x) \cdot x$$

Marginal Revenue

$$R'(x) = \frac{d}{dx} R(x) = p(x) + xp'(x)$$

Profit Function

$$P(x) = R(x) - C(x)$$

Marginal Profit Function

$$P'(x) = R'(x) - C'(x)$$

Average Profit Function

$$\bar{P}(x) = \frac{P(x)}{x}$$

Antiderivatives & Integration

Basic Rules

Power Rule for antiderivatives
$$y' = x^n \;\Rightarrow\; y = \frac{1}{n+1}x^n + C \Leftrightarrow n \neq -1$$

Exponential
$$y' = a^x \;\Rightarrow\; y = \frac{a^x}{\ln(a)} + C$$

Natural Log (case 1)
$$y' = \frac{1}{x} \;\Rightarrow\; y = \ln|x| + C$$

Natural Log (case 2)
$$y' = \frac{1}{ax+b} \;\Rightarrow\; y = \frac{1}{a}\ln|ax+b| + C$$

Natural Log (case 3)
$$y' = \frac{u'(x)}{u(x)} \;\Rightarrow\; y = \ln|u(x)| + C$$

Euler's Number (case 1)
$$y' = e^{ax} \;\Rightarrow\; y = \frac{1}{a}e^{ax} + C$$

Euler's Number (case 2)
$$y' = e^{ax+b} \;\Rightarrow\; y = \frac{1}{a}e^{ax+b} + C$$

Euler's Number (case 3)
$$y' = u'(x)e^{u(x)} \;\Rightarrow\; y = e^{u(x)} + C$$

Anti-Chain-Rule *Substitution Method*
$$y' = f'(g(x))g'(x) \;\Rightarrow\; y = f(g(x)) + C$$

Riemann Sum for Area Approximation

$$A \approx \lim_{n \to \infty} \sum_{i=1}^{n} f(x_i^*)\,\Delta x, \qquad \Delta x = \frac{b-a}{n}, \qquad x_i = a + i \cdot \Delta x$$

$$\sum_{i=1}^{n} c = cn$$

$$\sum_{i=1}^{n} cf(x_i) = c\sum_{i=1}^{n} f(x_i)$$

$$\sum_{i=1}^{n} [f(x_i) \pm g(x_i)] = \sum_{i=1}^{n} f(x_i) \pm \sum_{i=1}^{n} g(x_i)$$

$$\sum_{i=1}^{n} i = \frac{n(n+1)}{2}$$

$$\sum_{i=1}^{n} i^2 = \frac{n(n+1)(2n+1)}{6}$$

$$\sum_{i=1}^{n} i^3 = \left[\frac{n(n+1)}{2}\right]^2$$

Area Approximation Rules

Midpoint Rule

$$\int_a^b f(x)\,dx \approx \frac{b-a}{n}\left[f\left(\frac{x_1+x_2}{2}\right)+f\left(\frac{x_2+x_3}{2}\right)+\cdots\right]$$

Trapezoid Rule

$$\int_a^b f(x)\,dx \approx \frac{b-a}{2n}\left[f(x_1)+2f(x_2)+2f(x_3)+\cdots+2f(x_{n-1})+f(x_n)\right]$$

Simpson Rule

$$\int_a^b f(x)\,dx \approx \frac{b-a}{3n}\left[f(x_1)+4f(x_2)+2f(x_3)+4f(x_4)+\cdots+2f(x_{n-2})+4f(x_{n-1})+f(x_n)\right]$$

The Integral Notation $\int$

$$\lim_{n\to\infty}\sum_{i=1}^n f(x_i^*)\,\Delta x \equiv \int_a^b f(x)\,dx$$

Definite Integral Properties

$$\int_a^b f(x)\,dx = F(b)-F(a)$$

$$\int_a^a f(x)\,dx = 0$$

$$\int_{-a}^a f(x)\,dx = 0$$

$$\Leftrightarrow f(-x) = -f(x)\ (\text{odd})$$

$$\int_{-a}^a f(x)\,dx = 2\int_0^a f(x)$$

$$\Leftrightarrow f(-x) = f(x)\ (\text{even})$$

$$\int_a^b c\,dx = c(b-a)$$

$$\int_a^b cf(x)\,dx = c\int_a^b f(x)\,dx$$

$$\int_a^b [f(x)\pm g(x)]\,dx = \int_a^b f(x)\,dx \pm \int_a^b g(x)\,dx$$

$$\int_a^b f(x)\,dx = \int_a^k f(x)\,dx + \int_k^a f(x)\,dx$$

NOTE:

$$\int f(x) \cdot g(x)\, dx \neq \int g(x)\, dx \cdot \int f(x)\, dx \qquad \left| \quad \int_a^b f(x)\, dx = -\int_b^a f(x)\, dx \right.$$

Fundamental Theorems

Let $f(x) = u$ and $g(x) = v$ for the following:

i)
$$y = \int_u^v f(t)\, dt \quad \Rightarrow \quad y' = f(v) \cdot v' - f(u) \cdot u'$$

$$y = \int_a^v f(t)\, dt \quad \Rightarrow \quad y' = f(v) \cdot v' - f(a) \cdot a' = f(v) \cdot v' - 0 = f(v) \cdot v'$$

$$y = \int_u^b f(t)\, dt \quad \Rightarrow \quad y' = f(b) \cdot b' - f(u) \cdot u' = 0 - f(u) \cdot u' = -f(u) \cdot u'$$

Limit Definition of a Definite Integral

ii)
$$\lim_{n \to \infty} \sum_{i=1}^n f(x_i^*)\, \Delta x = \int_a^b f(x)\, dx = F(b) - F(a)$$

$$\Delta x = \frac{b - a}{n}, \qquad x_i = a + i \cdot \Delta x$$

Differential Equation (1ˢᵗ order)

$$y' = f'(x) \Rightarrow \frac{dy}{dx} = f'(x) \Rightarrow dy = f'(x)dx \Rightarrow \int dy = \int f'(x)\, dx$$

$$\Rightarrow \quad y + c_1 = f(x) + c_2 \Rightarrow y = f(x) + c_2 - c_1 = f(x) + c_3 \equiv f(x) + C$$

Common Integrals

$$\int dx = x + C$$

$$\int x^2 \, dx = \frac{1}{3}x^3 + C$$

$$\int e^x \, dx = e^x + C$$

$$\int \frac{1}{x+1} \, dx = \ln|x+1| + C$$

$$\int e^u u' \, du = e^u + C$$

$$\int u' \cos u \, du = \sin u + C$$

$$\int u' \csc u \sec u \, du = -\csc u + C$$

$$\int \frac{u'}{\sqrt{1-u^2}} \, du = \arcsin u + C$$

$$\int k \, dx = kx + C$$

$$\int x^n \, dx = \frac{1}{n+1}x^{n+1} + C$$

$$\Leftrightarrow n \neq -1$$

$$\int e^{ax} \, dx = \frac{1}{a}e^{ax} + C$$

$$\int \frac{1}{ax+b} \, dx = \frac{1}{a}\ln|ax+b| + C$$

$$\int \frac{u'}{u} \, du = \ln|u| + C$$

$$\int u' \sin u \, du = -\cos u + C$$

$$\int u' \sec u \tan u \, du = \sec u + C$$

$$\int \frac{-u'}{\sqrt{1-u^2}} \, du = \arccos u + C$$

$$\int x \, dx = \frac{1}{2}x^2 + C$$

$$\int \frac{1}{x} \, dx = \ln|x| + C$$

$$\int e^{ax+b} \, dx = \frac{1}{a}e^{ax+b} + C$$

$$\int f(u)u' \, du = F(u) + C$$

$$\int_a^b f(x) = F(b) - F(a)$$

$$\int u' \sec^2 u \, du = \tan u + C$$

$$\int u' \csc^2 u \, du = -\cot u + C$$

$$\int \frac{u'}{1+u^2} \, du = \arctan u + C$$

Definite Integral Rules

Substitution

$$\int_a^b f(g(x))g'(x)\,dx = \int_{g(a)}^{g(b)} f(u)\,du$$

Integration by Parts

$$\int_a^b f(x)g'(x)\,dx = f(x)g(x)|_a^b - \int_a^b g(x)f'(x)\,dx$$

Let

$u = f(x)$	$dv = g'(x)dx$
$du = f'(x)dx$	$v = g(x)$

Then

$$\int_a^b u\,dv = uv|_a^b - \int_a^b v\,du$$

INTEGRAL CALCULUS (CALCL II)

Parametric and Polar Operations

Notations

$$x = x(t), \qquad t \in [a,b]$$

$$x'(t) = \frac{dx}{dt} \equiv \dot{x}$$

$$y = y(t), \qquad t \in [a,b]$$

$$y'(t) = \frac{dy}{dt} \equiv \dot{y}$$

First Derivative

$$\frac{y'(t)}{x'(t)} = \frac{\frac{dy}{dt}}{\frac{dx}{dt}} = \frac{dy}{dt}\cdot\frac{dt}{dx} = \frac{dy}{dx}$$

Second Derivative

$$\frac{d^2y}{dx^2} = \frac{d}{dx}\frac{dy}{dx} = \frac{d}{dx}\frac{y'(t)}{x'(t)} = \frac{x'(t)\frac{d}{dx}y'(t) - y'(t)\frac{d}{dx}x'(t)}{[x'(t)]^2} = \frac{x'(t)\frac{d}{dx}\frac{dy}{dt} - y'(t)\frac{d}{dx}\frac{dx}{dt}}{[x'(t)]^2}$$

$$= \frac{x'(t)\frac{d}{dt}\frac{dy}{dx} - y'(t)\frac{d}{dt}\frac{dx}{dx}}{[x'(t)]^2} = \frac{x'(t)\frac{d}{dt}\frac{dy}{dx} - y'(t)\frac{d}{dt}(1)}{[x'(t)]^2} = \frac{x'(t)\frac{d}{dt}\frac{dy}{dx}}{[x'(t)]^2} = \frac{\frac{d}{dt}\frac{dy}{dx}}{x'(t)}$$

$$\therefore \frac{d^2y}{dx^2} = \frac{\frac{d}{dt}\frac{dy}{dx}}{\frac{dx}{dt}}$$

Trigonometric

$$x^2 + y^2 = r^2 \qquad \Big| \; x = r\cos\theta \qquad \Big| \; y = r\sin\theta \qquad \Big| \; \theta = \arctan\frac{y}{x}$$

Circle

$$\left[\frac{x-h}{r}\right]^2 + \left[\frac{y-k}{r}\right]^2 = 1 = (\cos\theta)^2 + (\sin\theta)^2 \Rightarrow \frac{x-h}{r} = \cos\theta \wedge \frac{y-k}{r} = \sin\theta, \qquad \theta \in [0, 2\pi]$$

Ellipse

$$\left[\frac{x-h}{a}\right]^2 + \left[\frac{y-k}{b}\right]^2 = 1 = (\cos\theta)^2 + (\sin\theta)^2 \Rightarrow \frac{x-h}{a} = \cos\theta \wedge \frac{y-k}{b} = \sin\theta, \qquad \theta \in [0, 2\pi]$$

Polar Derivative

$$\frac{dy}{dx} = \frac{\frac{dy}{d\theta}}{\frac{dr}{d\theta}} = \frac{\frac{d}{d\theta}r\sin\theta}{\frac{d}{d\theta}r\cos\theta} = \frac{r(\theta)\cos\theta + r'(\theta)\sin\theta}{r'(\theta)\cos\theta - r(\theta)\sin\theta}$$

Polar Equations for Ellipse

$\dfrac{x^2}{a^2} + \dfrac{y^2}{b^2} = 1$	$0 \le a < b$	$c^2 = a^2 - b^2$ Foci $(\pm c, 0)$ Vertices $(\pm a, 0)$
$\dfrac{x^2}{b^2} + \dfrac{y^2}{a^2} = 1$	$0 \le a < b$	$c^2 = a^2 - b^2$ Foci $(0, \pm c,)$ Vertices $(0, \pm a,)$

$e < 1$	$e = $ eccentricity, $d = $ diretrix	
$r(\theta) = \dfrac{ed}{a \pm e\cos\theta}$	$r(\theta) = \dfrac{ed}{a \pm e\sin\theta}$	$c^2 = a^2 - b^2$ $e = \dfrac{c}{a}$

Polar Equations for Hyperbola

$$\dfrac{x^2}{a^2} - \dfrac{y^2}{b^2} = 1$$	$c^2 = a^2 + b^2$ Foci $(\pm c, 0)$ Vertices $(\pm a, 0)$ Asymptotes $y = \pm\dfrac{b}{a}x$
$$\dfrac{y^2}{a^2} - \dfrac{x^2}{b^2} = 1$$	$c^2 = a^2 + b^2$ Foci $(0, \pm c,)$ Vertices $(0, \pm a,)$ Asymptotes $y = \pm\dfrac{a}{b}x$

$e > 11$	$e = $ eccentricity, $d = $ diretrix	$c^2 = a^2 + b^2$
$r(\theta) = \dfrac{ed}{a \pm e\cos\theta}$	$r(\theta) = \dfrac{ed}{a \pm e\sin\theta}$	$e = \dfrac{c}{a}$

Polar Equations for Parabola

$e = 1$	$e = $ eccentricity, $d = $ diretrix	$y^2 = 4px, \quad d = -p$ $x^2 = 4py, \quad d = -p$
$r(\theta) = \dfrac{d}{a \pm \cos\theta}$	$r(\theta) = \dfrac{d}{a \pm \sin\theta}$	

Antiderivatives & Integration

Basic Rules

Power Rule for antiderivatives	$y' = x^n \;\Rightarrow\; y = \dfrac{1}{n+1}x^n + C \Leftrightarrow n \neq -1$
Exponential	$y' = a^x \;\Rightarrow\; y = \dfrac{a^x}{\ln(a)} + C$
Natural Log (case 1)	$y' = \dfrac{1}{x} \;\Rightarrow\; y = \ln|x| + C$
Natural Log (case 2)	$y' = \dfrac{1}{ax+b} \;\Rightarrow\; y = \dfrac{1}{a}\ln|ax+b| + C$
Natural Log (case 3)	$y' = \dfrac{u'(x)}{u(x)} \;\Rightarrow\; y = \ln|u(x)| + C$
Euler's Number (case 1)	$y' = e^{ax} \;\Rightarrow\; y = \dfrac{1}{a}e^{ax} + C$
Euler's Number (case 2)	$y' = e^{ax+b} \;\Rightarrow\; y = \dfrac{1}{a}e^{ax+b} + C$
Euler's Number (case 3)	$y' = u'(x)e^{u(x)} \;\Rightarrow\; y = e^{u(x)} + C$
Anti-Chain-Rule *Substitution Method*	$y' = f'(g(x))g'(x) \;\Rightarrow\; y = f(g(x)) + C$

Riemann Sum for Area Approximation

$$A \approx \lim_{n \to \infty} \sum_{i=1}^{n} f(x_i^*)\, \Delta x, \qquad \Delta x = \frac{b-a}{n}, \qquad x_i = a + i \cdot \Delta x$$

$$\sum_{i=1}^{n} c = cn$$

$$\sum_{i=1}^{n} cf(x_i) = c \sum_{i=1}^{n} f(x_i)$$

$$\sum_{i=1}^{n} [f(x_i) \pm g(x_i)] = \sum_{i=1}^{n} f(x_i) \pm \sum_{i=1}^{n} g(x_i)$$

$$\sum_{i=1}^{n} i = \frac{n(n+1)}{2}$$

$$\sum_{i=1}^{n} i^2 = \frac{n(n+1)(2n+1)}{6}$$

$$\sum_{i=1}^{n} i^3 = \left[\frac{n(n+1)}{2}\right]^2$$

Area Approximation Rules

Midpoint Rule

$$\int_a^b f(x)\, dx \approx \frac{b-a}{n}\left[f\left(\frac{x_1 + x_2}{2}\right) + f\left(\frac{x_2 + x_3}{2}\right) + \cdots \right]$$

Trapezoid Rule

$$\int_a^b f(x)\, dx \approx \frac{b-a}{2n}\left[f(x_1) + 2f(x_2) + 2f(x_3) + \cdots + 2f(x_{n-1}) + f(x_n) \right]$$

The Integral Notation $\int$

$$\lim_{n \to \infty} \sum_{i=1}^{n} f(x_i^*)\, \Delta x \equiv \int_a^b f(x)\, dx$$

Definite Integral Properties

$$\int_a^b f(x)\, dx = F(b) - F(a)$$

$$\int_a^b c\, dx = c(b-a)$$

$$\int_a^a f(x)\,dx = 0$$

$$\int_{-a}^a f(x)\,dx = 0$$

$$\Leftrightarrow f(-x) = -f(x)\ \text{(odd)}$$

$$\int_{-a}^a f(x)\,dx = 2\int_0^a f(x)$$

$$\Leftrightarrow f(-x) = f(x)\ \text{(even)}$$

NOTE:

$$\int f(x)\cdot g(x)\,dx \neq \int g(x)\,dx \cdot \int f(x)\,dx$$

$$\int_a^b cf(x)\,dx = c\int_a^b f(x)\,dx$$

$$\int_a^b [f(x)\pm g(x)]\,dx = \int_a^b f(x)\,dx \pm \int_a^b g(x)\,dx$$

$$\int_a^b f(x)\,dx = \int_a^k f(x)\,dx + \int_k^a f(x)\,dx$$

$$\int_a^b f(x)\,dx = -\int_b^a f(x)\,dx$$

Fundamental Theorems

Let $f(x) = u$ and $g(x) = v$ for the following:

i)
$$y = \int_u^v f(t)dt \quad \Rightarrow \quad y' = f(v)\cdot v' - f(u)\cdot u'$$

$$y = \int_a^v f(t)dt \quad \Rightarrow \quad y' = f(v)\cdot v' - f(a)\cdot a' = f(v)\cdot v' - 0 = f(v)\cdot v'$$

$$y = \int_u^b f(t)dt \quad \Rightarrow \quad y' = f(b)\cdot b' - f(u)\cdot u' = 0 - f(u)\cdot u' = -f(u)\cdot u'$$

Limit Definition of a Definite Integral

ii)
$$\lim_{n\to\infty} \sum_{i=1}^n f(x_i^*)\,\Delta x = \int_a^b f(x)\,dx = F(b) - F(a)$$

$$\Delta x = \frac{b-a}{n}, \qquad x_i = a + i\cdot \Delta x$$

Differential Equation (1st order)

$$y' = f'(x) \Rightarrow \frac{dy}{dx} = f'(x) \Rightarrow dy = f'(x)dx \Rightarrow \int dy = \int f'(x)\,dx$$

$$\Rightarrow y + c_1 = f(x) + c_2 \Rightarrow y = f(x) + c_2 - c_1 = f(x) + c_3 \equiv f(x) + C$$

Common Integrals

$$\int dx = x + C$$

$$\int x^2\,dx = \frac{1}{3}x^3 + C$$

$$\int e^x\,dx = e^x + C$$

$$\int \frac{1}{x+1}\,dx = \ln|x+1| + C$$

$$\int e^u u'\,du = e^u + C$$

$$\int u' \cos u\,du = \sin u + C$$

$$\int u' \csc u \sec u\,du = -\csc u + C$$

$$\int \frac{u'}{\sqrt{1-u^2}}\,du = \arcsin u + C$$

$$\int k\,dx = kx + C$$

$$\int x^n\,dx = \frac{1}{n+1}x^{n+1} + C$$
$$\Leftrightarrow n \neq -1$$

$$\int e^{ax}\,dx = \frac{1}{a}e^{ax} + C$$

$$\int \frac{1}{ax+b}\,dx = \frac{1}{a}\ln|ax+b| + C$$

$$\int \frac{u'}{u}\,du = \ln|u| + C$$

$$\int u' \sin u\,du = -\cos u + C$$

$$\int u' \sec u \tan u\,du = \sec u + C$$

$$\int \frac{-u'}{\sqrt{1-u^2}}\,du = \arccos u + C$$

$$\int x\,dx = \frac{1}{2}x^2 + C$$

$$\int \frac{1}{x}\,dx = \ln|x| + C$$

$$\int e^{ax+b}\,dx = \frac{1}{a}e^{ax+b} + C$$

$$\int f(u)u'\,du = F(u) + C$$

$$\int_a^b f(x) = F(b) - F(a)$$

$$\int u' \sec^2 u\,du = \tan u + C$$

$$\int u' \csc^2 u\,du = -\cot u + C$$

$$\int \frac{u'}{1+u^2}\,du = \arctan u + C$$

Definite Integral Rules

Substitution

$$\int_a^b f(g(x))g'(x)\,dx = \int_{g(a)}^{g(b)} f(u)\,du$$

Integration by Parts

$$\int_a^b f(x)g'(x)\,dx = f(x)g(x)|_a^b - \int_a^b g(x)f'(x)\,dx$$

Let

$u = f(x)$	$dv = g'(x)dx$
$du = f'(x)dx$	$v = g(x)$

Then

$$\int_a^b u\,dv = uv|_a^b - \int_a^b v\,du$$

Trig Substitution

$\sqrt{a^2 - x^2}$	$\sqrt{a^2 + x^2}$	$\sqrt{x^2 - a^2}$
$1 - \sin^2\theta = \cos^2\theta$	$1 + \tan^2\theta = \sec^2\theta$	$\sec^2\theta - 1 = \tan^2\theta$
$x = a\sin\theta$	$x = a\tan\theta$	$x = a\sec\theta$
$\theta \in \left[-\dfrac{\pi}{2}, \dfrac{\pi}{2}\right]$	$\theta \in \left(-\dfrac{\pi}{2}, \dfrac{\pi}{2}\right)$	$\theta \in \left[0, \dfrac{\pi}{2}\right) \vee \theta \in \left[\pi, \dfrac{3\pi}{2}\right)$

Trig Identity

$$\int \tan x\,dx = \int \frac{\sin x}{\cos x}\,dx = -\int \frac{1}{\cos x} \cdot (-\sin x)\,dx, \qquad \frac{d}{dx}\ln[u(x)] = \frac{1}{u}\frac{du}{dx}$$

$$= -\ln|\cos x| + C = \ln\left|\frac{1}{\cos x}\right| + C = \ln|\sec x| + C$$

Partial Fractions

$$\frac{p(x)}{x(x+1)} = \frac{A}{x} + \frac{B}{x+1}$$

$$\frac{p(x)}{[x^2(x+1)]} = \frac{A}{x} + \frac{B}{x^2} + \frac{C}{x+1}$$

$$\frac{p(x)}{x(x^2+1)} = \frac{A}{x} + \frac{Bx+C}{x^2+1}$$

$$\frac{p(x)}{x(x^2+1)^2} = \frac{A}{x} + \frac{Bx+C}{x^2+1} + \frac{Dx+E}{(x^2+1)^2}$$

Integration Steps

Ask yourself the following questions:

1. Is the integrand in integratable form?
2. Can I perform a function or trig-identity manipulation?
3. Should I use U-Substitution or Trig-Substitution?
4. Integration by Parts?
5. Partial fraction decomposition?

*For a **definite integral** always check to see if the function is defined on the bounds*

Improper Integration

Infinite Bounds

$$\int_{-\infty}^{+\infty} f(x)\,dx = \int_{-\infty}^{0} f(x)\,dx + \int_{0}^{+\infty} f(x)\,dx = \lim_{t_1 \to -\infty} \int_{t_1}^{0} f(x)\,dx + \lim_{t_2 \to \infty} \int_{0}^{t_2} f(x)\,dx$$

Undefined Bounds

$$\int_{a}^{b} f(x)\,dx, x \in (a,b) \Rightarrow \lim_{t_1 \to a^-} \int_{t_1}^{0} f(x)\,dx + \lim_{t_2 \to b^+} \int_{0}^{t_2} f(x)\,dx$$

Areas, Volumes, and Curve Length

Area with respect to an axis

Cartesian

$x - axis$

$$A = \int_a^b f(x)\, dx \Leftrightarrow f(x) \geq 0 \; \forall_x \in [a, b]$$

$y - axis$

$$A = \int_c^d g(y)\, dy \Leftrightarrow g(y) \geq 0 \; \forall_y \in [c, d]$$

Area between curves

Given two curves $f \wedge g$ set them equal to each other to find all x-coordinates of intersection.

$$A = \int_a^b [f(x) - g(x)]\, dx \Leftrightarrow f(x) \geq g(x) \; \forall_x \in [a, b]$$

or

$$A = \int_{x_i}^{x^{i+1}} |f(x) - g(x)|\, dx = \left| \int_{x_1}^{x_2} f(x) - g(x)\, dx \right| + \left| \int_{x_2}^{x_3} f(x) - g(x)\, dx \right| + \cdots$$

Polar Area

$$A = \frac{1}{2} \int_{\theta_1}^{\theta_2} [r(\theta)]^2 \, d\theta \quad \wedge \quad A = \frac{1}{2} \int_{\theta_1}^{\theta_2} ([R(\theta)]^2 - [r(\theta)])^2 \, d\theta$$

Volume about an axis (Disk Method)

$x - axis$

$$V = \pi \int_a^b [f(x)]^2 \, dx \Leftrightarrow f(x) \geq 0 \; \forall_x \in [a, b]$$

$y - axis$

$$V = \pi \int_c^d [g(y)]^2 \, dy \Leftrightarrow g(y) \geq 0 \; \forall_y \in [c, d]$$

Volume between curves (Washer Method)

Given two curves $f \wedge g$ set them equal to each other to find all x-coordinates of intersection.

$$V = \pi \int_a^b ([f(x)]^2 - [g(x)]^2)\, dx \Leftrightarrow f(x) \geq g(x) \; \forall_x \in [a, b]$$

Cylindrical Shell Method

Rotate about $y - axis$

$$V = \int_a^b 2\pi x f(x)\, dx$$

Rotate about $x - axis$

$$V = \int_c^d 2\pi y g(y)\, dy$$

Arc Length

Cartesian

$$L = \int_a^b \sqrt{1 - [f'(x)]^2}\, dx$$

Polar

$$L = \int_{\theta_1}^{\theta_1} \sqrt{[r(\theta)]^2 - [r'(\theta)]^2}\, d\theta$$

Parametric

$$L = \int_{t_1}^{t_2} \sqrt{[x'(t)]^2 - [y'(t)]^2}\, dt$$

Surface Area

Cartesian

$$S_{x-axis} = \int_a^b 2\pi f(x)\, dl,$$

$$dl = \sqrt{1 - [f'(x)]^2}\, dx$$

Polar

$$S_{x-axis} = \int_{\theta_1}^{\theta_1} 2\pi r(\theta) \cos\theta\, dl$$

$$dl = \sqrt{[r(\theta)]^2 - [r'(\theta)]^2}\, d\theta$$

Parametric

$$S_{x-axis} = \int_{t_1}^{t_2} 2\pi y(t)\, dl,$$

$$dl = \sqrt{[x'(t)]^2 - [y'(t)]^2}\, d\theta$$

$$S_{y-axis} = \int_a^b 2\pi g(y)\, dl,$$

$$dl = \sqrt{1 - [g'(y)]^2}\, dy$$

$$S_{y-axis} = \int_{\theta_1}^{\theta_1} 2\pi r(\theta) \sin\theta\, dl$$

$$dl = \sqrt{[r(\theta)]^2 - [r'(\theta)]^2}\, d\theta$$

$$S_{y-axis} = \int_{t_1}^{t_2} 2\pi x(t)\, dl,$$

$$dl = \sqrt{[x'(t)]^2 - [y'(t)]^2}\, d\theta$$

Physics Applications

Center of Mass with Constant Density

x-coordinate

y-coordinate

$$\bar{x} = \frac{M_y}{m}$$

$$M_y = \rho \int_a^b x f(x)\, dx$$

$$m = \rho A = \rho \int_a^b f(x)\, dx,\ f(x) \geq 0 \in [a,b]$$

$$\therefore \bar{x} = \frac{1}{A} \int_a^b x f(x)\, dx$$

$$\bar{x} = \frac{1}{A} \int_a^b x[f(x) - g(x)]\, dx,\ f \geq g \in [a,b]$$

$$\bar{y} = \frac{M_x}{m}$$

$$M_x = \frac{\rho}{2} \int_a^b [f(x)]^2\, dx$$

$$m = \rho A = \rho \int_a^b f(x)\, dx,\ f(x) \geq 0 \in [a,b]$$

$$\therefore \bar{y} = \frac{1}{2A} \int_a^b [f(x)]^2\, dx$$

$$M_x = \frac{1}{2A} \int_a^b [f(x)]^2 - [g(x)]^2\, dx,\ f \geq g \in [a,b]$$

Sequences vs Series

Sequence

$$a_n = \{a_0, a_1, a_2, \dots\}$$

Series

$$\sum_{n=0}^{\infty} a_n = a_0 + a_1 + a_2 + \cdots$$

Sequence Tests

a_n **Converges**

$$\lim_{n \to \infty} a_n = L$$

a_n **Diverges**

$$\lim_{n \to \infty} a_n = \pm\infty \vee DNE$$

Series Tests

Test	Form	Condition	Diverges	Converges
Geometric	$\displaystyle\sum_{n=1}^{\infty} ar^{n-1}$		$\lvert r\rvert \geq 1$	$\lvert r\rvert < 1 \quad S = \dfrac{a}{1-r}$
P-Series	$\displaystyle\sum_{n=1}^{\infty} \dfrac{1}{n^p}$		$p \leq 1$	$p > 1$
Integral Test	$\displaystyle\sum_{n=1}^{\infty} a_n$	a_n is positive and decreasing on $[1, \infty)$	$\displaystyle\int_1^{\infty} f(x)dx = \infty$ $e.\,g.\ a_n = \dfrac{1}{n^2}$ $\Rightarrow f(x) = \dfrac{1}{x^2}$	$\displaystyle\int_1^{\infty} f(x)dx = k$
Comparison	$\displaystyle\sum_{n=1}^{\infty} a_n$	a_n, b_n are positive	$a_n \geq b_n\ \forall_n$ $\Leftrightarrow b_n$ diverges	$a_n \leq b_n \forall_n$ $\Leftrightarrow b_n$ converges

			Σb_n **Diverges**	Σb_n **Converges**
Limit Comparison	$\sum_{n=1}^{\infty} a_n$	a_n, b_n are positive $\lim_{n\to\infty} \dfrac{a_n}{b_n} = k, \quad k > 0$		
Alternating Series	$\sum_{n=1}^{\infty} (-1)^{n-1} c_n$	$c_n > 0$	Does not show divergence	$c_{n+1} \leq c_n \ \forall_n$ & $\lim_{n\to\infty} c_n = 0$
Ratio	$\sum_{n=1}^{\infty} a_n$		$\lim_{n\to\infty}\left\|\dfrac{a_{n+1}}{a_n}\right\| > 1$ or $= \infty$	$\lim_{n\to\infty}\left\|\dfrac{a_{n+1}}{a_n}\right\| < 1$
Root	$\sum_{n=1}^{\infty} a_n$		$\lim_{n\to\infty} \sqrt[n]{\|a_n\|} > 1$ or $= \infty$	$\lim_{n\to\infty} \sqrt[n]{\|a_n\|} < 1$

Test for Absolute/Conditional Convergence	**Absolutely Convergent**	**Conditionally Convergent**
If $\sum_{n=1}^{\infty} a_n$ Converges then	$\sum_{n=1}^{\infty} \|a_n\|$ Converges	$\sum_{n=1}^{\infty} \|a_n\|$ Diverges

If all else fails, perform "The nth Term for Divergence Test" i.e. if $\lim_{n\to\infty} a_n \neq 0$ or DNE then the sum diverges—*does not show convergence.*

Taylor series

$$f(x) \approx \frac{f^{(n)}(a)}{n!}(x-a)^n = f(x) + f'(x)(x-a) + \frac{f''(x)}{2!}(x-a)^2 + \frac{f'''(x)}{3!}(x-1)^3 + \cdots$$

Maclaurin Series

$$f(x) \approx \frac{f^{(n)}(0)}{n!}(x)^n = f(0) + f'(0)x + \frac{f''(0)}{2!}x^2 + \frac{f'''(0)}{3!}x^3 + \cdots$$

Power Series

$$\frac{1}{1-u} = \sum_{n=0}^{\infty} [u]^n$$

Radius/Interval of Converges

The ROC and interval of convergence for a function is found by putting f into it's power series representation, and then applying, in general, either "geometric series test", "ratio test", and or "root test". **Note**: The ratio/root test require you to plug the interval ends back in to the series, and use whatever test is necessary to find if the series is divergent/convergent at that end-point.

From $|x - a| < R$

$$I = [a - R, a + R] \qquad \Big| \; I = [a - R, a + R) \qquad \Big| \; I = (a - R, a + R] \qquad \Big| \; I = (a - R, a + R)$$

3D Calculus

Magnitude

$$\vec{v} = \mathbf{v} = \langle v_1, v_2, v_3 \rangle \;\; \Rightarrow \;\; |\vec{v}| = \|\mathbf{v}\| = \sqrt{v_1^2 + v_2^2 + v_3^2}$$

Unit Vectors

$$\hat{v} = \frac{\vec{v}}{|\vec{v}|} \;\; \equiv \;\; \hat{\mathbf{v}} = \frac{\mathbf{v}}{\|\mathbf{v}\|}$$

$$\hat{\imath} \equiv \mathbf{i} \qquad\qquad\qquad \Big| \; \hat{\jmath} \equiv \mathbf{j} \qquad\qquad\qquad \Big| \; \hat{k} \equiv \mathbf{k}$$
$$\hat{\imath} = \langle 1, 0, 0 \rangle \qquad\qquad \Big| \; \hat{\jmath} = \langle 0, 1, 0 \rangle \qquad\qquad \Big| \; \hat{k} = \langle 1, 0, 0 \rangle$$

Note:
$$\vec{v} = \langle v_1, v_2, v_3 \rangle = v_1 \langle 1, 0, 0 \rangle + v_2 \langle 0, 1, 0 \rangle + v_3 \langle 0, 0, 1 \rangle = v_1 \hat{\imath} + v_2 \hat{\jmath} + v_3 \hat{k} = v_1 \mathbf{i} + v_2 \mathbf{j} + v_3 \mathbf{k}$$

Dot/Cross Product

Dot

$$\vec{a} \cdot \vec{b} = \mathbf{a} \cdot \mathbf{b}$$

$$= \langle a_1, a_2, a_3 \rangle \cdot \langle b_1, b_2, b_3 \rangle$$

$$= a_1 b_1 + a_2 b_2 + a_3 b_3$$

Properties

$$\mathbf{a} \cdot \mathbf{a} = \|\mathbf{a}\|^2 \qquad\qquad\qquad \mathbf{a} \cdot \mathbf{b} = \mathbf{b} \cdot \mathbf{a}$$

$$\mathbf{a} \cdot (\mathbf{b} + \mathbf{c}) = \mathbf{a} \cdot \mathbf{b} + \mathbf{a} \cdot \mathbf{c} \qquad (\mathbf{ka}) \cdot \mathbf{b} = \mathrm{k}(\mathbf{a} \cdot \mathbf{b}) = \mathbf{a} \cdot (\mathbf{kb})$$

Cross

$$\vec{a} \times \vec{b} = \mathbf{a} \times \mathbf{b} = \langle a_1, a_2, a_3 \rangle \times \langle b_1, b_2, b_3 \rangle$$

$$= \begin{vmatrix} \hat{\imath} & \hat{\jmath} & \hat{k} \\ a_1 & a_2 & a_3 \\ b_1 & b_2 & b_3 \end{vmatrix}$$

$$= \begin{vmatrix} a_2 & a_3 \\ b_2 & b_3 \end{vmatrix} \vec{\imath} - \begin{vmatrix} a_1 & a_3 \\ b_1 & b_3 \end{vmatrix} \vec{\jmath} + \begin{vmatrix} a_1 & a_2 \\ b_1 & b_2 \end{vmatrix} \vec{k}$$

$$= [a_2 b_3 - b_2 a_3] \vec{\imath} - [a_1 b_3 - b_1 a_3] \vec{\jmath} + [a_1 b_2 - b_1 a_2] \vec{k}$$

Properties

$$\mathbf{a} \times \mathbf{b} = -\mathbf{b} \times \mathbf{a} \qquad (\mathbf{ka}) \times \mathbf{b} = \mathrm{k}(\mathbf{a} \times \mathbf{b}) \qquad \mathbf{a} \cdot (\mathbf{b} \times \mathbf{c}) = (\mathbf{a} \times \mathbf{b}) \cdot \mathbf{c}$$
$$= \mathbf{a} \times (\mathbf{kb})$$

$$(\mathbf{a} + \mathbf{b}) \times \mathbf{c} = \mathbf{a} \times \mathbf{c} + \mathbf{b} \times \mathbf{c} \qquad \mathbf{a} \times (\mathbf{b} + \mathbf{c}) = \mathbf{a} \times \mathbf{b} + \mathbf{a} \times \mathbf{c} \qquad \mathbf{a} \times (\mathbf{b} \times \mathbf{c}) = (\mathbf{a} \cdot \mathbf{c})\mathbf{b}$$
$$- (\mathbf{a} \cdot \mathbf{b})\mathbf{c}$$

Angles Between Vectors

$$\vec{a} \cdot \vec{b} = |\vec{a}||\vec{b}| \cos \theta \qquad\qquad\qquad |\vec{a} \times \vec{b}| = |\vec{a}||\vec{b}| \sin \theta$$

$$\Rightarrow \theta = \arccos \frac{\vec{a} \cdot \vec{b}}{|\vec{a}||\vec{b}|} \qquad\qquad\qquad \Rightarrow \theta = \arcsin \frac{|\vec{a} \times \vec{b}|}{|\vec{a}||\vec{b}|}$$

Projections

Scalar | **Vector**

$$\text{comp}_{\vec{a}}\vec{b} = \frac{\vec{a} \cdot \vec{b}}{|\vec{a}|} \qquad\qquad \text{proj}_{\vec{a}}\vec{b} = \frac{\vec{a} \cdot \vec{b}}{|\vec{a}|^2}\vec{a}$$

Areas/Volume

Triangle

$$A = \frac{1}{2}|\vec{a} \times \vec{b}|$$

Parallelogram

$$A = |\vec{a} \times \vec{b}|$$

Parallelepiped

$$V = |\vec{a} \cdot (\vec{b} \times \vec{c})|$$

Line

$$\mathcal{L}(t) = P_0 + t\vec{v}$$

$$= (x_0, y_0, z_0) + t\langle a, b, c\rangle$$

$$= \langle x_0 + at, y_0 + bt, z_0 + ct \rangle$$

$$= (x_0, y_0, z_0) + t\langle x - x_0, y - y_0, z - z_0\rangle$$

$$\vec{v} = \overrightarrow{P_1 P_2} = P_2 - P_1$$

$$= (x, y, z) - (x_0, y_0, z_0)$$

$$= \langle x - x_0, y - y_0, z - z_0\rangle$$

$$= \langle a, b, c\rangle$$

Line from tip to tip

A line segment from the tips two vectors beginning from the origin to $\vec{v}_1 \to \vec{v}_2$ is

$$\mathcal{L}(t) = (1 - t)\vec{v}_1 + t\vec{v}_2, \qquad t \in [0, 1]$$

Equation of a Plane

$$ax + by + cz = d \quad \Rightarrow \quad n = \langle a, b, c\rangle \perp \text{surface}$$

n is perpendicular to the surface	$\vec{v}$ is in the plane, $P_0 = (x_0, y_0, z_0)$ (point in plane)

$$n \perp \vec{v} \quad \Rightarrow \quad n \cdot \vec{v} = \langle a, b, c\rangle \cdot \langle x - x_0, y - y_0, z - z_0\rangle = a(x - x_0) + b(y - y_0) + c(z - z_0) = 0$$

Vector Functions
$$\vec{r}(t) = \langle r_1(t), r_2(t), r_3(t)\rangle = \langle f(t), g(t), h(t)\rangle$$

Limit	$\displaystyle\lim_{t \to a} \vec{r}(t) = \langle \lim_{t \to a} f(t) , \lim_{t \to a} g(t) , \lim_{t \to a} h(t) \rangle$
Derivative	$\displaystyle\frac{d\vec{r}}{dt} = \langle f'(t), g'(t), h'(t) \rangle$
Definite Integral	$\displaystyle\int_{t_1}^{t_2} \vec{r}(t)\, dt = \left(\int_{t_1}^{t_2} r_1(t)\, dt \right)\hat{\imath} + \left(\int_{t_1}^{t_2} r_2(t)\, dt \right)\hat{\jmath} + \left(\int_{t_1}^{t_2} r_3(t)\, dt \right)\hat{k}$
Indefinite Integral	$\displaystyle\int \vec{r}(t)\, dt = \left(\int r_1(t)\, dt \right)\hat{\imath} + \left(\int r_2(t)\, dt \right)\hat{\jmath} + \left(\int r_3(t)\, dt \right)\hat{k} + C$

Differentiation Rules

Note: $\vec{v}(t), \vec{u}(t), f(t)$

Function dot Vector

$$\frac{d}{dt}[f(t) \cdot \vec{u}(t)] = \vec{u}(t)\frac{df}{dt} + f(t)\frac{d\vec{u}}{dt}$$

Vector dot Vector

$$\frac{d}{dt}[\vec{u}(t) \cdot \vec{v}(t)] = \vec{v}(t) \cdot \frac{d\vec{u}}{dt} + \vec{u}(t) \cdot \frac{d\vec{v}}{dt}$$

Vector cross Vector

$$\frac{d}{dt}[\vec{u}(t) \times \vec{v}(t)] = \frac{d\vec{u}}{dt} \times \vec{v}(t) + \vec{u}(t) \times \frac{d\vec{v}}{dt}$$

Chain Rule

$$\frac{d}{dt}\vec{u}(f(t)) = \vec{u}'(f(t))f'(t)$$

Arc length

$$L = \int_{t_1}^{t_2} \sqrt{\left[\frac{dr_1}{dt}\right]^2 + \left[\frac{dr_2}{dt}\right]^2 + \left[\frac{dr_3}{dt}\right]^2}\, dt = \int_{t_1}^{t_2} \sqrt{[f'(t)]^2 + [g'(t)]^2 + [h'(t)]^2}\, dt = \int_{t_1}^{t_2} \left|\frac{d\vec{r}}{dt}\right| dt$$

Tangents

Unit Tangent Vector	$\mathbf{T}(t) = \dfrac{\mathbf{r}'(t)}{|\mathbf{r}'(t)|}, \qquad |\mathbf{r}'(t)| = \dfrac{ds}{dt}$
Curvature 1	$\kappa(t) = \left|\dfrac{d\mathbf{T}}{ds}\right| = \left|\dfrac{d\mathbf{T}}{dt}\dfrac{dt}{ds}\right| = \left|\dfrac{\frac{d\mathbf{T}}{dt}}{\frac{ds}{dt}}\right| = \dfrac{|\mathbf{T}'(t)|}{|\mathbf{r}'(t)|}$
Curvature 2 (vector function)	$\kappa(t) = \dfrac{|\mathbf{r}'(t) \times \mathbf{r}''(t)|}{|\mathbf{r}'(t)|^3}$
Curvature 3 (single variable)	$\kappa(x) = \dfrac{|f''(x)|}{(1 + [f'(x)]^2)^{\frac{3}{2}}}$
Curvature 4 (parametric)	$\kappa(t) = \dfrac{|x'(t)y''(t) - y'(t)x''(t)|}{\left[\left(x'(t)\right)^2 + \left(y'(t)\right)^2\right]^{\frac{3}{2}}}$
Normal Vector	$\mathbf{N}(t) = \dfrac{\mathbf{T}'(t)}{|\mathbf{T}'(t)|}$
Binormal Vector	$\mathbf{B}(t) = \mathbf{T}(t) \times \mathbf{N}(t)$

Tangential and Normal Components (acceleration)

Physics Notations

Position	$\vec{r}(t) \equiv \mathbf{r}(t)$
Velocity	$\vec{v}(t) = \vec{r}'(t) = \dfrac{d\vec{r}}{dt} = \dfrac{d\mathbf{r}}{dt} = \mathbf{r}'(t)$
Speed	$v = |\vec{v}(t)| = |\vec{r}'(t)|$
Acceleration	$\vec{a}(t) = \vec{v}'(t) = \vec{r}''(t)$
$\mathbf{T}(t) = \dfrac{\mathbf{r}'(t)}{|\mathbf{r}'(t)|} = \dfrac{\vec{v}(t)}{|\vec{v}(t)|} = \dfrac{\vec{v}}{v}$	$\vec{v} = v\mathbf{T} \Rightarrow \dfrac{d\vec{v}}{dt} = \vec{a} = v'\mathbf{T} + v\mathbf{T}'$
Curvature	$\kappa = \dfrac{|\mathbf{T}'|}{|\mathbf{r}'|} = \dfrac{|\mathbf{T}'|}{v} \Rightarrow \kappa v = |\mathbf{T}'|$
Tangential Component (acceleration)	$a_{\mathrm{T}} = \dfrac{d}{dt}|\vec{r}'| = \dfrac{dv}{dt} = v', \qquad v = |\vec{v}| = |\vec{r}'| \equiv \|\mathbf{r}'\|$
Normal Component (acceleration)	$a_{\mathrm{N}} = \kappa v^2$
Acceleration	$\boldsymbol{a} = v'\mathbf{T} + \kappa v^2\mathbf{N} = a_{\mathrm{T}}\mathbf{T} + a_{\mathrm{N}}\mathbf{N}$
Note:	$\mathbf{T} \cdot \mathbf{T} = 1 \wedge \mathbf{T} \cdot \mathbf{N} = 0$
Dot Product of Velocity and Acceleration	$\vec{v} \cdot \vec{a} = v\mathbf{T} \cdot (v'\mathbf{T} + \kappa v^2\mathbf{N}) = vv'\mathbf{T} \cdot \mathbf{T} + \kappa v^3\mathbf{T} \cdot \mathbf{N} = vv'$
Tangential Acceleration	$a_{\mathrm{T}} = v' = \dfrac{\vec{v} \cdot \vec{a}}{v} = \dfrac{\mathbf{r}'(t) \cdot \mathbf{r}''(t)}{|\mathbf{r}'(t)|}$
Normal Acceleration	$a_{\mathrm{N}} = \kappa v^2 = \dfrac{|\mathbf{r}'(t) \times \mathbf{r}''(t)|}{|\mathbf{r}'(t)|}$

Frenet-Serret Formulas

$$\frac{d\mathbf{T}}{ds} = \kappa\mathbf{N} \qquad\qquad \frac{d\mathbf{N}}{ds} = -\kappa\mathbf{T} + \tau\mathbf{B} \qquad\qquad \frac{d\mathbf{B}}{dx} = -\tau\mathbf{N}$$

Partial Derivatives

Given a multivariable function e.g. $f(x, y, z)$, then a partial derivative is the derivative with respect to a variable where the other variables are treating as constants i.e. *do not implicitly differentiate.*

$\dfrac{\partial f}{\partial x} = f_x = f_x(x, y, z)$	$\dfrac{\partial f}{\partial y} = f_y = f_y(x, y, z)$	$\dfrac{\partial f}{\partial z} = f_z = f_z(x, y, z)$
$\dfrac{\partial^2 f}{\partial x^2} = f_{xx}$	$\dfrac{\partial^2 f}{\partial y^2} = f_{yy}$	$\dfrac{\partial^2 f}{\partial z^2} = f_{zz}$

Mixed Partial

$$\frac{\partial^2 f}{\partial x \partial y} = f_{xy}, \qquad \frac{\partial^2 f}{\partial y \partial x} = f_{yx}$$

Tangent Plane

$$z - z_0 = f_x(x_0, y_0)(x - x_0) + f_y(x_0, y_0)(y - y_0)$$

Chain Rule

$$\frac{dz}{dt} = \frac{\partial z}{\partial x}\frac{dx}{dt} + \frac{\partial z}{\partial y}\frac{dy}{dt}, \qquad x = x(t) \wedge y = y(t)$$

$$\frac{\partial z}{\partial s} = \frac{\partial z}{\partial x}\frac{\partial x}{\partial s} + \frac{\partial z}{\partial y}\frac{\partial y}{\partial s}, \qquad \frac{\partial z}{\partial t} = \frac{\partial z}{\partial x}\frac{\partial x}{\partial t} + \frac{\partial z}{\partial y}\frac{\partial y}{\partial t}, \qquad x = x(s, t) \wedge y = y(s, t)$$

MULTIVARIABLE CALCULUS (CALC III)

Magnitude

$$\vec{v} = \mathbf{v} = \langle v_1, v_2, v_3 \rangle \;\Rightarrow\; |\vec{v}| = \|\mathbf{v}\| = \sqrt{v_1^2 + v_2^2 + v_3^2}$$

Unit Vectors

$$\hat{v} = \frac{\vec{v}}{|\vec{v}|} \;\equiv\; \hat{\mathbf{v}} \equiv \mathbf{u} = \frac{\mathbf{v}}{\|\mathbf{v}\|}$$

$\hat{\imath} \equiv \mathbf{i}$
$\hat{\imath} = \langle 1, 0, 0 \rangle$

$\hat{\jmath} \equiv \mathbf{j}$
$\hat{\jmath} = \langle 0, 1, 0 \rangle$

$\hat{k} \equiv \mathbf{k}$
$\hat{k} = \langle 1, 0, 0 \rangle$

Note:
$$\vec{v} = \langle v_1, v_2, v_3 \rangle = v_1 \langle 1, 0, 0 \rangle + v_2 \langle 0, 1, 0 \rangle + v_3 \langle 0, 0, 1 \rangle = v_1 \hat{\imath} + v_2 \hat{\jmath} + v_3 \hat{k} = v_1 \mathbf{i} + v_2 \mathbf{j} + v_3 \mathbf{k}$$

Dot/Cross Product

Dot

$$\vec{a} \cdot \vec{b} = \mathbf{a} \cdot \mathbf{b}$$

$$= \langle a_1, a_2, a_3 \rangle \cdot \langle b_1, b_2, b_3 \rangle$$

$$= a_1 b_1 + a_2 b_2 + a_3 b_3$$

Properties

$\mathbf{a} \cdot \mathbf{a} = \|\mathbf{a}\|^2$

$\mathbf{a} \cdot (\mathbf{b} + \mathbf{c}) = \mathbf{a} \cdot \mathbf{b} + \mathbf{a} \cdot \mathbf{c}$

$\mathbf{a} \cdot \mathbf{b} = \mathbf{b} \cdot \mathbf{a}$

$(k\mathbf{a}) \cdot \mathbf{b} = k(\mathbf{a} \cdot \mathbf{b}) = \mathbf{a} \cdot (k\mathbf{b})$

Cross

$$\vec{a} \times \vec{b} = \mathbf{a} \times \mathbf{b} = \langle a_1, a_2, a_3 \rangle \times \langle b_1, b_2, b_3 \rangle$$

$$= \begin{vmatrix} \hat{\imath} & \hat{\jmath} & \hat{k} \\ a_1 & a_2 & a_3 \\ b_1 & b_2 & b_3 \end{vmatrix}$$

$$= \begin{vmatrix} a_2 & a_3 \\ b_2 & b_3 \end{vmatrix} \vec{\imath} - \begin{vmatrix} a_1 & a_3 \\ b_1 & b_3 \end{vmatrix} \vec{\jmath} + \begin{vmatrix} a_1 & a_2 \\ b_1 & b_2 \end{vmatrix} \vec{k}$$

$$= [a_2 b_3 - b_2 a_3]\vec{\imath} - [a_1 b_3 - b_1 a_3]\vec{\jmath} + [a_1 b_2 - b_1 a_2]\vec{k}$$

Properties

$$\mathbf{a} \times \mathbf{b} = -\mathbf{b} \times \mathbf{a}$$

$$(k\mathbf{a}) \times \mathbf{b} = k(\mathbf{a} \times \mathbf{b})$$
$$= \mathbf{a} \times (k\mathbf{b})$$

$$\mathbf{a} \cdot (\mathbf{b} \times \mathbf{c}) = (\mathbf{a} \times \mathbf{b}) \cdot \mathbf{c}$$

$$(\mathbf{a} + \mathbf{b}) \times \mathbf{c} = \mathbf{a} \times \mathbf{c} + \mathbf{b} \times \mathbf{c}$$

$$\mathbf{a} \times (\mathbf{b} + \mathbf{c}) = \mathbf{a} \times \mathbf{b} + \mathbf{a} \times \mathbf{c}$$

$$\mathbf{a} \times (\mathbf{b} \times \mathbf{c}) = (\mathbf{a} \cdot \mathbf{c})\mathbf{b}$$
$$- (\mathbf{a} \cdot \mathbf{b})\mathbf{c}$$

Angles Between Vectors

$$\vec{a} \cdot \vec{b} = |\vec{a}||\vec{b}| \cos \theta$$
$$\Rightarrow \theta = \arccos \frac{\vec{a} \cdot \vec{b}}{|\vec{a}||\vec{b}|}$$

$$|\vec{a} \times \vec{b}| = |\vec{a}||\vec{b}| \sin \theta$$
$$\Rightarrow \theta = \arcsin \frac{|\vec{a} \times \vec{b}|}{|\vec{a}||\vec{b}|}$$

Projections

Scalar	Vector
$\text{comp}_{\vec{a}}\vec{b} = \dfrac{\vec{a} \cdot \vec{b}}{|\vec{a}|}$	$\text{proj}_{\vec{a}}\vec{b} = \dfrac{\vec{a} \cdot \vec{b}}{|\vec{a}|^2} \vec{a}$

Areas/Volume

Triangle

$$A = \frac{1}{2}|\vec{a} \times \vec{b}|$$

Parallelogram

$$A = |\vec{a} \times \vec{b}|$$

Parallelepiped

$$V = |\vec{a} \cdot (\vec{b} \times \vec{c})|$$

Line

$$\mathcal{L}(t) = P_0 + t\vec{v}$$
$$= (x_0, y_0, z_0) + t\langle a, b, c\rangle$$
$$= \langle x_0 + at, y_0 + bt, z_0 + ct \rangle$$
$$= (x_0, y_0, z_0) + t\langle x - x_0, y - y_0, z - z_0\rangle$$

$$\vec{v} = \overrightarrow{P_1P_2} = P_2 - P_1$$
$$= (x, y, z) - (x_0, y_0, z_0)$$
$$= \langle x - x_0, y - y_0, z - z_0\rangle$$
$$= \langle a, b, c\rangle$$

Line from tip to tip

A line segment from the tips two vectors beginning from the origin to $\vec{v}_1 \to \vec{v}_2$ is

$$\mathcal{L}(t) = (1-t)\vec{v}_1 + t\vec{v}_2, \qquad t \in [0,1]$$

Equation of a Plane

$$ax + by + cz = d \quad \Rightarrow \quad n = \langle a, b, c \rangle \perp \text{surface}$$

n is perpendicular to the surface	$\vec{v}$ is in the plane, $P_0 = (x_0, y_0, z_0)$ (point in plane)

$$n \perp \vec{v} \quad \Rightarrow \quad n \cdot \vec{v} = \langle a, b, c \rangle \cdot \langle x - x_0, y - y_0, z - z_0 \rangle = a(x - x_0) + b(y - y_0) + c(z - z_0) = 0$$

Vector Functions

$$\vec{r}(t) = \langle r_1(t), r_2(t), r_3(t) \rangle = \langle f(t), g(t), h(t) \rangle$$

Limit	$\lim\limits_{t \to a} \vec{r}(t) = \langle \lim\limits_{t \to a} f(t), \lim\limits_{t \to a} g(t), \lim\limits_{t \to a} h(t) \rangle$
Derivative	$\dfrac{d\vec{r}}{dt} = \langle f'(t), g'(t), h'(t) \rangle$
Definite Integral	$\int_{t_1}^{t_2} \vec{r}(t)\,dt = \left(\int_{t_1}^{t_2} r_1(t)\,dt \right)\hat{\imath} + \left(\int_{t_1}^{t_2} r_2(t)\,dt \right)\hat{\jmath} + \left(\int_{t_1}^{t_2} r_3(t)\,dt \right)\hat{k}$
Indefinite Integral	$\int \vec{r}(t)\,dt = \left(\int r_1(t)\,dt \right)\hat{\imath} + \left(\int r_2(t)\,dt \right)\hat{\jmath} + \left(\int r_3(t)\,dt \right)\hat{k} + C$

Differentiation Rules

Note: $\vec{v}(t), \vec{u}(t), f(t)$

Function dot Vector

$$\frac{d}{dt}[f(t) \cdot \vec{u}(t)] = \vec{u}(t)\frac{df}{dt} + f(t)\frac{d\vec{u}}{dt}$$

Vector dot Vector

$$\frac{d}{dt}[\vec{u}(t) \cdot \vec{v}(t)] = \vec{v}(t) \cdot \frac{d\vec{u}}{dt} + \vec{u}(t) \cdot \frac{d\vec{v}}{dt}$$

Vector cross Vector

$$\frac{d}{dt}[\vec{u}(t) \times \vec{v}(t)] = \frac{d\vec{u}}{dt} \times \vec{v}(t) + \vec{u}(t) \times \frac{d\vec{v}}{dt}$$

Chain Rule

$$\frac{d}{dt}\vec{u}(f(t)) = \vec{u}'(f(t))f'(t)$$

Arc length

$$L = \int_{t_1}^{t_2} \sqrt{\left[\frac{dr_1}{dt}\right]^2 + \left[\frac{dr_2}{dt}\right]^2 + \left[\frac{dr_3}{dt}\right]^2}\,dt = \int_{t_1}^{t_2} \sqrt{[f'(t)]^2 + [g'(t)]^2 + [h'(t)]^2}\,dt = \int_{t_1}^{t_2} \left|\frac{d\vec{r}}{dt}\right|\,dt$$

Tangents

Unit Tangent Vector	$$\mathbf{T}(t) = \frac{\mathbf{r}'(t)}{|\mathbf{r}'(t)|}, \qquad |\mathbf{r}'(t)| = \frac{ds}{dt}$$
Curvature 1	$$\kappa(t) = \left|\frac{d\mathbf{T}}{ds}\right| = \left|\frac{d\mathbf{T}}{dt}\frac{dt}{ds}\right| = \left|\frac{\frac{d\mathbf{T}}{dt}}{\frac{ds}{dt}}\right| = \frac{|\mathbf{T}'(t)|}{|\mathbf{r}'(t)|}$$
Curvature 2 (vector function)	$$\kappa(t) = \frac{|\mathbf{r}'(t) \times \mathbf{r}''(t)|}{|\mathbf{r}'(t)|^3}$$
Curvature 3 (single variable)	$$\kappa(x) = \frac{|f''(x)|}{(1 + [f'(x)]^2)^{\frac{3}{2}}}$$
Curvature 4 (parametric)	$$\kappa(t) = \frac{|x'(t)y''(t) - y'(t)x''(t)|}{\left[(x'(t))^2 + (y'(t))^2\right]^{\frac{3}{2}}}$$
Normal Vector	$$\mathbf{N}(t) = \frac{\mathbf{T}'(t)}{|\mathbf{T}'(t)|}$$
Binormal Vector	$$\mathbf{B}(t) = \mathbf{T}(t) \times \mathbf{N}(t)$$

Tangential and Normal Components (acceleration)

Physics Notations

Position	$\vec{r}(t) \equiv \mathbf{r}(t)$
Velocity	$\vec{v}(t) = \vec{r}'(t) = \dfrac{d\vec{r}}{dt} = \dfrac{d\mathbf{r}}{dt} = \mathbf{r}'(t)$
Speed	$v = |\vec{v}(t)| = |\vec{r}'(t)|$
Acceleration	$\vec{a}(t) = \vec{v}'(t) = \vec{r}''(t)$
$\mathbf{T}(t) = \dfrac{\mathbf{r}'(t)}{|\mathbf{r}'(t)|} = \dfrac{\vec{v}(t)}{|\vec{v}(t)|} = \dfrac{\vec{v}}{v}$	$\vec{v} = v\mathbf{T} \Rightarrow \dfrac{d\vec{v}}{dt} = \vec{a} = v'\mathbf{T} + v\mathbf{T}'$
Curvature	$\kappa = \dfrac{|\mathbf{T}'|}{|\mathbf{r}'|} = \dfrac{|\mathbf{T}'|}{v} \Rightarrow \kappa v = |\mathbf{T}'|$
Tangential Component (acceleration)	$a_{\mathrm{T}} = \dfrac{d}{dt}|\vec{r}'| = \dfrac{dv}{dt} = v', \qquad v = |\vec{v}| = |\vec{r}'| \equiv \|\mathbf{r}'\|$
Normal Component (acceleration)	$a_{\mathrm{N}} = \kappa v^2$
Acceleration	$\boldsymbol{a} = v'\mathbf{T} + \kappa v^2 \mathbf{N} = a_{\mathrm{T}}\mathbf{T} + a_{\mathrm{N}}\mathbf{N}$
Note:	$\mathbf{T} \cdot \mathbf{T} = 1 \wedge \mathbf{T} \cdot \mathbf{N} = 0$
Dot Product of Velocity and Acceleration	$\vec{v} \cdot \vec{a} = v\mathbf{T} \cdot (v'\mathbf{T} + \kappa v^2 \mathbf{N}) = vv'\mathbf{T} \cdot \mathbf{T} + \kappa v^3 \mathbf{T} \cdot \mathbf{N} = vv'$
Tangential Acceleration	$a_{\mathrm{T}} = v' = \dfrac{\vec{v} \cdot \vec{a}}{v} = \dfrac{\mathbf{r}'(t) \cdot \mathbf{r}''(t)}{|\mathbf{r}'(t)|}$
Normal Acceleration	$a_{\mathrm{N}} = \kappa v^2 = \dfrac{|\mathbf{r}'(t) \times \mathbf{r}''(t)|}{|\mathbf{r}'(t)|}$

Frenet-Serret Formulas

$$\frac{d\mathbf{T}}{ds} = \kappa\mathbf{N} \qquad\qquad \frac{d\mathbf{N}}{ds} = -\kappa\mathbf{T} + \tau\mathbf{B} \qquad\qquad \frac{d\mathbf{B}}{dx} = -\tau\mathbf{N}$$

Partial Derivatives

Given a multivariable function e.g. $f(x, y, z)$, then a partial derivative is the derivative with respect to a variable where the other variables are treating as constants i.e. *do not implicitly differentiate.*

$\dfrac{\partial f}{\partial x} = f_x = f_x(x, y, z)$	$\dfrac{\partial f}{\partial y} = f_y = f_y(x, y, z)$	$\dfrac{\partial f}{\partial z} = f_z = f_z(x, y, z)$
$\dfrac{\partial^2 f}{\partial x^2} = f_{xx}$	$\dfrac{\partial^2 f}{\partial y^2} = f_{yy}$	$\dfrac{\partial^2 f}{\partial z^2} = f_{zz}$

Mixed Partial

$$\frac{\partial^2 f}{\partial x \partial y} = f_{xy}, \qquad \frac{\partial^2 f}{\partial y \partial x} = f_{yx}$$

Equation of a Plane

$$ax + by + cz = d$$

Normal Vector

The normal vector $n = \langle a, b, c \rangle$, is extracted from the equation of a plane, and the normal vector is perpendicular to the surface.

Distance/Vector Between Points

Vector from two points

$$P_1(a, b, c) \wedge P_2(d, e, f) \quad \Rightarrow \quad \overrightarrow{P_1 P_2} = P_2 - P_1 = \langle d - a, e - b, f - c \rangle$$

$$\left| \overrightarrow{P_1 P_2} \right| = \sqrt{(d - a)^2 + (e - b)^2 + (f - c)^2}$$

Tangent Plane

$$z - z_0 = f_x(x_0, y_0)(x - x_0) + f_y(x_0, y_0)(y - y_0)$$

Equation of a sphere

$$(x - h)^2 + (y - k)^2 + (z - l)^2 = r^2, \text{center: } (h, k, l) \text{ radius: } r$$

Chain Rule

$$\frac{dz}{dt} = \frac{\partial z}{\partial x}\frac{dx}{dt} + \frac{\partial z}{\partial y}\frac{dy}{dt}, \qquad x = x(t) \wedge y = y(t)$$

$$\frac{\partial z}{\partial s} = \frac{\partial z}{\partial x}\frac{\partial x}{\partial s} + \frac{\partial z}{\partial y}\frac{\partial y}{\partial s}, \qquad \frac{\partial z}{\partial t} = \frac{\partial z}{\partial x}\frac{\partial x}{\partial t} + \frac{\partial z}{\partial y}\frac{\partial y}{\partial t}, \qquad x = x(s,t) \wedge y = y(s,t)$$

Gradient ∇f

The symbol ∇ is called *nabla* or **del**; ∂ is called *partial* or **del**. It would be appropriate to use "del" as del is for partial derivatives just as nabla is.

The gradient of f is noted as ∇f, and is equal the vector function of partials i.e.

$$\nabla f = \frac{\partial f}{\partial x}\mathbf{i} + \frac{\partial f}{\partial y}\mathbf{j} + \frac{\partial f}{\partial z}\mathbf{k}$$

Directional Derivative

Given $f(x,y,z)$, $\vec{v} = \langle v_1, v_2, v_3 \rangle$, and $P(x_0, y_0, z_0)$

$$D_{\mathbf{u}}f \equiv \nabla f(x_0, y_0, z_o) \cdot \mathbf{u} \equiv \nabla f(x_0, y_0, z_o) \cdot \frac{\vec{v}}{|\vec{v}|}$$

$$D_{\mathbf{u}}f = \frac{1}{|\vec{v}|}\langle f_x(x_0, y_0, z_o), f_y(x_0, y_0, z_o), f_z(x_0, y_0, z_o)\rangle \cdot \langle v_1, v_2, v_3 \rangle$$

Differentials

$$df = f_x(x,y)\Delta x + f_y(x,y)\Delta y + f_z(x,y)\Delta z$$

Implicit Differentiation

$$\frac{\partial z}{\partial x} = -\frac{\frac{\partial F}{\partial x}}{\frac{\partial F}{\partial z}} \quad \wedge \quad \frac{\partial z}{\partial y} = -\frac{\frac{\partial F}{\partial y}}{\frac{\partial F}{\partial z}}$$

Extrema

Given a three-dimensional function f, we can find the extrema by using partial derivatives, and derivative tests.

Process:

Set $f_x = 0$	Set $f_y = 0$	Solve for $(x, y) = (c_1, c_2)$ (critical point)
Evaluate $f_{xx}(c_1, c_2)$	f_{yy}	
f_{xy}	f_{yx}	True: $f_{xy} = f_{yx}$

$$D = \begin{bmatrix} f_{xx} & f_{xy} \\ f_{yx} & f_{yy} \end{bmatrix} = f_{xx}f_{yy} - [f_{xy}]^2$$

Local Min: $D > 0$ and $f_{xx}(c_1, c_2) > 0$

Local Max: $D > 0$ and $f_{xx}(c_1, c_2) < 0$

Saddle: $D < 0$

Lagrange Multipliers

These are like puzzles i.e. the set up is pretty straight forward, but you may need to make multiple attempts to find the right pattern.

2D

Given $f(x, y)$ (function) and $g(x, y) = k$ (constraint) then $\nabla f(x, y) = \lambda \nabla g(x, y)$

Solve the following system:

$f_x = \lambda g_x$ $\qquad \Big| \; f_y = \lambda g_y$ $\qquad \Big| \; g(x, y) = k$

3D

Given $f(x, y, z)$ (function) and $g(x, y, z) = k$ (constraint) then $\nabla f(x, y, z) = \lambda \nabla g(x, y, z)$

Solve the following system:

$f_x = \lambda g_x$ $\quad \Big| \; f_y = \lambda g_y$ $\quad \Big| \; f_z = \lambda g_z$ $\quad \Big| \; g(x, y, z) = k$

Once you find all possible values, then you simply plug them into f, and see which is largest/smallest. These are then your max/min.

Two Constraints

$$\nabla f(x, y, z) = \lambda \nabla g(x, y, z) + \mu \nabla h(x, y, z)$$

$f_x = \lambda g_x + \mu h_x$ $\quad \Big| \; f_y = \lambda g_y + \mu h_y$ $\quad \Big| \; f_z = \lambda g_z + \mu h_z$ $\quad \Big| \; g(x, y, z) = k_1$ $\quad \Big| \; h(x, y, z) = k_2$

Multiple Integrals

Double

$$\int_a^b \int_c^d f(x,y)\, dydx \equiv \iint_R f(x,y)\, dA, \qquad R = \{(x,y)|x \in [a,b], y \in [c,d]\} \equiv R = [a,b] \times [c,d]$$

Note 1:

$$\int_a^b \int_c^d f(x,y)\, dydx = \int_c^d \int_a^b f(x,y)\, dxdy \Leftrightarrow a \leq x \leq b \wedge c \leq y \leq d$$

Note 2: $f(x,y) = f(x)g(y)$

$$\int_a^b \int_c^d f(x,y)\, dydx = \int_a^b \int_c^d f(x)g(y)\, dydx = \int_c^d g(y)\, dy \int_a^b f(x)\, dx$$

Average Value

$$\frac{1}{d-c}\left(\frac{1}{b-a}\right) \int_a^b \int_c^d f(x,y)\, dydx$$

Type I

$$\iint_D f(x,y)\, dA = \int_a^b \int_{g_1(x)}^{g_2(x)} f(x,y)\, dydx, \qquad D = \{(x,y)|x \in [a,b], y \in [g_1(x), g_2(x)]\}$$

Type II

$$\iint_D f(x,y)\, dA = \int_c^d \int_{h_1(y)}^{h_2(y)} f(x,y)\, dxdy, \qquad D = \{(x,y)|x \in [h_1(y), h_2(y)], y \in [c,d]\}$$

Polar

$$r^2 = x^2 + y^2 \qquad\qquad | \ x = r\cos\theta \qquad\qquad | \ y = r\sin\theta$$

$$\iint_R f(x,y)\, dA = \int_{\theta_1}^{\theta_2} \int_{r_1}^{r_2} rf(r\cos\theta, r\sin\theta)\, drd\theta, \qquad R = \{(r,\theta)|r \in [r_1, r_2], \theta \in [\theta_1, \theta_2]\}$$

Note: Do not forget the extra r multiplied by f

Type III

f is continuous on a polar region

$$\iint_R f(x,y)\, dA = \int_{\theta_1}^{\theta_2} \int_{g_1(\theta)}^{g_2(\theta)} f(r\cos\theta, r\sin\theta)\, r\, dr d\theta,$$

$$R = \{(r,\theta) | r \in [g_1(\theta), g_2(\theta)], \theta \in [\theta_1, \theta_2]\}$$

Moments & Center of Mass

Moments

M_x $\qquad \left| \iint_D y\rho(x,y)\, dA \right.$

M_y $\qquad \left| \iint_D x\rho(x,y)\, dA \right.$

Center of mass

$\bar{x} = \dfrac{M_y}{m}$ $\qquad \left| \dfrac{1}{m}\iint_D y\rho(x,y)\, dA, \quad m = \iint_D \rho(x,y)\, dA \right.$

$\bar{y} = \dfrac{M_x}{m}$ $\qquad \left| \dfrac{1}{m}\iint_D x\rho(x,y)\, dA, \quad m = \iint_D \rho(x,y)\, dA \right.$

Moment of Inertia

I_x $\qquad \left| \iint_D y^2\rho(x,y)\, dA \right.$

I_y $\qquad \left| \iint_D x^2\rho(x,y)\, dA \right.$

I_0 (about origin) $\qquad \left| \iint_D (x^2 + y^2)\rho(x,y)\, dA \right.$

Surface Area

$z = f(x,y), (x,y) \in D$, and f_x, f_y are continuous

$$A_s = \iint_D \sqrt{1 + \left(\frac{\partial z}{\partial x}\right)^2 + \left(\frac{\partial z}{\partial y}\right)^2}\, dA = \iint_R \sqrt{1 + \left(f_x(x,y)\right)^2 + \left(f_y(x,y)\right)^2}\, dA$$

Triple Integrals

$$\iiint_R f(x,y,z)\, dV, \qquad R = \{(x,y,z)|[x_1,x_2] \times [y_1,y_2] \times [z_1,z_2]\} \equiv \int_{z_1}^{z_2} \int_{y_1}^{y_2} \int_{x_1}^{x_2} f(x,y,z)\, dx\, dy\, dz$$

Type IV:

$$\iiint_E f(x,y,z)\, dV = \iint_D \left[\int_{g_1(x,y)}^{g_2(x,y)} f(x,y,z)\, dz \right] dA$$

Type V:

$$\iiint_E f(x,y,z)\, dV = \int_{x_1}^{x_2} \int_{h_1(x)}^{h_2(x)} \int_{g_1(x,y)}^{g_2(x,y)} f(x,y,z)\, dz\, dy\, dx$$

Type VI:

$$\iiint_E f(x,y,z)\, dV = \int_{y_1}^{y_2} \int_{u_1(y)}^{u_2(y)} \int_{g_1(x,y)}^{g_2(x,y)} f(x,y,z)\, dz\, dx\, dy$$

Moments & Center of Mass

Moments

M_{xy} $\displaystyle\iiint_E z\rho(x,y,z)\, dV$

M_{yz} $\displaystyle\iiint_E x\rho(x,y,z)\, dV$

M_{xz} $\displaystyle\iiint_E y\rho(x,y,z)\, dV$

Center of Mass

The centroid of E is the center of mass $(\bar{x}, \bar{y}, \bar{z})$ for constant density.

$$m = \iiint_E \rho(x,y,z)\, dV$$

$$\bar{x} = \frac{M_{yz}}{m} \qquad \bar{y} = \frac{M_{xz}}{m} \qquad \bar{z} = \frac{M_{xy}}{m}$$

Moments of Inertia

$$I_x = \iiint_E (y^2 + z^2)\rho(x,y,z)\, dV \quad I_y = \iiint_E (x^2 + z^2)\rho(x,y,z)\, dV \quad I_z = \iiint_E (x^2 + y^2)\rho(x,y,z)\, dV$$

Cylindrical Coordinates

$$r^2 = x^2 + y^2 \qquad \tan\theta = \frac{y}{x} \qquad x = r\cos\theta \qquad y = r\sin\theta \qquad z = z$$

$$\iiint_E f(x,y,z)\, dV = \int_{\theta_1}^{\theta_2} \int_{g_1(\theta)}^{g_2(\theta)} \int_{h_1(r\cos\theta, r\sin\theta)}^{h_2(r\cos\theta, r\sin\theta)} rf(r\cos\theta, r\sin\theta, z)\, dz\, dr\, d\theta$$

Note: Do not forget the extra r

Spherical Coordinates

$$x = \rho\sin\phi\cos\theta \qquad y = \rho\sin\phi\sin\theta \qquad z = \rho\cos\phi \qquad \rho^2 = x^2 + y^2 + z^2$$

$$E = \{(\rho, \theta, \phi)\,|\,\rho \in [\rho_1, \rho_2], \theta \in [\theta_1, \theta_2], \phi \in [\phi_1, \phi_2]\}$$

$$\iiint_E f(x,y,z)\, dV = \int_{\phi_1}^{\phi_2} \int_{\theta_1}^{\theta_2} \int_{\rho_1}^{\rho_2} f(\rho\sin\phi\cos\theta, \rho\sin\phi\sin\theta, \rho\cos\phi)\rho^2\sin\phi\, d\rho\, d\theta\, d\phi$$

Change of Variables

2D Jacobian

$$\frac{\partial(x,y)}{\partial(u,v)} = \begin{vmatrix} \dfrac{\partial x}{\partial u} & \dfrac{\partial x}{\partial v} \\ \dfrac{\partial y}{\partial u} & \dfrac{\partial y}{\partial v} \end{vmatrix} = \frac{\partial x}{\partial u}\frac{\partial y}{\partial v} - \frac{\partial x}{\partial v}\frac{\partial y}{\partial u}, \qquad x = x(u,v) \wedge y = y(u,v)$$

$$\iint_R f(x,y)\, dA = \int_S f(x(u,v), y(u,v))\, \text{abs}\left\{\frac{\partial(x,y)}{\partial(u,v)}\right\} du\, dv$$

Note: Do not confuse the determinant with the absolute value i.e.

$$\begin{vmatrix} \dfrac{\partial x}{\partial u} & \dfrac{\partial x}{\partial v} \\ \dfrac{\partial y}{\partial u} & \dfrac{\partial y}{\partial v} \end{vmatrix} \neq \left|\frac{\partial(x,y)}{\partial(u,v)}\right| = \text{abs}\left\{\begin{vmatrix} \dfrac{\partial x}{\partial u} & \dfrac{\partial x}{\partial v} \\ \dfrac{\partial y}{\partial u} & \dfrac{\partial y}{\partial v} \end{vmatrix}\right\}$$

3D Jacobian

$$J = \begin{vmatrix} \dfrac{\partial x}{\partial u} & \dfrac{\partial x}{\partial v} & \dfrac{\partial x}{\partial w} \\[2mm] \dfrac{\partial y}{\partial u} & \dfrac{\partial y}{\partial v} & \dfrac{\partial y}{\partial w} \\[2mm] \dfrac{\partial z}{\partial u} & \dfrac{\partial z}{\partial v} & \dfrac{\partial z}{\partial w} \end{vmatrix}, \qquad x = x(u,v,w) \wedge y = y(u,v,w) \wedge z = z(u,v,w)$$

$$\iiint_V f(x,y,z)\, dV \Rightarrow dV = |J|\, du\, dv\, dw, \qquad J = \frac{\partial(x,y)}{\partial(u,v)}$$

Line Integrals

General

Smooth

$$\int_C f(x,y)\, ds = \int_{t_1}^{t_2} f\big(x(t),y(t)\big)\sqrt{[x'(t)]^2 + [y'(t)]^2}\, dt$$

Not Smooth

$$\int_C f(x,y)\, ds = \int_{C_1} f(x,y)\, ds + \int_{C_2} f(x,y)\, ds + \cdots \int_{C_n} f(x,y)\, ds$$

x, y Derivatives

Respect to x

$$\int_C f(x,y)\, dx \qquad\qquad \int_{t_1}^{t_2} f\big(x(t),y(t)\big)x'(t)\, dt$$

Respect to y

$$\int_C f(x,y)\, dy \qquad\qquad \int_{t_1}^{t_2} f\big(x(t),y(t)\big)y'(t)\, dt$$

Note:

Changing direction of x, y

$$\int_{-C} f(x,y)\, ds = -\int_C f(x,y)\, ds$$

Arc length

$$\int_{-C} f(x,y)\, ds = \int_C f(x,y)\, ds$$

Vector form

$$\int_C f(x,y,z)\, ds = \int_{t_1}^{t_2} f\big(x(t),y(t),z(t)\big)\sqrt{[x'(t)]^2 + [y'(t)]^2 + [z'(t)]^2}\, dt$$

$$\because \mathbf{r}(t) = \langle x(t), y(t), z(t) \rangle \wedge \|\mathbf{r}(t)\| = \sqrt{[x'(t)]^2 + [y'(t)]^2 + [z'(t)]^2}$$

$$\therefore \int_{t_1}^{t_2} f\big(x(t), y(t), z(t)\big) \sqrt{[x'(t)]^2 + [y'(t)]^2 + [z'(t)]^2}\, dt = \int_{t_1}^{t_2} f\big(\mathbf{r}(t)\big) \|\mathbf{r}(t)\|\, dt$$

Respect to z

$$\int_{t_1}^{t_2} f\big(x(t), y(t), z(t)\big) z'(t)\, dt$$

Multiple Functions P, Q, R

$$\int_C P(x, y, z)\, dx + Q(x, y, z) dy + R(x, y, z) dz = \int_{t_1}^{t_2} \big[g_1(t) + g_2(t) + g_{3(t)}\big]\, dt$$

Work

Case I

$$W = \int_C \mathbf{F}(x, y, z) \cdot \mathbf{T}(x, y, z)\, ds$$

Case II

$$W = \int_C \mathbf{F} \cdot \mathbf{T}\, ds$$

Case III

$$W = \int_{t_1}^{t_2} \left[\mathbf{F}\big(\mathbf{r}(t)\big) \cdot \frac{\mathbf{r}'(t)}{\|\mathbf{r}'(t)\|}\right] \|\mathbf{r}'(t)\|\, dt$$

Case IV

$$W = \int_{t_1}^{t_2} \mathbf{F}\big(\mathbf{r}(t)\big) \cdot \mathbf{r}'(t)\, dt$$

Case V

$$W = \int_C \mathbf{F}\big(\mathbf{r}(t)\big) \cdot d\mathbf{r}$$

Case VI

$$W = \int_C P dx + Q dy + R dz, \qquad \mathbf{F} = \langle P, Q, R \rangle$$

Gradient Line Integral

Case I: Fundamental Theorem

$$\int_C \nabla f \cdot d\mathbf{r} = f\big(\mathbf{r}(t_2)\big) - f\big(\mathbf{r}(t_1)\big)$$

Case II

$$\int_C \nabla f \cdot d\mathbf{r} = f(x_2, y_2, z_2) - f(x_1, y_1, z_1)$$

Case III

$$\int_{t_1}^{t_2} \nabla f(\mathbf{r}(t)) \cdot \mathbf{r}'(t)\, dt = \int_{t_1}^{t_2} \left[\frac{\partial f}{\partial x} \frac{dx}{dt} + \frac{\partial f}{\partial y} \frac{dy}{dt} + \frac{\partial f}{\partial z} \frac{dz}{dt} \right] dt$$

Case IV

$$\int_{t_1}^{t_2} \frac{d}{dt} f(\mathbf{r}(t))\, dt = f(\mathbf{r}(t_2)) - f(\mathbf{r}(t_1))$$

Conservative Vector Field

$$\nabla f = \mathbf{F}(x, y) = \langle P(x, y), Q(x, y) \rangle \ \wedge \ \frac{\partial P}{\partial y} = \frac{\partial Q}{\partial x}$$

Green's Theorem

$$\int_C P\, dx + Q\, dy = \iint_D \left[\frac{\partial Q}{\partial x} - \frac{\partial P}{\partial y} \right] dA$$

Curl ∇

Note: gradient of f is ∇f, and curl/divergence of f is $\nabla \times \nabla f$ and $\nabla \cdot \nabla f$, where ∇ (nabla) is referred to as del.

$$\nabla = \frac{\partial}{\partial x}\mathbf{i} + \frac{\partial}{\partial y}\mathbf{j} + \frac{\partial}{\partial z}\mathbf{k} \equiv \langle \partial_x, \partial_y, \partial_z \rangle$$

$$\nabla \times \nabla f = \nabla \times \mathbf{F} = \begin{vmatrix} \mathbf{i} & \mathbf{j} & \mathbf{k} \\ \partial_x & \partial_y & \partial_z \\ \partial_x^f & \partial_y^f & \partial_z^f \end{vmatrix}, \qquad \langle \partial_x^f, \partial_y^f, \partial_z^f \rangle \equiv \frac{\partial f}{\partial x}\mathbf{i} + \frac{\partial f}{\partial y}\mathbf{j} + \frac{\partial f}{\partial}\mathbf{k}$$

Conservative if curl $\mathbf{F} = 0$

Divergence

$$\nabla \cdot \nabla f = \nabla \cdot \mathbf{F} = \langle \partial_x, \partial_y, \partial_z \rangle \cdot \langle \partial_x^f, \partial_y^f, \partial_z^f \rangle$$

Stokes Theorem

$$\int_C \nabla f \cdot d\mathbf{r} = \int_C \mathbf{F} \cdot d\mathbf{r} = \iint_S \nabla \times \mathbf{F} \cdot d\mathbf{S} = \iint_S \text{curl } \mathbf{F} \cdot d\mathbf{S}$$

Divergence Theorem

$$\iint_S \mathbf{F} \cdot d\mathbf{S} = \iiint_E \nabla \cdot \nabla f \, d\mathbf{V} = \iiint_E \nabla \cdot \mathbf{F} \, dV = \iiint_E \operatorname{div} \mathbf{F} \, dV$$

PreCalculus Review

Arithmetic

$$ab \pm ac = a(b \pm c) = (b \pm c)a$$

$$\frac{\left(\frac{a}{b}\right)}{c} = \frac{a}{bc}$$

$$\frac{a}{b} \pm \frac{c}{d} = \frac{ad \pm bc}{bd}$$

$$\frac{a - b}{c - d} = \frac{b - a}{d - c}$$

$$\frac{ab + ac}{a} = b + c, a \neq 0$$

$$a\left(\frac{b}{c}\right) = \frac{ab}{c}$$

$$\frac{a}{\left(\frac{b}{c}\right)} = \left(\frac{a}{1}\right) \cdot \left(\frac{c}{b}\right) = \frac{ac}{b}$$

$$\frac{a \pm b}{c} = \frac{a}{c} \pm \frac{b}{c}$$

$$\frac{\left(\frac{a}{b}\right)}{\left(\frac{c}{d}\right)} = \frac{a}{b} \cdot \frac{d}{c} = \frac{ad}{bc}$$

Exponential

$$a^1 = a \qquad a^0 = 1 \qquad a^{-n} = \frac{1}{a^n} \qquad \frac{1}{a^{-n}} = a^n \qquad a^n a^m = a^{n+m}$$

$$\frac{a^n}{a^m} = a^{n-m} \qquad \left(\frac{a}{b}\right)^n = \frac{a^n}{b^n} \qquad \left(\frac{a}{b}\right)^{-n} = \frac{b^n}{a^n} \qquad (a^n)^{\frac{1}{m}} = \left(a^{\frac{1}{m}}\right)^n \qquad (a^n)^m = (a^m)^n$$

Radicals

$$\sqrt[m]{\sqrt[n]{a}} = \sqrt[mn]{a} = a^{\frac{1}{mn}} \qquad \sqrt[n]{a^n} = a, n \text{ is odd} \qquad \sqrt[n]{a^n} = |a|, n \text{ is even}$$

$$\sqrt{a} = \sqrt[2]{a} = \sqrt[2]{a^1} = a^{\frac{1}{2}} \qquad \sqrt[n]{a^m} = a^{\frac{m}{n}} \qquad \sqrt[n]{\frac{a}{b}} = \frac{\sqrt[n]{a}}{\sqrt[n]{b}} = \frac{a^{\frac{1}{n}}}{b^{\frac{1}{n}}} = \left(\frac{a}{b}\right)^{\frac{1}{n}}$$

Fractions

$$\frac{a}{b} \pm \frac{c}{d} = \frac{ad \pm bc}{bd}$$

$$\frac{g(x)}{f(x)} \pm \frac{h(x)}{r(x)} = \frac{[g(x)r(x)] \pm [f(x)h(x)]}{f(x)r(x)}$$

Logarithmic

$$\frac{\ln(b)}{\ln(a)} = \log_a b \qquad y = \log_b x \Leftrightarrow x = b^y \qquad e \approx 2.72 \qquad \log_a a = 1$$

$$\log_a 1 = 0 \qquad \log_a a^u = u \qquad \log_e u = \ln u \qquad \log_a u^b = b \log_a u$$

$$\log_a uv = \log_a u + \log_a v \qquad \log_a \frac{u}{v} = \log_a u - \log_a v \qquad \log_a b = \frac{\ln(b)}{\ln(a)}$$

$$v = \ln u \Rightarrow u = e^v \qquad v = e^u \Rightarrow u = \ln v \qquad e = \sum_{n=0}^{\infty} \frac{1}{n!}$$

$$\ln a = \text{undefined}, a \le 0 \qquad \ln 1 = 0 \qquad \ln e^u = u \Rightarrow e^{\ln u} = u$$

$$\ln e^1 = 1 \Rightarrow e^{\ln(1)} = 1 \qquad \ln u^b = b \ln u \qquad \ln uv = \ln u + \ln v \qquad \ln \frac{u}{v} = \ln u - \ln v$$

Other Formulas/Equations

Quadratic Formula

$$ax^2 + bx + c = 0 \quad \Rightarrow \quad x = \frac{-b \pm \sqrt{b^2 - 4ac}}{2a}$$

Discriminant

Two Real Solutions	$b^2 - 4ac > 0$
Repeated Solution	$b^2 - 4ac = 0$
Complex Solution ($x = \alpha \pm \beta i$)	if $b^2 - 4ac < 0$

Complete the Square

$$y = ax^2 + bx + c \quad \Rightarrow \quad y = a\left(x + \frac{b}{2a}\right)^2 + c - \frac{b^2}{4a}$$

Other Formulas

Distance Formula	Midpoint Formula

$$D = \sqrt{(x - x_0)^2 + (y - y_0)^2}$$	$$M = \left(\frac{x + x_0}{2}, \frac{y + y_0}{2}\right)$$
Equation of a Line $$slope = m = \frac{y_2 - y_1}{x_2 - x_1}$$	$$y = mx + b$$ $$(y_2 - y_1) = m(x_2 - x_1)$$ $$Ax + By = C$$
Equation of Parabola Vertex: (h, k)	$$y = ax^2 + bx + c$$ $$y = a(x - h)^2 + k$$
Equation of Circle Center: (h, k) Radius: r	$$(x - h)^2 + (y - k)^2 = r^2$$
Equation of Ellipse Right Point: $(h + a, k)$ Left Point: $(h - a, k)$ Top Point: $(h, k + b)$ Bottom Point: $(h, k - b)$	$$\frac{(x - h)^2}{a^2} + \frac{(y - k)^2}{b^2} = 1$$
Equation of Hyperbola Center: (h, k) Slope: $\pm\frac{b}{a}$ Asymptotes: $y = \pm\frac{b}{a}(x - h) + k$ Vertices: $(h + a, k), (h - a, k)$	$$\frac{(x - h)^2}{a^2} - \frac{(y - k)^2}{b^2} = 1$$
Equation of Hyperbola Center: (h, k) Slope: $\pm\frac{b}{a}$ Asymptotes: $y = \pm\frac{b}{a}(x - h) + k$ Vertices: $(h, k + b), (h, k - b)$	$$\frac{(y - k)^2}{a^2} - \frac{(x - h)^2}{b^2} = 1$$

Areas

Square: $A = L^2 = W^2$ Rectangle: $A = L \cdot W$ Circle: $A = \pi \cdot r^2$

Ellipse: $A = \pi \cdot ab$ Triangle: $A = \frac{1}{2}b \cdot h$ Trapezoid: $A = \frac{1}{2}(a + b) \cdot h$

Parallelogram: $b \cdot h$ Rhombus: $A = \frac{pq}{2}$, p and q are the diagonals

Surface Areas

Cube: $A_s = 6L^2 = 6W^2$ Box: $A_s = 2(LW + WH + HL)$ Sphere: $A_s = 4\pi r^2$

Cone: $A_s = \pi r\left(r + \sqrt{h^2 + r^2}\right)$ Cylinder: $2\pi rh + 2\pi r^2$

Volumes

Cube: $V = L^3 = W^3$ Box: $V = L \cdot W \cdot H$ Sphere: $V = \frac{4}{3}\pi \cdot r^3$

Cone: $V = \frac{1}{3}\pi \cdot r^2 h$ Ellipsoid: $V = \frac{4}{3}\pi \cdot abc$, a, b, c are the radii

Domain Restrictions

$y = \dfrac{u}{v}$, $v \neq 0$ $y = \sqrt{u}$, $u \geq 0$ $y = \ln u$, $u > 0$

$y = a^u$, none $y = \sqrt[n]{u}$ none if n is odd, $u \geq 0$ if n is even

Right Triangle

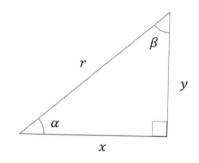

$$x^2 + y^2 = r^2 \quad \Leftrightarrow \quad r = \sqrt{x^2 + y^2}$$

$$\cos\alpha = \frac{x}{r} \qquad\qquad\qquad \cos\beta = \frac{y}{r}$$

$$\tan\alpha = \frac{y}{x} \qquad\qquad\qquad \tan\beta = \frac{x}{y}$$

$$\sin\alpha = \frac{y}{r} \qquad\qquad\qquad \sin\beta = \frac{x}{r}$$

$$x = r\cos\alpha \qquad\qquad\qquad y = r\cos\beta$$

$$y = r\sin\alpha \qquad\qquad\qquad x = r\sin\beta$$

$$\alpha = \arctan\left(\frac{y}{x}\right) = \tan^{-1}\left(\frac{y}{x}\right) \qquad \beta = \arctan\left(\frac{x}{y}\right) = \tan^{-1}\left(\frac{x}{y}\right)$$

Reciprocal Identities

$$\sin\theta = \frac{1}{\csc\theta} \qquad \csc\theta = \frac{1}{\sin\theta} \qquad \tan\theta = \frac{1}{\cot\theta}$$

$$\csc\theta = \frac{1}{\sec\theta} \qquad \sec\theta = \frac{1}{\cos\theta} \qquad \cot\theta = \frac{1}{\tan\theta}$$

$$\tan\theta = \frac{\sin\theta}{\cos\theta} \qquad \cot\theta = \frac{\cos\theta}{\sin\theta}$$

Double Angle Formulas

$$\sin(2\theta) = 2\sin\theta\cos\theta \qquad\qquad \cos(2\theta) = 1 - 2\sin^2\theta$$

$$\cos 2\theta = \cos^2 \theta - \sin^2 \theta \qquad \cos 2\theta = 2\cos^2 \theta - 1$$

$$\cos 2\theta = 1 - 2\sin^2 \theta \qquad \tan 2\theta = \frac{2\tan\theta}{1-\tan^2\theta} \text{Officia}$$

Half Angle Formulas

$$\sin^2 \theta = \frac{1}{2}[1 - \cos(2\theta)] \qquad \cos^2 \theta = \frac{1}{2}[1 + \cos(2\theta)] \qquad \tan^2 \theta = \frac{1 - \cos(2\theta)}{1 + \cos(2\theta)}$$

Sum and Difference Formulas

$$\sin(\alpha \pm \beta) = \sin\alpha \cos\beta \pm \cos\alpha \sin\beta$$

$$\cos(\alpha \pm \beta) = \cos\alpha \cos\beta \mp \sin\alpha \sin\beta$$

$$\tan(\alpha \pm \beta) = \frac{\tan\alpha \pm \tan\beta}{1 \mp \tan\alpha \tan\beta}$$

Product to Sum Formulas

$\sin\alpha \sin\beta = \frac{1}{2}[\cos(\alpha - \beta) - \cos(\alpha + \beta)]$	$\cos\alpha \cos\beta = \frac{1}{2}[\cos(\alpha - \beta) + \cos(\alpha + \beta)]$
$\sin\alpha \cos\beta = \frac{1}{2}[\sin(\alpha + \beta) + \sin(\alpha - \beta)]$	$\cos\alpha \sin\beta = \frac{1}{2}[\sin(\alpha + \beta) - \sin(\alpha - \beta)]$

Sum to Product Formulas

$\sin\alpha + \sin\beta = 2\sin\left[\frac{\alpha + \beta}{2}\right]\cos\left[\frac{\alpha - \beta}{2}\right]$	$\sin\alpha - \sin\beta = 2\cos\left[\frac{\alpha + \beta}{2}\right]\sin\left[\frac{\alpha - \beta}{2}\right]$
$\cos\alpha + \cos\beta = 2\cos\left[\frac{\alpha + \beta}{2}\right]\cos\left[\frac{\alpha - \beta}{2}\right]$	$\cos\alpha - \cos\beta = -2\sin\left[\frac{\alpha + \beta}{2}\right]\sin\left[\frac{\alpha - \beta}{2}\right]$

Unit Circle

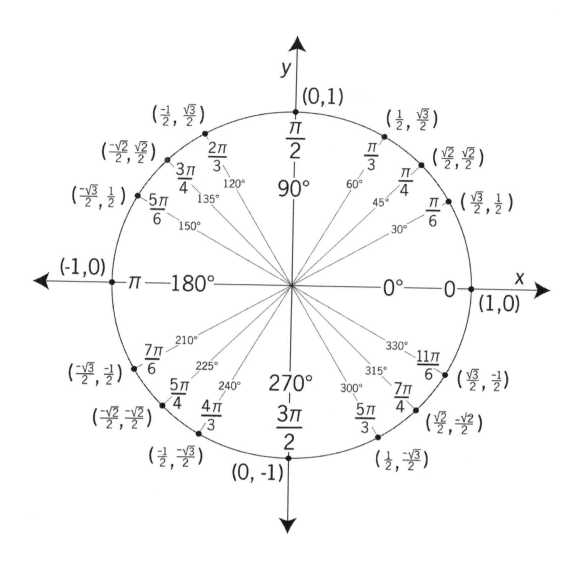

Pre-CALC III Reference

Derivative Rules (prime notations)

Derivative of a Constant	$(c)' = 0$
Power Rule	$(x^n)' = nx^{n-1}$
Constant Multiple Rule	$(cu)' = cu'$
Product Rule	$[uv]' = uv' + vu'$
Quotient Rule	$\left[\dfrac{u}{v}\right]' = \dfrac{vu' - uv'}{v^2}$
Chain Rule	$[u(v)]' = u'(v) \cdot v'$

Exponential and Logarithmic

	Operator	Prime
exp{u}	$\dfrac{d}{dx} e^{f(x)} = e^{f(x)} \cdot f'(x)$	$(e^u)' = e^u \cdot u'$
Natural Log	$\dfrac{d}{dx} \ln f(x) = \dfrac{f'(x)}{f(x)}$	$[\ln(u)]' = \dfrac{u'}{u}$
Base Log Note: $\log_b a \equiv \frac{\ln a}{\ln b}$	$\dfrac{d}{dx} \log_b f(x) = \dfrac{1}{\ln b} \cdot \dfrac{f'(x)}{f(x)}$	$[\log_b u]' = \dfrac{1}{\ln b} \cdot \dfrac{u'}{u}$
Exponential	$\dfrac{d}{dx} a^{f(x)} = a^{f(x)} f'(x) \ln a$	$(a^u)' = a^u u' \ln a$

Inverse Function Derivative

$$\frac{d}{dx} f^{-1}(x)\bigg|_a = \frac{1}{f'(f^{-1}(a))}, \qquad f^{-1}(a) = b \Leftrightarrow f(b) = a$$

Trig Derivatives

Standard

$(\sin u)' = \cos u \cdot u'$	$(\cos u)' = -\sin u \cdot u'$	$(\tan u)' = \sec^2 u \cdot u'$
$(\csc u)' = -\csc u \cot u \cdot u'$	$(\sec u)' = \sec u \tan u \cdot u'$	$(\cot u)' = -\csc^2 u \cdot u'$

Inverse

$(\sin^{-1} u)' = \dfrac{u'}{\sqrt{1-u^2}}$	$(\cos^{-1} u)' = -\dfrac{u'}{\sqrt{1-u^2}}$	$(\tan^{-1} u)' = \dfrac{u'}{1+u^2}$
$(\csc^{-1} u)' = -\dfrac{u'}{|u|\sqrt{u^2-1}}$	$(\sec^{-1} u)' = \dfrac{u'}{|u|\sqrt{u^2-1}}$	$(\cot^{-1} u)' = -\dfrac{u'}{1+u^2}$

Common Derivatives

Operator

$\dfrac{d}{dx}y = \dfrac{dy}{dx}$	$\dfrac{d}{dx}x^n = nx^{n-1}$	$\dfrac{d}{dx}y^n = ny^{n-1}\dfrac{dy}{dx}$
$\dfrac{d}{dx}e^x = e^x$	$\dfrac{d}{dx}e^{f(x)} = e^{f(x)}f'(x)$	$\dfrac{d}{dx}\ln x = \dfrac{1}{x}$
$\dfrac{d}{dx}\ln f(x) = \dfrac{f'(x)}{f(x)}$	$\dfrac{d}{dx}a^x = a^x \ln a$	$\dfrac{d}{dx}a^{f(x)} = a^{f(x)}f'(x)\ln a$
$\dfrac{d}{dx}(\sin x) = \cos x$	$\dfrac{d}{dx}(\csc x) = -\csc x \cot x$	$\dfrac{d}{dx}(\cos x) = -\sin x$
$\dfrac{d}{dx}(\sec x) = \sec x \tan x$	$\dfrac{d}{dx}(\tan x) = \sec^2 x$	$\dfrac{d}{dx}(\cot x) = -\csc^2 x$
$\dfrac{d}{dx}\sin^{-1} x = \dfrac{1}{\sqrt{1-x^2}}$	$\dfrac{d}{dx}\csc^{-1} x = \dfrac{-1}{|x|\sqrt{x^2-1}}$	$\dfrac{d}{dx}\cos^{-1} x = \dfrac{-1}{\sqrt{1-x^2}}$
$\dfrac{d}{dx}\sec^{-1} x = \dfrac{1}{|x|\sqrt{x^2-1}}$	$\dfrac{d}{dx}\tan^{-1} x = \dfrac{1}{1+x^2}$	$\dfrac{d}{dx}\cot^{-1} x = \dfrac{-1}{1+x^2}$
$\dfrac{d}{dx}\sinh x = \cosh x$	$\dfrac{d}{dx}\operatorname{csch} x = -\operatorname{csch} x \coth x$	$\dfrac{d}{dx}\cosh x = \sinh x$
$\dfrac{d}{dx}\operatorname{sech} x = -\operatorname{sech} x \tanh x$	$\dfrac{d}{dx}\tanh x = \operatorname{sech}^2 x$	$\dfrac{d}{dx}\coth x = -\operatorname{csch}^2 x$

Prime

$$[e^u]' = u'e^u$$

$$[\ln u]' = \frac{u'}{u}$$

$$[a^u]' = u'a^u \ln a$$

$$[\sin u]' = u' \cos u$$

$$[\cos u]' = -u' \sin u$$

$$[\tan u]' = u' \sec^2 u$$

$$[\csc u]' = -u' \csc u \cot u$$

$$[\sec u]' = u' \sec u \tan u$$

$$[\cot u]' = -u' \csc^2 u$$

$$[\arcsin u]' = \frac{u'}{\sqrt{1-u^2}}$$

$$[\arccos u]' = \frac{-u'}{\sqrt{1-u^2}}$$

$$[\arctan u]' = \frac{u'}{1+u^2}$$

$$[\operatorname{arccsc} u]' = \frac{-u'}{|u|\sqrt{u^2-1}}$$

$$[\operatorname{arcsec} u]' = \frac{u'}{|u|\sqrt{u^2-1}}$$

$$[\operatorname{arccot} u]' = \frac{-u'}{1+u^2}$$

Implicit Differentiation

$\dfrac{d}{d[x]}[y]$ *Always pay attention to the variables*	$\dfrac{dy}{dx} = y'$
$\dfrac{d}{dx}y^2$	$2(y)^{2-1}\dfrac{d}{dx}y = 2yy'$
Chain/Power Rule	$\dfrac{d}{dx}y^n = ny^{n-1}\dfrac{dy}{dx} \equiv ny^{n-1}y'$
Chain/Product	$\dfrac{d}{dx}(xy) = x\dfrac{dy}{dx} + y\dfrac{dx}{dx} \equiv xy' + y$
Chain/Quotient	$\dfrac{d}{dx}\left(\dfrac{x}{y}\right) = \dfrac{y\dfrac{dx}{dx} - x\dfrac{dy}{dx}}{y^2} \equiv \dfrac{y - xy'}{y^2}$
Logarithmic	$\dfrac{d}{dx}\ln y = \dfrac{y'}{y}$
Exponential	$\dfrac{d}{dx}a^y = y'a^y \ln a$
Euler's Number	$\dfrac{d}{dx}e^y = y'e^y$
Trigonometric	$\dfrac{d}{dx}\sin y = \cos y \cdot \dfrac{dy}{dx} = \cos y \cdot y'$

Tangent Line

$$f(x,y) = 0, \qquad P(a,b) \quad \Rightarrow \quad y_T = f'(a,b)(x-a) + b$$

Related Rates

The idea for related rates, in general, is to find the equation that relates geometrically to the question, implicitly differentiate it, and then plug in the given variables and solve for the unknown. Here are a few examples i.e. just use the equation/formula that mimics the object in question.

Right triangle	$a^2 + b^2 = c^2 \Rightarrow aa'(t) + bb'(t) = cc'(t)$
Circle	$A = \pi r^2 \Rightarrow \dfrac{dA}{dt} = 2\pi r r' r(t)$
Sphere	$V = \dfrac{4}{3}\pi r^3 \Rightarrow V'(t) = 4\pi r^2 \dfrac{dr}{dt}$

Hyperbolic Functions

Notation

$$\sinh x = \frac{e^x - e^{-x}}{2}$$

$$\operatorname{csch} x = \frac{2}{e^x + e^{-x}}$$

$$\tanh x = \frac{e^x - e^{-x}}{e^x + e^{-x}}$$

$$\operatorname{sech} x = \frac{2}{e^x + e^{-x}}$$

$$\cosh x = \frac{e^x + e^{-x}}{2}$$

$$\coth x = \frac{e^x + e^{-x}}{e^x - e^{-x}}$$

Identities

$$\sinh(-x) = -\sinh x \qquad \cosh(-x) = \cosh x$$

$$\cosh^2 x - \sinh^2 x = 1 \qquad 1 - \tanh^2 x = \operatorname{sech}^2 x$$

$$\sinh(x + y) = \sinh x \cosh y + \cosh x \sinh y$$

$$\cosh(x + y) = \cosh x \cosh y + \sinh x \sinh y$$

$$\sinh^{-1} x = \ln\left[x + \sqrt{x^2 + 1}\right], \qquad -\infty \le x \le \infty$$

$$\cosh^{-1} x = \ln\left[x + \sqrt{x^2 - 1}\right], \qquad x \ge 1$$

$$\tanh^{-1} x = \frac{1}{2}\ln\left[\frac{1 + x}{1 - x}\right], \qquad -1 < x < 1$$

Derivatives

Standard

$[\sinh u]' = u' \cosh u$	$[\cosh u]' = u' \sinh u$	$[\tanh u]' = u' \operatorname{sech}^2 u$
$[\operatorname{csch} u]' = -u' \operatorname{csch} u \coth u$	$[\operatorname{sech} u]' = -u' \operatorname{sech} u \tanh u$	$[\coth u]' = -u' \operatorname{csch}^2 u$

Inverse

$[\sinh^{-1} u]' = \dfrac{u'}{\sqrt{1 + u^2}}$	$[\cosh^{-1} u]' = \dfrac{u'}{\sqrt{u^2 - 1}}$	$[\tanh^{-1} u]' = \dfrac{u'}{1 - u^2}$
$[\operatorname{csch}^{-1} u]' = -\dfrac{u'}{|u|\sqrt{1 + u^2}}$	$[\operatorname{sech}^{-1} u]' = -\dfrac{u'}{u\sqrt{1 - u^2}}$	$[\coth^{-1} u]' = \dfrac{u'}{1 - u^2}$

Antiderivatives & Integration

Basic Rules

Power Rule for antiderivatives
$$y' = x^n \;\Rightarrow\; y = \frac{1}{n + 1}x^n + C \Leftrightarrow n \neq -1$$

Exponential
$$y' = a^x \;\Rightarrow\; y = \frac{a^x}{\ln(a)} + C$$

Natural Log (case 1)
$$y' = \frac{1}{x} \;\Rightarrow\; y = \ln|x| + C$$

Natural Log (case 2)
$$y' = \frac{1}{ax + b} \;\Rightarrow\; y = \frac{1}{a}\ln|ax + b| + C$$

Natural Log (case 3)
$$y' = \frac{u'(x)}{u(x)} \;\Rightarrow\; y = \ln|u(x)| + C$$

Euler's Number (case 1)
$$y' = e^{ax} \;\Rightarrow\; y = \frac{1}{a}e^{ax} + C$$

Euler's Number (case 2)
$$y' = e^{ax+b} \;\Rightarrow\; y = \frac{1}{a}e^{ax+b} + C$$

Euler's Number (case 3)
$$y' = u'(x)e^{u(x)} \;\Rightarrow\; y = e^{u(x)} + C$$

Anti-Chain-Rule *Substitution Method*
$$y' = f'(g(x))g'(x) \;\Rightarrow\; y = f(g(x)) + C$$

Riemann Sum for Area Approximation

$$A \approx \lim_{n \to \infty} \sum_{i=1}^{n} f(x_i^*)\,\Delta x, \qquad \Delta x = \frac{b - a}{n}, \qquad x_i = a + i \cdot \Delta x$$

$$\sum_{i=1}^{n} c = cn$$

$$\sum_{i=1}^{n} i = \frac{n(n+1)}{2}$$

$$\sum_{i=1}^{n} cf(x_i) = c \sum_{i=1}^{n} f(x_i)$$

$$\sum_{i=1}^{n} i^2 = \frac{n(n+1)(2n+1)}{6}$$

$$\sum_{i=1}^{n} [f(x_i) \pm g(x_i)] = \sum_{i=1}^{n} f(x_i) \pm \sum_{i=1}^{n} g(x_i)$$

$$\sum_{i=1}^{n} i^3 = \left[\frac{n(n+1)}{2} \right]^2$$

Area Approximation Rules

Midpoint Rule

$$\int_a^b f(x)\, dx \approx \frac{b-a}{n} \left[f\left(\frac{x_1 + x_2}{2} \right) + f\left(\frac{x_2 + x_3}{2} \right) + \cdots \right]$$

Trapezoid Rule

$$\int_a^b f(x)\, dx \approx \frac{b-a}{2n} \left[f(x_1) + 2f(x_2) + 2f(x_3) + \cdots + 2f(x_{n-1}) + f(x_n) \right]$$

The Integral Notation $\int$

$$\lim_{n \to \infty} \sum_{i=1}^{n} f(x_i^*) \, \Delta x \equiv \int_a^b f(x) \, dx$$

Definite Integral Properties

$$\int_a^b f(x) \, dx = F(b) - F(a)$$

$$\int_a^a f(x) \, dx = 0$$

$$\int_{-a}^a f(x) \, dx = 0$$
$$\Leftrightarrow f(-x) = -f(x) \text{ (odd)}$$

$$\int_{-a}^a f(x) \, dx = 2 \int_0^a f(x)$$
$$\Leftrightarrow f(-x) = f(x) \text{ (even)}$$

NOTE:

$$\int f(x) \cdot g(x) \, dx \neq \int g(x) \, dx \cdot \int f(x) \, dx$$

$$\int_a^b c \, dx = c(b - a)$$

$$\int_a^b cf(x) \, dx = c \int_a^b f(x) \, dx$$

$$\int_a^b [f(x) \pm g(x)] \, dx = \int_a^b f(x) \, dx \pm \int_a^b g(x) \, dx$$

$$\int_a^b f(x) \, dx = \int_a^k f(x) \, dx + \int_k^a f(x) \, dx$$

$$\int_a^b f(x) \, dx = - \int_b^a f(x) \, dx$$

Fundamental Theorems

Let $f(x) = u$ and $g(x) = v$ for the following:

i)
$$y = \int_u^v f(t) dt \quad \Rightarrow \quad y' = f(v) \cdot v' - f(u) \cdot u'$$

$$y = \int_a^v f(t) dt \quad \Rightarrow \quad y' = f(v) \cdot v' - f(a) \cdot a' = f(v) \cdot v' - 0 = f(v) \cdot v'$$

$$y = \int_u^b f(t) dt \quad \Rightarrow \quad y' = f(b) \cdot b' - f(u) \cdot u' = 0 - f(u) \cdot u' = -f(u) \cdot u'$$

Limit Definition of a Definite Integral

$$ii) \qquad \lim_{n \to \infty} \sum_{i=1}^{n} f(x_i^*)\, \Delta x = \int_a^b f(x)\, dx = F(b) - F(a)$$

$$\Delta x = \frac{b-a}{n}, \qquad x_i = a + i \cdot \Delta x$$

Differential Equation (1st order)

$$y' = f'(x) \;\Rightarrow\; \frac{dy}{dx} = f'(x) \;\Rightarrow\; dy = f'(x)dx \;\Rightarrow\; \int dy = \int f'(x)\, dx$$

$$\Rightarrow\; y + c_1 = f(x) + c_2 \;\Rightarrow\; y = f(x) + c_2 - c_1 = f(x) + c_3 \equiv f(x) + C$$

Common Integrals

$$\int dx = x + C \qquad\qquad \int k\, dx = kx + C \qquad\qquad \int x\, dx = \frac{1}{2}x^2 + C$$

$$\int x^2\, dx = \frac{1}{3}x^3 + C \qquad \int x^n\, dx = \frac{1}{n+1}x^{n+1} + C \qquad \int \frac{1}{x}\, dx = \ln|x| + C$$

$$\Leftrightarrow n \neq -1$$

$$\int e^x\, dx = e^x + C \qquad \int e^{ax}\, dx = \frac{1}{a}e^{ax} + C \qquad \int e^{ax+b}\, dx = \frac{1}{a}e^{ax+b} + C$$

$$\int \frac{1}{x+1}\, dx = \ln|x+1| + C \quad \int \frac{1}{ax+b}\, dx = \frac{1}{a}\ln|ax+b| + C \quad \int f(u)u'\, du = F(u) + C$$

$$\int e^u u'\, du = e^u + C \qquad \int \frac{u'}{u}\, du = \ln|u| + C \qquad \int_a^b f(x) = F(b) - F(a)$$

$$\int u' \cos u\, du = \sin u + C \qquad \int u' \sin u\, du = -\cos u + C \qquad \int u' \sec^2 u\, du = \tan u + C$$

$$\int u' \csc u \sec u\, du = -\csc u + C \quad \int u' \sec u \tan u\, du = \sec u + C \quad \int u' \csc^2 u\, du = -\cot u + C$$

$$\int \frac{u'}{\sqrt{1-u^2}}\, du = \arcsin u + C \quad \int \frac{-u'}{\sqrt{1-u^2}}\, du = \arccos u + C \quad \int \frac{u'}{1+u^2}\, du = \arctan u + C$$

Definite Integral Rules

Substitution

$$\int_a^b f(g(x))g'(x)\,dx = \int_{g(a)}^{g(b)} f(u)\,du$$

Integration by Parts

$$\int_a^b f(x)g'(x)\,dx = f(x)g(x)\big|_a^b - \int_a^b g(x)f'(x)\,dx$$

Let

$u = f(x)$	$dv = g'(x)dx$
$du = f'(x)dx$	$v = g(x)$

Then

$$\int_a^b u\,dv = uv\big|_a^b - \int_a^b v\,du$$

Trig Substitution

$\sqrt{a^2 - x^2}$

$1 - \sin^2\theta = \cos^2\theta$

$x = a\sin\theta$

$\theta \in \left[-\dfrac{\pi}{2}, \dfrac{\pi}{2}\right]$

$\sqrt{a^2 + x^2}$

$1 + \tan^2\theta = \sec^2\theta$

$x = a\tan\theta$

$\theta \in \left(-\dfrac{\pi}{2}, \dfrac{\pi}{2}\right)$

$\sqrt{x^2 - a^2}$

$\sec^2\theta - 1 = \tan^2\theta$

$x = a\sec\theta$

$\theta \in \left[0, \dfrac{\pi}{2}\right) \vee \theta \in \left[\pi, \dfrac{3\pi}{2}\right)$

Trig Identity

$$\int \tan x\,dx = \int \frac{\sin x}{\cos x}\,dx = -\int \frac{1}{\cos x}\cdot(-\sin x)\,dx, \qquad \frac{d}{dx}\ln[u(x)] = \frac{1}{u}\frac{du}{dx}$$

$$= -\ln|\cos x| + C = \ln\left|\frac{1}{\cos x}\right| + C = \ln|\sec x| + C$$

Partial Fractions

$$\frac{p(x)}{x(x+1)} = \frac{A}{x} + \frac{B}{x+1}$$

$$\frac{p(x)}{x(x^2+1)} = \frac{A}{x} + \frac{Bx+C}{x^2+1}$$

$$\frac{p(x)}{[x^2(x+1)]} = \frac{A}{x} + \frac{B}{x^2} + \frac{C}{x+1}$$

$$\frac{p(x)}{x(x^2+1)^2} = \frac{A}{x} + \frac{Bx+C}{x^2+1} + \frac{Dx+E}{(x^2+1)^2}$$

PHYSICS INFO

Basic symbols

Note: A bold letter i.e. $\boldsymbol{v}$ is the same as saying $\vec{v}$. Vector-hats are usually done by hand, and bold are generally used in print (probably because the vector hat was not on a typewriter in the past). Both will be used throughout this text.

Time	t
Position	$\vec{r}(t) = \boldsymbol{r}(t) = \langle r_1(t), r_2(t), r_3(t) \rangle$ $\|\vec{r}(t)\| = s$
Velocity	$\vec{v} = \boldsymbol{v} = \dfrac{d\vec{r}}{dt} = \dfrac{d\boldsymbol{r}}{dt} = \langle r'_1(t), r'_2(t), r'_3(t) \rangle$ $\|\vec{v}\| = \|\boldsymbol{v}\| = \dfrac{ds}{dt} = s'(t) = \dot{s} = v(t) = v$
Acceleration	$\vec{a} = \boldsymbol{a} = \dfrac{d\vec{v}}{dt} = \dfrac{d\boldsymbol{v}}{dt} = \dfrac{d^2\vec{r}}{dt^2} = \dfrac{d^2\boldsymbol{r}}{dt^2} = \langle r''_1(t), r''_2(t), r''_3(t) \rangle$ $\|\vec{a}\| = \|\boldsymbol{a}\| = \|\boldsymbol{v}'\| = \dfrac{d^2 s}{dt^2} = \ddot{s} = \dfrac{dv}{dt} = \dot{v} = v'(t) = a(t) = a$

Deriving formulas

Starting with *constant* acceleration

$$\frac{dv}{dt} = a \quad \Rightarrow \quad dv = a\,dt \quad \Rightarrow \quad \int dv = \int a\,dt \quad \Rightarrow \quad v = at + v_0$$

Now velocity

$$\frac{ds}{dt} = v = at + v_0 \quad \Rightarrow \quad \int ds = \int at + v_0\,dt \quad \Rightarrow \quad s = \frac{1}{2}at^2 + v_0 t + s_0$$

$$s = \frac{1}{2}at^2 + v_0 t + s_0 = \begin{cases} \Delta x = v_{0,x} t + \dfrac{1}{2} a_x t^2 \\ \Delta y = v_{0,y} t + \dfrac{1}{2} a_y t^2 \end{cases}$$

Most formulas are already derived in a physics book so even though calculus may be a prerequisite, it may not really be used in problem solving.

Units

System International Units (S.I. Units)

Meters (m) | Seconds (s) | Kilograms (kg)

Note: Units are not italicized, as variables are e.g. $m = 16$kg and $\Delta x = 10$m: m is the variable for mass, where m is the unit of measurement for meters.

Unit conversion

Unit conversion is pretty straightforward; let's look at an example.

Example

Convert 100 meters per second to inches per hours

Find the appropriate relations and solve for 1 so that when the product cancels out the units:

$$1\text{m} = 100\text{cm} \Rightarrow 1 = \frac{100\text{cm}}{1\text{m}} \quad \Big| \quad 1\text{in} = 2.54\text{cm} \Rightarrow 1 = \frac{1\text{in}}{2.54\text{cm}} \quad \Big| \quad 3600\text{s} = 1\text{hr} \Rightarrow 1 = \frac{3600\text{s}}{1\text{hr}}$$

$$100\frac{\text{m}}{\text{s}}\left(\frac{100\text{cm}}{1\text{m}}\right)\left(\frac{1\text{in}}{2.54\text{cm}}\right)\left(\frac{3600\text{s}}{1\text{hr}}\right) = \frac{100 \cdot 100 \cdot 3600}{2.54}\frac{\text{in}}{\text{hr}} = \frac{100 \cdot 100 \cdot 3600}{2.54}\frac{\text{in}}{\text{hr}} = 1.42 \times 10^7 \frac{\text{in}}{\text{hr}}$$

To sum up unit conversion, just make sure you have the appropriate relations, and then set them equal to 1 (1 multiplied by any thing is still the same thing) in the order of canceling units.

Vectors

Notation

$$\vec{a} = \langle a_1, a_2 \rangle \text{ in 2D} \quad \text{or} \quad \vec{a} = \langle a_1, a_2, a_3 \rangle \text{ in 3D}$$

Addition/Subtraction

$$\vec{a} \pm \vec{b} = \langle a_1, a_2 \rangle \pm \langle b_1, b_2 \rangle = \langle a_1 \pm b_1, a_2 \pm b_2 \rangle$$

$$\vec{a} \pm \vec{b} = \langle a_1, a_2, a_3 \rangle \pm \langle b_1, b_2, b_3 \rangle = \langle a_1 \pm b_1, a_2 \pm b_2, a_3 \pm b_3 \rangle$$

Visually

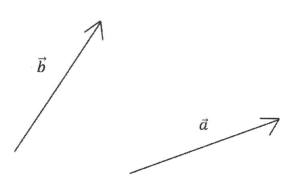

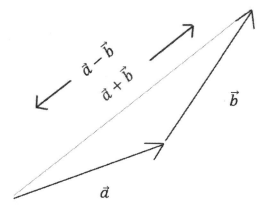

Dot Product

$$\vec{a} \cdot \vec{b} = \langle a_1, a_2 \rangle \cdot \langle b_1, b_2 \rangle = a_1 b_1 + a_2 b_2$$

$$\vec{a} \cdot \vec{b} = \langle a_1, a_2, a_3 \rangle \cdot \langle b_1, b_2, b_3 \rangle = a_1 b_1 + a_2 b_2 + a_3 b_3$$

Cross Product

$$\vec{a} \times b = -\vec{b} \times \vec{a}$$

$$\vec{a} \times \vec{b} = \begin{vmatrix} \hat{\imath} & \hat{\jmath} & \hat{k} \\ a_1 & a_2 & a_3 \\ b_1 & b_2 & b_3 \end{vmatrix}$$

$$= \hat{\imath} \begin{vmatrix} a_2 & a_3 \\ b_2 & b_3 \end{vmatrix} - \hat{\jmath} \begin{vmatrix} a_1 & a_3 \\ b_1 & b_3 \end{vmatrix} + \hat{k} \begin{vmatrix} a_1 & a_2 \\ b_1 & b_2 \end{vmatrix}$$

$$= \hat{\imath}[(a_2)(b_3) - (a_3)(b_2)] - \hat{\jmath}[(a_1)(b_3) - (a_3)(b_1)] + \hat{k}[(a_1)(b_2) - (a_2)(b_1)]$$

$\hat{\imath}, \hat{\jmath},$ and $\hat{k}$ are called **unit vectors**. A unit vector, is a vector of length 1

$$\hat{\imath} = \langle 1, 0, 0 \rangle, \qquad \hat{\jmath} = \langle 0, 1, 0 \rangle, \qquad \hat{k} = \langle 0, 0, 1 \rangle$$

$$= \langle (a_2)(b_3) - (a_3)(b_2), 0, 0 \rangle - \langle 0, (a_1)(b_3) - (a_3)(b_1), 0 \rangle + \langle 0, 0, (a_1)(b_2) - (a_2)(b_1) \rangle$$

$$= \langle (a_2)(b_3) - (a_3)(b_2), (a_1)(b_3) - (a_3)(b_1), (a_1)(b_2) - (a_2)(b_1) \rangle$$

Magnitude or Length of a vector

A bold letter is a vector i.e. $\vec{a} = \boldsymbol{a} = \langle a_1, a_2, a_3 \rangle$

$$2D, \qquad \|\boldsymbol{a}\| = |\vec{a}| = a = \sqrt{a_1^2 + a_2^2}$$

$$3D, \qquad |\vec{a}| = \|\boldsymbol{a}\| = a = \sqrt{a_1^2 + a_2^2 + a_3^2}$$

Unitizing a vector

To make the vector be of length 1 but preserve the direction.

$$2D, \qquad \hat{a} = \frac{\vec{a}}{|\vec{a}|} = \frac{\langle a_1, a_2 \rangle}{\sqrt{a_1^2 + a_2^2}}$$

$$3D, \qquad \hat{a} = \frac{\vec{a}}{|\vec{a}|} = \frac{\langle a_1, a_2, a_3 \rangle}{\sqrt{a_1^2 + a_2^2 + a_3^2}}$$

Resultant Vector

$$\vec{R} = \vec{a} + \vec{b}$$

In physics you will be usually be given the vector e.g. (e.g. = for example) $\vec{v}$ ($\vec{v}$ = velocity)

The resultant vector, v would be a vector that can be broken into a x and y component.

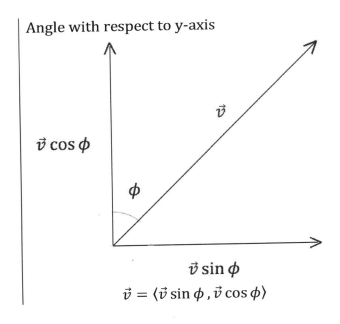

| Angle with respect to x-axis | Angle with respect to y-axis |

$$\vec{v} = \langle \vec{v} \cos\theta, \vec{v} \sin\theta \rangle \qquad \vec{v} = \langle \vec{v} \sin\phi, \vec{v} \cos\phi \rangle$$

$$\vec{v}, \quad \begin{cases} v_x = \vec{v}\cos\theta, \vec{v}_x = \langle \vec{v}\cos\theta, 0\rangle \\ v_y = \vec{v}\sin\theta, \vec{v}_y = \langle 0, \vec{v}\sin\theta\rangle \end{cases} \qquad \vec{v}, \quad \begin{cases} v_x = \vec{v}\sin\phi, \vec{v}_x = \langle \vec{v}\sin\phi, 0\rangle \\ v_y = \vec{v}\cos\phi, \vec{v}_y = \langle 0, \vec{v}\cos\phi\rangle \end{cases}$$

$$\vec{R} = \vec{v} = \vec{v}_x + \vec{v}_y = \langle \vec{v}\cos\theta, 0\rangle + \langle 0, \vec{v}\sin\theta\rangle = \langle \vec{v}\cos\theta, \vec{v}\sin\theta\rangle$$

$$|\vec{v}| = \sqrt{(\vec{v}\cos\theta)^2 + (\vec{v}\sin\theta)^2} = \sqrt{\vec{v}^2\cos^2\theta + \vec{v}^2\sin^2\theta} = \sqrt{\vec{v}^2(\cos^2\theta + \sin^2\theta)} = \sqrt{\vec{v}^2(1)} = v$$

This may be slightly confusing with the notation because of the vectors but in physics, you will be given a number for the vector i.e. $\vec{v} = -25\frac{m}{s}, \theta = 25°$ (a vector has magnitude and direction, which means it can be $\vec{v} = \langle\left(-25\frac{m}{s}\right)\cos 25°, \left(-25\frac{m}{s}\right)\sin 25°\rangle$ or for magnitude $\|\vec{v}\| = v = 25\frac{m}{s}$.

Summing it up

Since we are always working with numbers in general, not vector notation i.e. $\langle a_1, \dots\rangle$, and we are in a physics course, we can simply refer to distance, velocity, and acceleration without any vector hats i.e. $\vec{v}$ ... so velocity is v, acceleration is a, and distance is either x or y (in calculus distance is s). For the time being.

$$v, \begin{cases} v_x = v\cos\theta \\ v_y = v\sin\theta \end{cases}, \quad a, \begin{cases} a_x = a\cos\theta \\ a_y = a\sin\theta \end{cases}, \quad \Delta x = x - x_0, \quad \Delta y = y - y_0$$

$$\text{For some vector } A, \begin{cases} A_x = A\cos\theta \\ A_y = A\sin\theta \end{cases}$$

$$\text{Resultant vector: } R = \sqrt{[\Sigma A_x]^2 + [\Sigma A_y]^2}, \, A \text{ is any vector}$$

The example on the next page is a problem usually found around chapters 3-5. The problem demonstrates how to relate a free body diagram to a Cartesian coordinate system. This is extremely important to understand. Most students struggle with this, so make sure to take the time to understand it fully.

Free Body Diagram

A 250-N force is directed horizontally to push a 29-kg box up an inclined plane at a constant speed. Determine the magnitude of the normal force, FN, and the coefficient of kinetic friction. The angle of the incline is 27 degrees.

Step 1) Identify the unknowns, and the givens.

Given

Force	$\vec{F} = 250\text{N}$	Angle	$\theta = 27°$
		Gravity	$g = 9.81\dfrac{m}{s^2}$
Mass	$m = 29\text{kg}$	Weight	$w = 29 * 9.81\text{N}$

Step 2) Free Body Diagram.

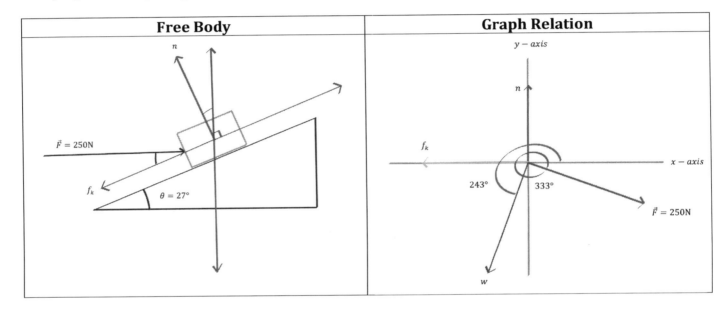

Free Body	Graph Relation

Step 3) Locate all related equations. $\sum \vec{F} = 0 \ \wedge \ \mu_k = \dfrac{f_k}{n}$

x-direction

$\vec{F_x} = \vec{F}\cos\theta_1 = 250\cos 333° \, \text{N}$

$w_x = mg\cos\theta_2 = (29)(9.81)\cos 243° \, \text{N}$

$\sum F_x = f_k + \vec{F}\cos\theta_1 + mg\cos\theta_2 = 0$

$\Rightarrow f_k = -(250\cos 333° + (29)(9.81)\cos 243°)\text{N}$

$\Rightarrow F_k \approx -93.59587378\text{N} \Rightarrow |F_k| = f_k = 94\text{N}$

y-direction

$\vec{F_y} = \vec{F}\sin\theta_1 = 250\sin 333° \, \text{N}$

$w_y = mg\sin\theta_2 = (29)(9.81)\sin 243° \, \text{N}$

$\sum F_y = n + \vec{F}\sin\theta_1 + mg\sin\theta_2 = 0$

$\Rightarrow n = -(250\sin 333° + (29)(9.81)\sin 243°)\text{N}$

$\Rightarrow n \approx 366.980071 \Rightarrow |n| = 367\text{N}$

Step 4) Plug in all values

$$\therefore |n| = 367\text{N}, \quad \mu_k = \left|\frac{F_k}{n}\right| = \frac{f_k}{n} = \left|\frac{\vec{F}\cos\theta_1 + mg\cos\theta_2}{\vec{F}\sin\theta_1 + mg\sin\theta_2}\right| = \left|\frac{-93.59587378}{366.980071}\right| \approx 0.26$$

Average velocity (straight-line)

$$v_{\mathrm{av}} \equiv \bar{v} \ (v \text{ bar}) = \frac{\Delta s}{\Delta t} = \frac{s - s_0}{t - t_0} = \frac{s_2 - s_1}{t_2 - t_1}$$

Note: "s" (italicized) is the standard variable for distance/displacement in calculus, where "s" (not italicized) is the unit for time t. Often in physics, "d" will be used for distance/displacement but in calculus, the d is reserved for derivatives, which is why we will stick with x and y to represent distances.

x-direction	y-direction
$\bar{v}_x \equiv v_{\mathrm{av}-x} = \dfrac{x - x_0}{t - t_0} = \dfrac{\Delta x}{\Delta t}$	$\bar{v}_y \equiv v_{\mathrm{av}-y} = \dfrac{y - y_0}{t - t_0} = \dfrac{\Delta y}{\Delta t}$

Note: x_0 may be referred to as x-initial, x-naught or x-subzero.

Instantaneous velocity (Calculus)

Limit Definition	$v = \lim\limits_{\Delta t \to 0} \dfrac{\Delta s}{\Delta t}$, $\qquad$ straight $-$ line
	$v = \lim\limits_{\Delta t \to 0} \dfrac{s(t + \Delta t) - s(t)}{\Delta t}$, $\qquad$ curve
x-direction	$v_x = \lim\limits_{\Delta t \to 0} \dfrac{\Delta x}{\Delta t}$, $\qquad$ straight $-$ line
	$= \lim\limits_{\Delta t \to 0} \dfrac{x(t + \Delta t) - x(t)}{\Delta t}$
y-direction	$v_y = \lim\limits_{\Delta t \to 0} \dfrac{\Delta y}{\Delta t}$, $\qquad$ straight $-$ line
	$= \lim\limits_{\Delta t \to 0} \dfrac{y(t + \Delta t) - y(t)}{\Delta t}$, $\qquad$ curve
Operator Notation	$v = \dfrac{d}{dt} s(t) = \dfrac{ds}{dt} = s'(t) \equiv \dot{s}$
x-direction	$v_x = \dfrac{d}{dt} x(t) = \dfrac{dx}{dt} = x'(t) \equiv \dot{x}$
y-direction	$v_y = \dfrac{d}{dt} y(t) = \dfrac{dy}{dt} = y'(t) \equiv \dot{y}$

Note: When you have a function $y = f(x)$, it can be separated into "parametric equations" $y = y(t)$ and $x = x(t)$, which gives two new graphing systems.

Parametric Equation Graphing Example

$$y(x) = \begin{cases} +\sqrt{25 - x^2} \\ -\sqrt{25 - x^2} \end{cases}$$

$$x^2 + y^2 = 25$$

$$\Rightarrow \left(\frac{x}{5}\right)^2 + \left(\frac{y}{5}\right)^2 = 1 = \cos^2 t + \sin^2 t$$

$$\Rightarrow x(t) = 5\cos t \wedge y(t) = 5\sin t, \qquad t \in [0, 2\pi]$$

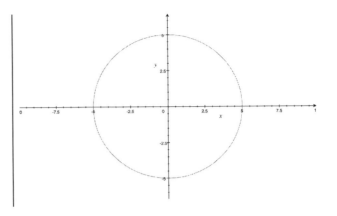

Average Acceleration (straight-line)

$$\bar{a} \equiv a_{\text{av}} = \frac{v - v_0}{t - t_0} = \frac{\Delta v}{\Delta t}$$

Instantaneous Acceleration (Calculus)

Acceleration	$a = \lim\limits_{\Delta t \to 0} \dfrac{v(\Delta t - t) - v(t)}{\Delta t} = \dfrac{dv}{dt} = \dot{v} = \dfrac{d}{dt}\left(\dfrac{ds}{dt}\right) = \ddot{s}$
x-direction	$a_x = \dfrac{dv_x}{dt} = \dfrac{d}{dt}\left(\dfrac{dx}{dt}\right)$
y-direction	$a_y = \dfrac{dv_y}{dt} = \dfrac{d}{dt}\left(\dfrac{dy}{dt}\right)$

Formulas (one-dimensional)

Note: The following formulas can be used in the y-direction as well but be careful because in the y-direction a may be equal to gravity and or the velocity may not be constant i.e. depending on how the coordinates are chosen in reference to the object(s) in question.

Velocity:
Acceleration is constant in x-direction

$$v_x = v_{x,0} + a_x t$$

Average Velocity:
a is constant in x-direction

$$v_{\text{av}-x} = v_{x,0} + \frac{1}{2}a_x t$$

Distance:
a is constant in x-direction

$$\Delta x = x - x_0 = v_{x,0}t + \frac{1}{2}a_x t^2$$

Velocity:
a is constant in x-direction

$$v_x^2 = v_{x,0}^2 + 2a_x \Delta x$$

$$v_f^2 = v_i^2 + 2ad$$

Distance:
a is constant in x-direction

$$\Delta x = x - x_0 = \left(\frac{v_x + v_{x,0}}{2}\right)t$$

$$d_f - d_i = \left(\frac{v_f + v_i}{2}\right)t$$

Note: $v_{x,0}$ is read as the initial velocity in the x-direction

Integration Derivations (Calculus)

Note: A derivative is the "rate-of-change," were a derivation is to derive something.

$$\frac{dv}{dt} = a \qquad \Rightarrow \quad \int dv = \int a\, dt \quad \Rightarrow \quad v = at + v_0$$

$$\frac{ds}{dt} = v = at + v_0 \quad \Rightarrow \quad ds = (at + v_0)dt \quad \Rightarrow \quad s - s_0 = \frac{at^2}{2} + v_0 t$$

Vector Notations

$$\mathbf{r} = x(t)\mathbf{i} + y(t)\mathbf{j} + z(t)\mathbf{k} \equiv \vec{r} = x(t)\hat{\imath} + y(t)\hat{\jmath} + z(t)\hat{k}$$

$$x(t)\hat{\imath} + y(t)\hat{\jmath} + z(t)\hat{k} = x(t)\langle 1,0,0\rangle + y(t)\langle 0,1,0\rangle + z(t)\langle 0,0,1\rangle = \langle x(t), y(t), z(t)\rangle$$

$$\therefore \vec{r} = x(t)\hat{\imath} + y(t)\hat{\jmath} + z(t)\hat{k} = \langle x(t), y(t), z(t)\rangle$$

Vector Derivatives

$$\vec{v} = \frac{d\vec{r}}{dt} = \frac{dx}{dt}\hat{\imath} + \frac{dy}{dt}\hat{\jmath} + \frac{dz}{dt}\hat{k} = \langle x'(t), y'(t), z'(t)\rangle = \langle \dot{x}, \dot{y}, \dot{z}\rangle$$

$$\vec{a} = \frac{d\vec{v}}{dt} = \frac{d^2\vec{r}}{dt^2} = \frac{d^2\vec{x}}{dt^2}\hat{\imath} + \frac{d^2\vec{y}}{dt^2}\hat{\jmath} + \frac{d^2\vec{z}}{dt^2}\hat{k} = \langle x''(t), y''(t), z''(t)\rangle = \langle \ddot{x}, \ddot{y}, \ddot{z}\rangle$$

Note: Sometimes you will see a derivative such as $x'(t) = v_x = \frac{dx}{dt}$, but in three-dimensional calculus, $v_x = \frac{\partial v}{\partial x}$, which is the partial derivative of v with respect to x. Just pay attention to what each book defines notations as, as they may not always be consistent.

$$\therefore \vec{v} = \frac{d\vec{r}}{dt} = \frac{dx}{dt}\hat{\imath} + \frac{dy}{dt}\hat{\jmath} + \frac{dz}{dt}\hat{k} = \langle x'(t), y'(t), z'(t) \rangle \equiv \langle v_x, v_y, v_z \rangle$$

$$\vec{a} = \frac{d^2\vec{r}}{dt^2} = \frac{d^2\vec{x}}{dt^2}\hat{\imath} + \frac{d^2\vec{y}}{dt^2}\hat{\jmath} + \frac{d^2\vec{z}}{dt^2}\hat{k} = \langle a_x, a_y, a_z \rangle$$

Magnitude of vector

$$\|v\| = |\vec{v}| = v = \sqrt{\left(x'(t)\right)^2 + \left(y'(t)\right)^2 + \left(z'(t)\right)^2}$$

Projectile Motion

$x = (v_0 \cos(\theta_0))t$	$y = (v_0 \sin(\theta_0))t - \frac{1}{2}gt^2$
$v_x = v_0 \cos(\theta_0)$	$v_y = v_0 \sin(\theta_0) - gt$
$y = (\tan\theta_0)x - \dfrac{gx^2}{2v_0^2 \cos^2(\theta_0)}$	$t = \dfrac{v_0 \sin(\theta_0) \pm \sqrt{v_0^2 \sin^2(\theta_0) - 2gy}}{g}$

Circular Motion

T is the period, R is the radius

Uniform circular motion	$a_{\text{rad}} = \dfrac{v^2}{R}$
Uniform circular motion	$v = \dfrac{2\pi R}{T}$
Uniform circular motion	$a_{\text{rad}} = \dfrac{4\pi^2 R}{T^2}$
Uniform circular motion	$R = \dfrac{v^2}{a_{\text{rad}}}$
Uniform circular motion	$a_{\text{tan}} = \dfrac{d|\vec{v}|}{dt}$
Non-uniform circular motion	$a_{\text{tan}} = \left|\dfrac{d\vec{v}}{dt}\right|$

Uniform circular motion	$\left|\dfrac{d\vec{v}}{dt}\right| = \dfrac{a^2}{r}$
Non-uniform circular motion	$\left|\dfrac{d\vec{v}}{dt}\right| = \sqrt{(a_{\text{rad}})^2 + (a_{\text{tan}})^2}$

Force

Resultant vector $\vec{R}$ (the sum of all vectors)

$$\vec{R}_x = \vec{F}_{x,1} + \vec{F}_{x,2} + \vec{F}_{x,3} + \cdots = \sum \vec{F}_x \qquad \vec{R}_y = \vec{F}_{y,1} + \vec{F}_{y,2} + \vec{F}_{y,3} + \cdots = \sum \vec{F}_y$$

$$\vec{R} = \vec{F}_1 + \vec{F}_2 + \vec{F}_3 + \cdots = \sum \vec{F} \;\Rightarrow\; |\vec{R}| = F = \sqrt{\left(\vec{R}_x\right)^2 + \left(\vec{R}_y\right)^2} = \sqrt{\left(\sum \vec{F}_x\right)^2 + \left(\sum \vec{F}_y\right)^2}$$

Newton's First Law of Motion

A body acted on, with zero net force, moves with constant velocity and no acceleration.

Newton unit N

$$N = kg \cdot \frac{m}{s^2} \text{ (mass(times)acceleration)}$$

Newton's Second Law of Motion

If a force is acted on a body, then the body accelerates, and the direction of acceleration is the same as the net forces direction.

$$\sum \vec{F} = m\vec{a}$$

Formulas

Weight	$w = mg$, (mass)(gravity)	
		$\vec{w} = m\vec{a}$
Force acting on another **Force**	$\vec{F}_{1,2} = -\vec{F}_{2,1}$	

LINEAR ALGEBRA

Rank of matrix and pivots

$[1 \quad 1], \qquad rank(A_1) = 1$

$\qquad\qquad\qquad\qquad\qquad\qquad\qquad [1 \quad 1], \qquad rank(A_8) = 1$

$\begin{bmatrix} 1 \\ 1 \end{bmatrix}, \qquad rank(A_2) = 1$

$\qquad\qquad\qquad\qquad\qquad\qquad\qquad \begin{bmatrix} 1 \\ 0 \end{bmatrix}, \qquad rank(A_9) = 1$

$[1 \quad 1 \quad 1], \qquad rank(A_3) = 1$

$\qquad\qquad\qquad\qquad\qquad\qquad\qquad [1 \quad 1 \quad 1], \qquad rank(A_{10}) = 1$

$\begin{bmatrix} 1 \\ 1 \\ 1 \end{bmatrix}, \qquad rank(A_4) = 1$

$\qquad\qquad\qquad\qquad\qquad\qquad\qquad \begin{bmatrix} 1 \\ 0 \\ 0 \end{bmatrix}, \qquad rank(A_{11}) = 1$

$\begin{bmatrix} 1 & 0 \\ 0 & 1 \end{bmatrix}, \qquad rank(A_5) = 2$

$\qquad\qquad\qquad\qquad\qquad\qquad\qquad \begin{bmatrix} 1 & 1 & 1 \\ 1 & 1 & 1 \\ 1 & 1 & 1 \end{bmatrix}, \qquad rank(A_{12}) = 1$

$\begin{bmatrix} 1 & 0 & 0 \\ 0 & 1 & 1 \end{bmatrix}, \qquad rank(A_6) = 2$

$\qquad\qquad\qquad\qquad\qquad\qquad\qquad \begin{bmatrix} 1 & 1 & 1 \\ 1 & 1 & -1 \\ 1 & 1 & 1 \end{bmatrix}, \qquad rank(A_{13}) = 2$

$\begin{bmatrix} 1 & 0 \\ 0 & 0 \\ 0 & 1 \end{bmatrix}, \qquad rank(A_7) = 2$

$\qquad\qquad\qquad\qquad\qquad\qquad\qquad \begin{bmatrix} 1 & 1 & 1 \\ 0 & 1 & 1 \\ 0 & 0 & 1 \end{bmatrix}, \qquad rank(A_{14}) = 3$

Note: max rank is the smaller dimension of $n \times m$ e.g. 3×7 means that 3 is the highest possible rank. It goes with the transpose as well i.e. 7×3 still has a highest rank of 3.

$$A = \begin{bmatrix} 1 & 2 & 1 & 1 & 1 & 1 \\ -1 & -2 & 1 & 1 & 1 & 1 \end{bmatrix} \overset{R1 + R2 \Leftarrow R2}{\underset{\sim}{}} \begin{bmatrix} 1 & 2 & 1 & 1 & 1 & 1 \\ 0 & 0 & 2 & 2 & 2 & 2 \end{bmatrix} \Rightarrow rank(A) = 2$$

$$Ax = b \Rightarrow \begin{bmatrix} 3 & 2 & 3 & | & 1 \\ 1 & 3 & 3 & | & 3 \\ 3 & 2 & 1 & | & 1 \end{bmatrix} \sim \begin{bmatrix} 1 & 0 & 0 & | & -\frac{3}{7} \\ 0 & 1 & 0 & | & \frac{8}{7} \\ 0 & 0 & 1 & | & 0 \end{bmatrix}, \qquad rank(A) = 3 \quad i.e. \quad A = full\ rank$$

Length of a vector and the unit vector

Given a vector $x = \vec{x} = (x_1, x_2, x_3, \ldots, x_n) = \begin{bmatrix} x_1 \\ x_2 \\ x_3 \\ \vdots \\ x_n \end{bmatrix}$

The length of the vector is the magnitude of the vector

$$\|x\| \equiv |\vec{x}| = \sqrt{x_1^2 + x_2^2 + x_3^2 + \cdots + x_n^2}$$

Ex:

Find the length of $(1,2,3,4)$

$$(1,2,3,4) = \begin{bmatrix} 1 \\ 2 \\ 3 \\ 4 \end{bmatrix} \Rightarrow |(1,2,3,4)| = \sqrt{1^2 + 2^2 + 3^2 + 4^2} = \sqrt{1 + 4 + 9 + 16} = \sqrt{30} \text{ units}$$

Ex:

From the vector above, find its unit vector.

$$\frac{\vec{v}}{|\vec{v}|} = \frac{v}{\|v\|} \quad \Rightarrow \quad \left|\frac{\vec{v}}{|\vec{v}|}\right| = \left\|\frac{v}{\|v\|}\right\| = 1 \text{ units}$$

$$\frac{x}{\|x\|} = \frac{1}{\sqrt{1+4+9+16}} \begin{bmatrix} 1 \\ 2 \\ 3 \\ 4 \end{bmatrix} = \frac{(1,2,3,4)}{\sqrt{30}} = \left(\frac{1}{\sqrt{30}}, \frac{2}{\sqrt{30}}, \frac{3}{\sqrt{30}}, \frac{4}{\sqrt{30}}\right)$$

$$\left|\frac{\vec{x}}{|\vec{x}|}\right| = \sqrt{\left(\left(\frac{1}{\sqrt{30}}\right)^2 + \left(\frac{2}{\sqrt{30}}\right)^2 + \left(\frac{3}{\sqrt{30}}\right)^2 + \left(\frac{4}{\sqrt{30}}\right)^2\right)} = \sqrt{\frac{1}{30} + \frac{4}{30} + \frac{9}{30} + \frac{16}{30}} = \sqrt{\frac{30}{30}} = 1 \text{ units}$$

Solutions of Augmented Matrices

Consider the basic scenario i.e. remember from algebra when you have $ax + by = c$ and $dx + ey = f$? Remember that these two lines either lye on each other, intersect or never touch, and this means they have either a unique solution, infinite solutions, on no solution. The same goes with $ax + by + cz = d$, except this is a plane.

For $\mathbb{R}^3$, consider the following system and its three possible solutions after reduction:

Coefficient Matrix

$$ax + by + cz = d$$
$$ex + fy + gy = h \quad \Rightarrow \quad \begin{bmatrix} a & b & c \\ e & f & g \\ i & j & k \end{bmatrix} \begin{bmatrix} x \\ y \\ z \end{bmatrix} = \begin{bmatrix} d \\ h \\ l \end{bmatrix} \quad \Rightarrow \quad \begin{bmatrix} a & b & c & d \\ e & f & g & h \\ i & j & k & l \end{bmatrix}$$
$$ix + jy + kz = l$$

$$\text{The Coefficient Matrix} = \begin{bmatrix} a & b & c \\ e & f & g \\ i & j & k \end{bmatrix}$$

Unique Solution

$$\sim \begin{bmatrix} 1 & 0 & 0 & * \\ 0 & 1 & 0 & * \\ 0 & 0 & 1 & * \end{bmatrix} \Rightarrow \begin{bmatrix} x \\ y \\ z \end{bmatrix} = \begin{bmatrix} * \\ * \\ * \end{bmatrix}$$

In $2D/3D$ here is a single point of intersection

Infinite Solution

$$\sim \begin{bmatrix} 1 & 0 & 0 & * \\ 0 & 1 & 0 & * \\ 0 & 0 & 0 & 0 \end{bmatrix} \Rightarrow \begin{bmatrix} x \\ y \\ z \end{bmatrix} = \begin{bmatrix} * \\ * \\ 0 \end{bmatrix} + s \begin{bmatrix} 0 \\ 0 \\ 1 \end{bmatrix}$$

In $3D$ two planes lie on top of each other
In $2D$ two lines lie on top of each other

No Solution

$$\sim \begin{bmatrix} 1 & 0 & 0 & * \\ 0 & 1 & 0 & * \\ 0 & 0 & 0 & * \end{bmatrix} \Rightarrow \begin{bmatrix} x \\ y \\ 0 \end{bmatrix} = \begin{bmatrix} * \\ * \\ * \end{bmatrix}$$

Two planes/lines never touch

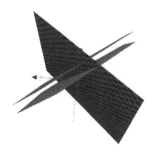

Solving System of Equations

$$x_2 + x_4 = 5 \wedge x_3 - 4x_4 = 4$$

I like to set up a matrix for this problem, and solve the matrix i.e.

$$x_2 + x_4 = 5 \Rightarrow 0x_1 + x_2 + 0x_3 + x_4 = 5$$

$$x_3 - 4x_4 = 4 \Rightarrow 0x_1 + 0x_2 + x_3 - 4x_4 = 4$$

$$\Rightarrow \begin{bmatrix} 0 & 1 & 0 & 1 & | & 5 \\ 0 & 0 & 1 & -4 & | & 4 \end{bmatrix} \Rightarrow \begin{bmatrix} 0 & 0 & 0 & 0 & | & 0 \\ 0 & 1 & 0 & 1 & | & 5 \\ 0 & 0 & 1 & -4 & | & 4 \\ 0 & 0 & 0 & 0 & | & 0 \end{bmatrix}$$

This helps to see the pivots, and identify that $x_1 \wedge x_4$ are free variables. Which means you can set them equal to themselves.

$$\begin{bmatrix} 0 & 0 & 0 & 0 & | & 0 \\ 0 & 1 & 0 & 1 & | & 5 \\ 0 & 0 & 1 & -4 & | & 4 \\ 0 & 0 & 0 & 0 & | & 0 \end{bmatrix} \Rightarrow x = \begin{matrix} x_1 \\ x_2 \\ x_3 \\ x_4 \end{matrix} = \begin{matrix} x_1 \\ 5 - x_4 \\ 4 + 4x_4 \\ x_4 \end{matrix} = \begin{matrix} 0 + x_1 + 0x_4 \\ 5 + 0x_1 - x_4 \\ 4 + 0x_1 + 4x_4 \\ 0 + 0x_1 + x_4 \end{matrix} = \begin{pmatrix} 0 \\ 5 \\ 4 \\ 0 \end{pmatrix} + \begin{pmatrix} 1 \\ 0 \\ 0 \\ 0 \end{pmatrix} x_1 + \begin{pmatrix} 0 \\ -1 \\ 4 \\ 1 \end{pmatrix} x_4$$

You can choose $x_1 \wedge x_4 = s \wedge t$ since they are free

$$\therefore x = \begin{pmatrix} 0 \\ 5 \\ 4 \\ 0 \end{pmatrix} + s \begin{pmatrix} 1 \\ 0 \\ 0 \\ 0 \end{pmatrix} + t \begin{pmatrix} 0 \\ -1 \\ 4 \\ 1 \end{pmatrix} = \{s, 5 - t, 4 + 4t, t\}$$

Gauss Jordan Augmented Matrix

$$\begin{aligned} 2x - y &= 2 \\ x + 2y &= 11 \\ 2x + 3y &= 18 \end{aligned} \Rightarrow \begin{bmatrix} 2 & -1 & | & 2 \\ 1 & 2 & | & 11 \\ 2 & 3 & | & 18 \end{bmatrix}$$

$$R2 \Leftarrow \frac{1}{2}R1 - R2 \wedge R3 \Leftarrow R1 - R3 \Rightarrow \begin{bmatrix} 2 & -1 & | & 2 \\ 0 & -\frac{5}{2} & | & -10 \\ 0 & -4 & | & -16 \end{bmatrix}$$

$$R2 \Leftarrow -\frac{2}{5}R2 \wedge R3 \Leftarrow -\frac{1}{4}R3 \Rightarrow \begin{bmatrix} 2 & -1 & | & 2 \\ 0 & 1 & | & 4 \\ 0 & 1 & | & 4 \end{bmatrix}$$

$$R3 \Leftarrow R2 - R3 \Rightarrow \begin{bmatrix} 2 & -1 & | & 2 \\ 0 & 1 & | & 4 \\ 0 & 0 & | & 0 \end{bmatrix}$$

$$R1 \Leftarrow R1 + R2 \Rightarrow \begin{bmatrix} 2 & 0 & | & 6 \\ 0 & 1 & | & 4 \\ 0 & 0 & | & 0 \end{bmatrix}$$

$$R1 \Leftarrow \frac{1}{2}R1 \Rightarrow \begin{bmatrix} 1 & 0 & | & 3 \\ 0 & 1 & | & 4 \\ 0 & 0 & | & 0 \end{bmatrix} \Rightarrow I_2 x = \begin{bmatrix} 3 \\ 4 \end{bmatrix} \Rightarrow \begin{aligned} x &= 3 \\ y &= 4 \end{aligned}$$

$$\therefore (x, y) = (3, 4)$$

Row Operation Rules and Guidelines for Solve a System of Matrices

Solve the system of equations rref [{-1/4,1,0,1},{1,0,1,2},{3,-1,1,2}]

$$\begin{aligned} -\frac{1}{4}x + y &= 1 \\ x + z &= 2 \\ 3x - y + z &= 2 \end{aligned} \Rightarrow \begin{bmatrix} -\frac{1}{4} & 1 & 0 & | & 1 \\ 1 & 0 & 1 & | & 2 \\ 3 & -1 & 1 & | & 2 \end{bmatrix}$$

Always go in the following order unless a zero already exists and or a row operation makes it exist.

$$1^{st} \begin{bmatrix} * & * & * & * & | & * \\ 1 & * & * & * & | & * \\ 2 & 4 & * & * & | & * \\ 3 & 5 & 6 & * & | & * \end{bmatrix}, 2^{nd} \begin{bmatrix} * & 12 & 11 & 9 & | & * \\ 0 & * & 10 & 8 & | & * \\ 0 & 0 & * & 7 & | & * \\ 0 & 0 & 0 & * & | & * \end{bmatrix}, 3^{rd} \begin{bmatrix} 1 & 0 & 0 & 0 & | & * \\ 0 & 1 & 0 & 0 & | & * \\ 0 & 0 & 1 & 0 & | & * \\ 0 & 0 & 0 & 1 & | & * \end{bmatrix}$$

General allowed operations when solve a system (not the same for a matrix A)

1. Row swapping $R1 \Leftrightarrow R2$ (means swap row 1 with row 2)

2. Divide/multiply a Row $\frac{1}{5}R2 \wedge -3R4$ (means divide row 2 by 5 and multiply row 4 by -3)

3. Adding/subtracting scaled rows $5R1 + R2 \Leftarrow R2$ (means the new row 2 = 5[row 1] + [row 2])

$$\begin{bmatrix} -\frac{1}{4} & 1 & 0 & | & 1 \\ 1 & 0 & 1 & | & 2 \\ 3 & -1 & 1 & | & 2 \end{bmatrix}$$

Take a look at the matrix. First multiply row 1 by -4 and then swap row 2 and row 3

$$-4R1 = -4\begin{bmatrix} -\frac{1}{4} & 1 & 0 & 1 \end{bmatrix} = \begin{bmatrix} 1 & -4 & 0 & -4 \end{bmatrix} \Leftarrow R1$$

$$R2 \Leftrightarrow R3$$

$$\begin{bmatrix} 1 & -4 & 0 & | & -4 \\ 3 & -1 & 1 & | & 2 \\ 1 & 0 & 1 & | & 2 \end{bmatrix}$$

Now eliminate 3 and 1 from column 1

$$-3R1 + R2 = -3\begin{bmatrix} 1 & -4 & 0 & -4 \end{bmatrix} + \begin{bmatrix} 3 & -1 & 1 & 2 \end{bmatrix} = \begin{bmatrix} 0 & 11 & 1 & 14 \end{bmatrix} \Leftarrow R2$$

$$-R1 + R3 = (-1)\begin{bmatrix} 1 & -4 & 0 & -4 \end{bmatrix} + \begin{bmatrix} 1 & 0 & 1 & 2 \end{bmatrix} = \begin{bmatrix} 0 & 4 & 1 & 6 \end{bmatrix} \Leftarrow R3$$

$$\begin{bmatrix} 1 & -4 & 0 & | & -4 \\ 0 & 11 & 1 & | & 14 \\ 0 & 4 & 1 & | & 6 \end{bmatrix}$$

Now eliminate 4 from column 2

$$-\frac{4}{11}R2 + R3 = -\frac{4}{11}\begin{bmatrix} 0 & 11 & 1 & 14 \end{bmatrix} + \begin{bmatrix} 0 & 4 & 1 & 6 \end{bmatrix} = \begin{bmatrix} 0 & 0 & \frac{7}{11} & \frac{10}{11} \end{bmatrix} \Leftarrow R3$$

$$\begin{bmatrix} 1 & -4 & 0 & | & -4 \\ 0 & 11 & 1 & | & 14 \\ 0 & 0 & \frac{7}{11} & | & \frac{10}{11} \end{bmatrix}$$

Multiply row 2 by $\frac{1}{11}$ and row 3 by $\frac{11}{7}$

$$\frac{1}{11}R2 = \begin{bmatrix} 0 & 1 & \frac{1}{11} & \frac{14}{11} \end{bmatrix}$$

$$\frac{11}{7}R3 = \begin{bmatrix} 0 & 0 & 1 & \frac{10}{7} \end{bmatrix}$$

$$\begin{bmatrix} 1 & -4 & 0 & \bigg| & \frac{-4}{} \\ 0 & 1 & \frac{1}{11} & \bigg| & \frac{14}{11} \\ 0 & 0 & 1 & \bigg| & \frac{10}{7} \end{bmatrix} \Rightarrow$$

$$x - 4y = -4 \Rightarrow x = 4\left(\frac{8}{7}\right) - 4 = \frac{4}{7}$$

$$y + \frac{1}{11}z = \frac{14}{11} \Rightarrow y = \frac{14}{11} - \frac{1}{11}\left(\frac{10}{7}\right) = \frac{8}{7}$$

$$z = \frac{10}{7}$$

$$\therefore \boldsymbol{x} = \begin{pmatrix} \frac{4}{7} \\ \frac{8}{7} \\ \frac{10}{7} \end{pmatrix} = \frac{1}{7}\begin{pmatrix} 4 \\ 8 \\ 10 \end{pmatrix} = \frac{2}{7}\begin{pmatrix} 2 \\ 4 \\ 5 \end{pmatrix}$$

Echelon Forms: EF, REF, RREF

$$\begin{array}{c} x_2 - x_1 - x_3 = 2 \\ 2x_1 - x_2 = 2 \\ 2x_1 + x_2 + x_3 = 2 \end{array} \Rightarrow \begin{bmatrix} -1 & 1 & -1 & \bigg| & 2 \\ 2 & -1 & 0 & \bigg| & 2 \\ 2 & 1 & 1 & \bigg| & 2 \end{bmatrix}$$

Echelon Form
aka **ef**

$$\begin{bmatrix} -1 & 1 & -1 & \bigg| & 2 \\ 2 & -1 & 0 & \bigg| & 2 \\ 2 & 1 & 1 & \bigg| & 2 \end{bmatrix} \begin{array}{c} 2R1 + R2 \Leftarrow R2 \\ 2R1 + R3 \Leftarrow R3 \\ \sim \end{array} \begin{bmatrix} -1 & 1 & -1 & \bigg| & 2 \\ 0 & 1 & -2 & \bigg| & 6 \\ 0 & 3 & -1 & \bigg| & 6 \end{bmatrix} \begin{array}{c} -3R2 + R3 \Leftarrow R3 \\ \sim \end{array} \begin{bmatrix} -1 & 1 & -1 & \bigg| & 2 \\ 0 & 1 & -2 & \bigg| & 6 \\ 0 & 0 & 5 & \bigg| & -12 \end{bmatrix}$$

Reduced Echelon Form
aka **ref**

$$\begin{bmatrix} -1 & 1 & -1 & \bigg| & 2 \\ 0 & 1 & -2 & \bigg| & 6 \\ 0 & 0 & 5 & \bigg| & -12 \end{bmatrix} \begin{array}{c} -R1 \Leftarrow R1 \\ \frac{1}{5}R3 \Leftarrow R3 \\ \sim \end{array} \begin{bmatrix} 1 & -1 & 1 & \bigg| & 2 \\ 0 & 1 & -2 & \bigg| & 6 \\ 0 & 0 & 1 & \bigg| & -\frac{12}{5} \end{bmatrix}$$

Reduced Row Echelon Form
aka **rref**

$$\begin{bmatrix} 1 & -1 & 1 & -2 \\ 0 & 1 & -2 & 6 \\ 0 & 0 & 1 & -\dfrac{12}{5} \end{bmatrix} \begin{array}{l} 2R3 + R2 \Leftarrow R2 \\ -R3 + R1 \Leftarrow R1 \\ \sim \end{array} \begin{bmatrix} 1 & -1 & 0 & \dfrac{2}{5} \\ 0 & 1 & 0 & \dfrac{6}{5} \\ 0 & 0 & 1 & -\dfrac{12}{5} \end{bmatrix} \begin{array}{l} R2 + R1 \Leftarrow R1 \\ \sim \end{array} \begin{bmatrix} 1 & 0 & 0 & \dfrac{8}{5} \\ 0 & 1 & 0 & \dfrac{6}{5} \\ 0 & 0 & 1 & -\dfrac{12}{5} \end{bmatrix}$$

[{-1,1,-1,2},{2,-1,0,2},{2,1,1,2}]

Linear Dependence

Linear combination

Say you have $\mathcal{B} = \{u, v, w\}$, write it as a linear combination. All that means is $ux_1 + vx_2 + wx_3$

Now to verify linear independence/dependence set the combination equal to zero. If there is a unique solution, the vectors are linearly independent else dependent i.e. if $u, v,$ or w can be written as a linear combination of the others e.g. $u = v - w$ or $v = u + 2w$ then they are dependent.

Different ways to verify dependency of vectors

Ex 1: Set u,v,w Linearly Dependent

Are the sets linear dependent/independent? ($\mathcal{B}$ denotes basis. $\mathcal{W}$ is generally subset/space)

$$\mathcal{W}_1 = \{u - 2v + w, w + v - u, 2w - v\}$$

(it can easily be seen that $(u - 2v + w) + (w + v - u) = 2w - v$, which means the set is dependent)

$$\mathcal{W}_1 : (u - 2v + w)x_1 + (w + v - u)x_2 + (2w - v)x_3$$

$$= [u - 2v + w \quad -u + v + w \quad 0u - v + 2w] \begin{bmatrix} x_1 \\ x_2 \\ x_3 \end{bmatrix}$$

$$= \left[[u \quad v \quad w] \begin{bmatrix} 1 \\ -2 \\ 1 \end{bmatrix} \quad [u \quad v \quad w] \begin{bmatrix} -1 \\ 1 \\ 1 \end{bmatrix} \quad [u \quad v \quad w] \begin{bmatrix} 0 \\ -1 \\ 2 \end{bmatrix} \right] \begin{bmatrix} x_1 \\ x_2 \\ x_3 \end{bmatrix}$$

$$= [u \quad v \quad w] \begin{bmatrix} 1 & -1 & 0 \\ -2 & 1 & -1 \\ 1 & 1 & 2 \end{bmatrix} \begin{bmatrix} x_1 \\ x_2 \\ x_3 \end{bmatrix}$$

$$\text{rref} \begin{bmatrix} 1 & -1 & 0 \\ -2 & 1 & -1 \\ 1 & 1 & 2 \end{bmatrix} = \begin{bmatrix} 1 & 0 & 1 \\ 0 & 1 & 1 \\ 0 & 0 & 0 \end{bmatrix}, \qquad \text{not full rank} \therefore \text{LD}$$

Ex 2: Set u,v,w Linearly Independent

$$W_2 = \{u, v + 2u, u - 2v\}$$

$$ux_1 + (v + 2u)x_2 + (u - 2v + w)x_3 = 0 \Rightarrow$$

$$=$$

$$= \begin{bmatrix} [u & v & w] \begin{bmatrix} 1 \\ 0 \\ 0 \end{bmatrix} & [u & v & w] \begin{bmatrix} 2 \\ 1 \\ 0 \end{bmatrix} & [u & v & w] \begin{bmatrix} 1 \\ -2 \\ 1 \end{bmatrix} \end{bmatrix} \begin{bmatrix} x_1 \\ x_2 \\ x_3 \end{bmatrix}$$

$$= [u \quad v \quad w] \begin{bmatrix} 1 & 2 & 1 \\ 0 & 1 & -2 \\ 0 & 0 & 1 \end{bmatrix} \begin{bmatrix} x_1 \\ x_2 \\ x_3 \end{bmatrix}$$

$$\text{rref} \begin{bmatrix} 1 & 2 & 1 \\ 0 & 1 & -2 \\ 0 & 0 & 1 \end{bmatrix}, \qquad \text{full rank} \therefore \text{ LI}$$

Ex 3: Vectors Linearly Independent

Determine if the set is linearly independent or dependent

$$w = \left\{ \begin{pmatrix} 1 \\ 2 \\ 3 \end{pmatrix}, \begin{pmatrix} 3 \\ 2 \\ 1 \end{pmatrix}, \begin{pmatrix} 1 \\ 1 \\ -1 \end{pmatrix} \right\}$$

$$ux_1 + vx_2 + wx_3 = \begin{pmatrix} 1 \\ 2 \\ 3 \end{pmatrix} x_1 + \begin{pmatrix} 3 \\ 2 \\ 1 \end{pmatrix} x_2 + \begin{pmatrix} 1 \\ 1 \\ -1 \end{pmatrix} x_3 = 0 \quad (Ax = 0)$$

$$\text{rref} \left(\begin{bmatrix} 1 & 3 & 1 & | & 0 \\ 2 & 2 & 1 & | & 0 \\ 3 & 1 & -1 & | & 0 \end{bmatrix} \right) = \begin{bmatrix} 1 & 0 & 0 & | & 0 \\ 0 & 1 & 0 & | & 0 \\ 0 & 0 & 1 & | & 0 \end{bmatrix}$$

This is a full rank matrix therefore it is a linearly independent set of vetors.

Ex 4: Vectors Linearly D
ependent

Determine if the set is linearly independent or dependent

$$w = \left\{ \begin{pmatrix} 1 \\ 2 \\ 3 \end{pmatrix}, \begin{pmatrix} 3 \\ 2 \\ 1 \end{pmatrix}, \begin{pmatrix} -3 \\ -6 \\ -9 \end{pmatrix} \right\}$$

$$\begin{bmatrix} 1 & 3 & -3 & | & 0 \\ 2 & 2 & -6 & | & 0 \\ 3 & 1 & -9 & | & 0 \end{bmatrix}$$

$$Ax = 0 \Rightarrow A^T A^{-1} Ax = A^T A^{-1} 0 \Rightarrow A^T(I)x = 0 \Rightarrow A^T x = 0$$

$$\therefore \begin{bmatrix} 1 & 2 & 3 & | & 0 \\ 3 & 2 & 1 & | & 0 \\ -3 & -6 & -9 & | & 0 \end{bmatrix} \quad R1 = -3R3 \quad \therefore \quad \text{LD} \quad \text{i.e.} \quad \text{not full rank}$$

$$3R1 + R2 \Leftarrow R3 \quad \Rightarrow \quad \begin{bmatrix} 1 & 2 & 3 & | & 0 \\ 3 & 2 & 1 & | & 0 \\ -3 & -6 & -9 & | & 0 \end{bmatrix} \sim \begin{bmatrix} 1 & 2 & 3 & | & 0 \\ 3 & 2 & 1 & | & 0 \\ 0 & 0 & 0 & | & 0 \end{bmatrix}$$

Ex 5: Polynomials

Determine if the set is linearly independent or dependent

$$p_1 = x^2 + x, p_2 = x - x^2, p_3 = 1$$

Don't be scared of the polynomial, just follow the rules, and it will work itself out!

(note: $p(x) = ax^2 + bx + c$ or higher order polynomials)

$$(x^2 + x)v_1 + (x - x^2)v_2 + (1)v_3 = 0$$

$$[x^2 + x \quad x - x^2 \quad 1] \begin{bmatrix} v_1 \\ v_2 \\ v_3 \end{bmatrix} = \begin{bmatrix} 0 \\ 0 \\ 0 \end{bmatrix} \Rightarrow$$

$$[x^2 + x + 0 \quad -x^2 + x + 0 \quad 0x^2 + 0x + 1] \begin{bmatrix} v_1 \\ v_2 \\ v_3 \end{bmatrix} = \begin{bmatrix} 0 \\ 0 \\ 0 \end{bmatrix} \Rightarrow [x^2 \quad x \quad 1] \begin{bmatrix} 1 & -1 & 0 \\ 1 & 1 & 0 \\ 0 & 0 & 1 \end{bmatrix} \begin{bmatrix} v_1 \\ v_2 \\ v_3 \end{bmatrix} = \begin{bmatrix} 0 \\ 0 \\ 0 \end{bmatrix}$$

$$-R1 + R2 \Rightarrow \begin{bmatrix} 1 & -1 & 0 \\ 0 & 2 & 0 \\ 0 & 0 & 1 \end{bmatrix}$$

Full rank and linearly independent

Ex 6: (M_(2x2))

$$w = \left\{ \begin{bmatrix} 1 & 0 \\ 1 & 1 \end{bmatrix}, \begin{bmatrix} 1 & 1 \\ 0 & 1 \end{bmatrix}, \begin{bmatrix} 1 & 0 \\ 0 & 1 \end{bmatrix}, \begin{bmatrix} 1 & 0 \\ 1 & 0 \end{bmatrix} \right\}$$

$$\begin{bmatrix} 1 & 0 \\ 1 & 1 \end{bmatrix} x_1 + \begin{bmatrix} 1 & 1 \\ 0 & 1 \end{bmatrix} x_2 + \begin{bmatrix} 1 & 0 \\ 0 & 1 \end{bmatrix} x_3 + \begin{bmatrix} 1 & 0 \\ 1 & 0 \end{bmatrix} x_4 = 0$$

$$\begin{bmatrix} x_1 & 0 \\ x_1 & x_1 \end{bmatrix} + \begin{bmatrix} x_2 & x_2 \\ 0 & x_2 \end{bmatrix} + \begin{bmatrix} x_3 & 0 \\ 0 & x_3 \end{bmatrix} + \begin{bmatrix} x_4 & 0 \\ x_4 & 0 \end{bmatrix} = 0$$

$$\begin{bmatrix} x_1 + x_2 + x_3 + x_4 & x_2 \\ x_1 + x_4 & x_1 + x_2 + x_3 \end{bmatrix} = \begin{bmatrix} 0 & 0 \\ 0 & 0 \end{bmatrix}$$

$$\begin{matrix} x_1 + x_2 + x_3 + x_4 = 0 \\ x_2 = 0 \\ x_1 + x_4 = 0 \\ x_1 + x_2 + x_3 = 0 \end{matrix} \Rightarrow \begin{bmatrix} 1 & 1 & 1 & 1 & | & 0 \\ 0 & 1 & 0 & 0 & | & 0 \\ 1 & 0 & 0 & 1 & | & 0 \\ 1 & 1 & 1 & 0 & | & 0 \end{bmatrix} \sim \begin{bmatrix} 1 & 0 & 0 & 0 & | & 0 \\ 0 & 1 & 0 & 0 & | & 0 \\ 0 & 0 & 1 & 0 & | & 0 \\ 0 & 0 & 0 & 1 & | & 0 \end{bmatrix}$$

This is a full rank matrix, therefore it is a linearly independent set of 2X2 matrices

Column Space - Row Space - Null Space - Kernel

$$A = \begin{bmatrix} -3 & 9 & -2 & -7 \\ 2 & -6 & 4 & 8 \\ 3 & -9 & -2 & 2 \end{bmatrix}$$

Step 1 rref(A) rref[{-3,9,-2,-7},{2,-6,4,8},{3,-9,-2,2}]

$$\begin{bmatrix} -3 & 9 & -2 & -7 \\ 2 & -6 & 4 & 8 \\ 3 & -9 & -2 & 2 \end{bmatrix} \sim \begin{bmatrix} 1 & -3 & 0 & \frac{3}{2} \\ 0 & 0 & 1 & \frac{5}{4} \\ 0 & 0 & 0 & \frac{4}{0} \end{bmatrix}$$

Identify Row Space

$$\begin{bmatrix} 1 & -3 & 0 & 3/2 \\ 0 & 0 & 1 & 5/4 \\ 0 & 0 & 0 & 0 \end{bmatrix} \Rightarrow \mathcal{B}_{RS} = \left\{ \begin{pmatrix} 1 \\ -3 \\ 0 \\ 3/2 \end{pmatrix}, \begin{pmatrix} 0 \\ 0 \\ 1 \\ 5/4 \end{pmatrix} \right\}$$

Identify Column Space

$$\begin{bmatrix} -3 & 9 & -2 & -7 \\ 2 & -6 & 4 & 8 \\ 3 & -9 & -2 & 2 \end{bmatrix} \sim \begin{bmatrix} 1 & -3 & 0 & 3/2 \\ 0 & 0 & 1 & 5/4 \\ 0 & 0 & 0 & 0 \end{bmatrix} \Rightarrow \mathcal{B}_{CS} = \left\{ \begin{pmatrix} -3 \\ 2 \\ 3 \end{pmatrix}, \begin{pmatrix} -2 \\ 4 \\ -2 \end{pmatrix} \right\}$$

Check you work i.e. Note: CS*RS=A

$$\begin{bmatrix} -3 & -2 \\ 2 & 4 \\ 3 & -2 \end{bmatrix} \begin{bmatrix} 1 & -3 & 0 & 3/2 \\ 0 & 0 & 1 & 5/4 \end{bmatrix} = \begin{bmatrix} -3 & 9 & -2 & -7 \\ 2 & -6 & 4 & 8 \\ 3 & -9 & -2 & 2 \end{bmatrix}$$

Null Space (Kernel)

$$\begin{bmatrix} -3 & 9 & -2 & -7 \\ 2 & -6 & 4 & 8 \\ 3 & -9 & -2 & 2 \end{bmatrix} \sim \begin{bmatrix} 1 & -3 & 0 & 3/2 \\ 0 & 0 & 1 & 5/4 \\ 0 & 0 & 0 & 0 \end{bmatrix} \Rightarrow \mathcal{B}_{NS} = \left\{ \begin{pmatrix} 3 \\ 1 \\ 0 \\ 0 \end{pmatrix}, \begin{pmatrix} -6 \\ 0 \\ -5 \\ 4 \end{pmatrix} \right\}$$

You can extract the null space quickly by changing the sign of the non-pivot element and adding a pivot where the pivot would line up to an identity matrix but this is how to compute it:

The 'Null Space' is the solution to $A\boldsymbol{x} = \boldsymbol{0}$

$$\begin{bmatrix} 1 & -3 & 0 & 3/2 \\ 0 & 0 & 1 & 5/4 \\ 0 & 0 & 0 & 0 \end{bmatrix} \begin{bmatrix} x_1 \\ x_2 \\ x_3 \\ x_4 \end{bmatrix} = \begin{bmatrix} 0 \\ 0 \\ 0 \end{bmatrix} \Rightarrow \begin{matrix} x_1 - 3x_2 + \dfrac{3}{2}x_4 = 0 \\ x_2 = x_2 \ free \\ x_3 + \dfrac{5}{4}x_4 = 0 \\ x_4 = x_4 \ free \end{matrix} \Rightarrow \begin{matrix} x_1 = 3x_2 - \dfrac{3}{2}x_4 \\ x_2 = x_2 + 0x_4 \\ x_3 = 0x_2 - \dfrac{5}{4}x_4 \\ x_4 = 0x_2 + x_4 \end{matrix}$$

$$\Rightarrow \quad \boldsymbol{x} = \begin{pmatrix} 3 \\ 1 \\ 0 \\ 0 \end{pmatrix} x_2 + \begin{pmatrix} -\dfrac{3}{2} \\ 0 \\ -\dfrac{5}{4} \\ 1 \end{pmatrix} x_4, \quad x_2 = 1 \wedge x_4 = 4 \Rightarrow \mathcal{B}_{NS} = \left\{ \begin{pmatrix} 3 \\ 1 \\ 0 \\ 0 \end{pmatrix}, \begin{pmatrix} -6 \\ 0 \\ -5 \\ 4 \end{pmatrix} \right\}$$

Check your work A*NS=0:

$$\begin{bmatrix} -3 & 9 & -2 & -7 \\ 2 & -6 & 4 & 8 \\ 3 & -9 & -2 & 2 \end{bmatrix} \begin{bmatrix} 3 & -6 \\ 1 & -5 \\ 0 & 0 \\ 0 & 4 \end{bmatrix} = \begin{bmatrix} 0 & 0 \\ 0 & 0 \\ 0 & 0 \end{bmatrix} = \boldsymbol{0}$$

LUD Decomposition and Elementary Matrices

$$A = \begin{bmatrix} 1 & 2 & 1 \\ 3 & 2 & 1 \\ 1 & 2 & 4 \end{bmatrix}, \qquad A = LUD = ? \quad (note) \begin{bmatrix} * & 6th & 5th \\ 1st & * & 4th \\ 2nd & 3rd & * \end{bmatrix} \wedge \begin{bmatrix} * & 12th & 11th & 9th \\ 1st & * & 10th & 8th \\ 2nd & 4th & * & 7th \\ 3rd & 5th & 6th & * \end{bmatrix}$$

$$\begin{bmatrix} 1 & 2 & 1 \\ 3 & 2 & 1 \\ 1 & 2 & 4 \end{bmatrix} \quad \begin{matrix} -3R1 + R2 = [-3 \ \ -6 \ \ -3] + [3 \ \ 2 \ \ 1] = [0 \ \ -4 \ \ -2] \Leftarrow R2 \\ (-1)R1 + R3 = [-1 \ \ -2 \ \ -1] + [1 \ \ 2 \ \ 4] = [0 \ \ 0 \ \ 3] \Leftarrow R3 \end{matrix}$$

$$\Rightarrow \begin{bmatrix} 1 & 2 & 1 \\ 0 & -4 & -2 \\ 0 & 0 & 3 \end{bmatrix} \vee E_1 A = \begin{bmatrix} 1 & 0 & 0 \\ -3 & 1 & 0 \\ -1 & 0 & 1 \end{bmatrix} \begin{bmatrix} 1 & 2 & 1 \\ 3 & 2 & 1 \\ 1 & 2 & 4 \end{bmatrix} = \begin{bmatrix} 1 & 2 & 1 \\ 0 & -4 & -2 \\ 0 & 0 & 3 \end{bmatrix}$$

$$\Rightarrow \begin{bmatrix} 1 & 2 & 1 \\ 0 & -4 & -2 \\ 0 & 0 & 3 \end{bmatrix} \quad \frac{2}{3}R3 + R2 = [0 \ \ 0 \ \ 2] + [0 \ -4 \ -2] = [0 \ -4 \ \ 0] \Leftarrow R2$$
$$-\frac{1}{3}R3 + R1 = [0 \ \ 0 \ -1] + [1 \ \ 2 \ \ 1] = [1 \ \ 2 \ \ 0] \Leftarrow R1$$

$$\Rightarrow \begin{bmatrix} 1 & 2 & 0 \\ 0 & -4 & 0 \\ 0 & 0 & 3 \end{bmatrix} \quad \frac{1}{2}R2 + R1 = [0 \ -2 \ \ 0] + [1 \ \ 2 \ \ 0] = [1 \ \ 0 \ \ 0] \Leftarrow R1$$

$$\Rightarrow \begin{bmatrix} 1 & 0 & 0 \\ 0 & -4 & 0 \\ 0 & 0 & 3 \end{bmatrix} \vee E_3 E_2 E_1 A = \begin{bmatrix} 1 & \frac{1}{2} & 0 \\ 0 & 1 & 0 \\ 0 & 0 & 1 \end{bmatrix} \begin{bmatrix} 1 & 0 & -\frac{1}{3} \\ 0 & 1 & \frac{2}{3} \\ 0 & 0 & 1 \end{bmatrix} \begin{bmatrix} 1 & 0 & 0 \\ -3 & 1 & 0 \\ -1 & 0 & 1 \end{bmatrix} \begin{bmatrix} 1 & 2 & 1 \\ 3 & 2 & 1 \\ 1 & 2 & 4 \end{bmatrix} = \begin{bmatrix} 1 & 0 & 0 \\ 0 & -4 & 0 \\ 0 & 0 & 3 \end{bmatrix} = D$$

$$L = \begin{bmatrix} 1 & 0 & 0 \\ 3 & 1 & 0 \\ 1 & 0 & 1 \end{bmatrix}, \qquad U = \begin{bmatrix} 1 & -\frac{1}{2} & \frac{1}{3} \\ 0 & 1 & -\frac{2}{3} \\ 0 & 0 & 1 \end{bmatrix}, \qquad D = \begin{bmatrix} 1 & 0 & 0 \\ 0 & -4 & 0 \\ 0 & 0 & 3 \end{bmatrix}$$

$$\therefore A = LUD = \begin{bmatrix} 1 & 0 & 0 \\ 3 & 1 & 0 \\ 1 & 0 & 1 \end{bmatrix} \begin{bmatrix} 1 & -\frac{1}{2} & \frac{1}{3} \\ 0 & 1 & -\frac{2}{3} \\ 0 & 0 & 1 \end{bmatrix} \begin{bmatrix} 1 & 0 & 0 \\ 0 & -4 & 0 \\ 0 & 0 & 3 \end{bmatrix} = \begin{bmatrix} 1 & 2 & 1 \\ 3 & 2 & 1 \\ 1 & 2 & 4 \end{bmatrix}$$

Transpose

$$(n \times m)^T = (m \times n)$$

Ex 1:

$$\begin{bmatrix} 1 \\ 2 \\ 3 \\ 4 \\ 5 \end{bmatrix}^T = \begin{bmatrix} 1 & 2 & 3 & 4 & 5 \end{bmatrix}$$

Ex 2:

$$\begin{bmatrix} 1 & 2 & 3 \\ 1 & 3 & 2 \end{bmatrix}^T = \begin{bmatrix} 1 & 1 \\ 2 & 3 \\ 3 & 2 \end{bmatrix}$$

Ex 3:

$$\begin{bmatrix} 1 & 2 & 3 \\ 4 & 5 & 6 \\ 7 & 8 & 9 \end{bmatrix}^T = \begin{bmatrix} 1 & 4 & 7 \\ 2 & 5 & 8 \\ 3 & 6 & 9 \end{bmatrix}$$

Ex 4:

$$(AB)^T = B^T A^T$$

$$[(4 \times 3)(3 \times 5)]^T = (3 \times 5)^T (4 \times 3)^T = (5 \times 3)(3 \times 4) = (5 \times 4)$$

Symmetric matrix for A=LDU=LDL^T

$$A = \begin{bmatrix} 1 & 3 & 4 \\ 3 & 1 & 3 \\ 4 & 3 & -1 \end{bmatrix}$$

$$E_1 A = \begin{bmatrix} 1 & 0 & 0 \\ -3 & 1 & 0 \\ -4 & 0 & 1 \end{bmatrix} \begin{bmatrix} 1 & 3 & 4 \\ 3 & 1 & 3 \\ 4 & 3 & -1 \end{bmatrix} = \begin{bmatrix} 1 & 3 & 4 \\ 0 & -8 & -9 \\ 0 & -9 & -17 \end{bmatrix}$$

$$E_2(E_1A) = \begin{bmatrix} 1 & 0 & 0 \\ 0 & 1 & 0 \\ 0 & -\dfrac{9}{8} & 1 \end{bmatrix} \begin{bmatrix} 1 & 3 & 4 \\ 0 & -8 & -9 \\ 0 & -9 & -17 \end{bmatrix} = \begin{bmatrix} 1 & 3 & 4 \\ 0 & -8 & -9 \\ 0 & 0 & -\dfrac{55}{8} \end{bmatrix}$$

$$A = LDL^T = LDU = \begin{bmatrix} 1 & 0 & 0 \\ 3 & 1 & 0 \\ 4 & \dfrac{9}{8} & 1 \end{bmatrix} \begin{bmatrix} 1 & 0 & 0 \\ 0 & -8 & 0 \\ 0 & 0 & -\dfrac{55}{8} \end{bmatrix} \begin{bmatrix} 1 & 0 & 0 \\ 3 & 1 & 0 \\ 4 & \dfrac{9}{8} & 1 \end{bmatrix}^T$$

$$\therefore A = \begin{bmatrix} 1 & 0 & 0 \\ 3 & 1 & 0 \\ 4 & \dfrac{9}{8} & 1 \end{bmatrix} \begin{bmatrix} 1 & 0 & 0 \\ 0 & -8 & 0 \\ 0 & 0 & -\dfrac{55}{8} \end{bmatrix} \begin{bmatrix} 1 & 3 & 4 \\ 0 & 1 & \dfrac{9}{8} \\ 0 & 0 & 1 \end{bmatrix}$$

Matrix addition and subtraction

$$(n \times m) \pm (n \times m) = (n \times m)$$

Ex 1:

$$A = \begin{bmatrix} 1 & 2 & 1 \\ 1 & 1 & 1 \end{bmatrix} \wedge B = \begin{bmatrix} 1 & 1 & 1 \\ 1 & 2 & 1 \end{bmatrix}, \qquad A + B = ?$$

$$A + B = \begin{bmatrix} 1 & 2 & 1 \\ 1 & 1 & 1 \end{bmatrix} + \begin{bmatrix} 1 & 1 & 1 \\ 1 & 2 & 1 \end{bmatrix} = \begin{bmatrix} 1+1 & 2+1 & 1+1 \\ 1+1 & 1+2 & 1+1 \end{bmatrix} = \begin{bmatrix} 2 & 3 & 2 \\ 2 & 3 & 2 \end{bmatrix}$$

Ex 2:

$$C = \begin{bmatrix} 1 & 2 \\ 2 & 2 \\ 2 & 2 \end{bmatrix} \wedge D = \begin{bmatrix} 1 & 1 \\ 1 & 1 \\ 1 & 1 \end{bmatrix}, \qquad C - D = ?$$

$$C - D = \begin{bmatrix} 1 & 2 \\ 2 & 2 \\ 2 & 2 \end{bmatrix} - \begin{bmatrix} 1 & 1 \\ 1 & 1 \\ 1 & 1 \end{bmatrix} = \begin{bmatrix} 1-1 & 2-1 \\ 2-1 & 2-1 \\ 2-1 & 2-1 \end{bmatrix} = \begin{bmatrix} 0 & 1 \\ 1 & 1 \\ 1 & 1 \end{bmatrix}$$

Ex 3:

$$(A + B)^T - 5(C - D) = ?$$

$$\begin{bmatrix} 2 & 3 & 2 \\ 2 & 3 & 2 \end{bmatrix}^T - 5\begin{bmatrix} 0 & 1 \\ 1 & 1 \\ 1 & 1 \end{bmatrix} = \begin{bmatrix} 2 & 2 \\ 3 & 3 \\ 2 & 2 \end{bmatrix} - \begin{bmatrix} 0 & 5 \\ 5 & 5 \\ 5 & 5 \end{bmatrix} = \begin{bmatrix} 2 & -3 \\ -2 & -2 \\ -3 & -3 \end{bmatrix}$$

Multiply the matrices (2x2)(2x3)

$$(m \times n)(n \times p) = (m \times p)$$

$$(2 \times 2)(2 \times 3) = (2 \times 3)$$

$$\begin{bmatrix} 1 & 5 \\ -1 & 2 \end{bmatrix}\begin{bmatrix} 1 & 5 & 0 \\ 4 & 0 & 2 \end{bmatrix} = \begin{bmatrix} [1 \ \ 5]\begin{bmatrix}1\\4\end{bmatrix} & [1 \ \ 5]\begin{bmatrix}5\\0\end{bmatrix} & [1 \ \ 5]\begin{bmatrix}0\\2\end{bmatrix} \\ [-1 \ \ 2]\begin{bmatrix}1\\4\end{bmatrix} & [-1 \ \ 2]\begin{bmatrix}5\\0\end{bmatrix} & [-1 \ \ 2]\begin{bmatrix}0\\2\end{bmatrix} \end{bmatrix}$$

$$= \begin{bmatrix} (1)(1) + (5)(4) & (1)(5) + (5)(0) & (1)(0) + (5)(2) \\ (-1)(1) + (2)(4) & (-1)(5) + (2)(0) & (-1)(0) + (2)(2) \end{bmatrix}$$

$$= \begin{bmatrix} 21 & 5 & 10 \\ 7 & -5 & 4 \end{bmatrix}$$

Matrix Multiplication (mxn)(nxp)

$$(m \times n)(n \times p) = (m \times p)$$

Matrix multiplication is kind of like a giant 'dot product'

This is the row by column method

Ex 1:

$$(2 \times 2)(2 \times 1) = (2 \times 1): \quad \begin{bmatrix} 1 & 2 \\ 1 & 1 \end{bmatrix}\begin{bmatrix} 3 \\ 1 \end{bmatrix} = \begin{bmatrix} [1 \ \ 2]\begin{bmatrix}3\\1\end{bmatrix} \\ [1 \ \ 1]\begin{bmatrix}3\\1\end{bmatrix} \end{bmatrix} = \begin{bmatrix} (1)(3) + (2)(1) \\ (1)(3) + (1)(1) \end{bmatrix} = \begin{bmatrix} 5 \\ 4 \end{bmatrix}$$

Ex 2:

$$(2 \times 3)(3 \times 1) = (2 \times 1): \quad \begin{bmatrix} 1 & 2 & 2 \\ 2 & 1 & 2 \end{bmatrix}\begin{bmatrix} 1 \\ 3 \\ 1 \end{bmatrix} = \begin{bmatrix} [1 \quad 2 \quad 2]\begin{bmatrix} 1 \\ 3 \\ 1 \end{bmatrix} \\ [2 \quad 1 \quad 2]\begin{bmatrix} 1 \\ 3 \\ 1 \end{bmatrix} \end{bmatrix} = \begin{bmatrix} (1)(1) + (2)(3) + (2)(1) \\ (2)(1) + (1)(3) + (2)(1) \end{bmatrix} = \begin{bmatrix} 9 \\ 7 \end{bmatrix}$$

Ex 3:

$$(3 \times 3)(1x3) = DNE: \quad \begin{bmatrix} 1 & 3 & 2 \\ 1 & 2 & 2 \\ 1 & 1 & 2 \end{bmatrix}[1 \quad 2 \quad 3]$$

Ex 4:

$$(3 \times 3)(1x3)^T = (3 \times 3)(3 \times 1) = (3 \times 1): \quad \begin{bmatrix} 1 & 3 & 2 \\ 1 & 2 & 2 \\ 1 & 1 & 2 \end{bmatrix}[1 \quad 2 \quad 3]^T = \begin{bmatrix} 1 & 3 & 2 \\ 1 & 2 & 2 \\ 1 & 1 & 2 \end{bmatrix}\begin{bmatrix} 1 \\ 2 \\ 3 \end{bmatrix} =$$

$$\begin{bmatrix} [1 \quad 3 \quad 2]\begin{bmatrix} 1 \\ 2 \\ 3 \end{bmatrix} \\ [1 \quad 2 \quad 2]\begin{bmatrix} 1 \\ 2 \\ 3 \end{bmatrix} \\ [1 \quad 1 \quad 2]\begin{bmatrix} 1 \\ 2 \\ 3 \end{bmatrix} \end{bmatrix} = \begin{bmatrix} (1)(1) + (3)(2) + (2)(3) \\ (1)(1) + (2)(2) + (2)(3) \\ (1)(1) + (1)(2) + (2)(3) \end{bmatrix} = \begin{bmatrix} 13 \\ 11 \\ 9 \end{bmatrix}$$

Ex 5:

$$(2 \times 3)(3 \times 3) = (2 \times 3): \quad \begin{bmatrix} 1 & 4 & 1 \\ 3 & 1 & 1 \end{bmatrix}\begin{bmatrix} 1 & 4 & 3 \\ 2 & 1 & 1 \\ 1 & 2 & 2 \end{bmatrix}$$

$$= \begin{bmatrix} [1 \quad 4 \quad 1]\begin{bmatrix} 1 \\ 2 \\ 1 \end{bmatrix} & [1 \quad 4 \quad 1]\begin{bmatrix} 4 \\ 1 \\ 2 \end{bmatrix} & [1 \quad 4 \quad 1]\begin{bmatrix} 3 \\ 1 \\ 2 \end{bmatrix} \\ [3 \quad 1 \quad 1]\begin{bmatrix} 1 \\ 2 \\ 1 \end{bmatrix} & [3 \quad 1 \quad 1]\begin{bmatrix} 4 \\ 1 \\ 2 \end{bmatrix} & [3 \quad 1 \quad 1]\begin{bmatrix} 3 \\ 1 \\ 2 \end{bmatrix} \end{bmatrix}$$

$$= \begin{bmatrix} (1)(1) + (4)(2) + (1)(1) & (1)(4) + (4)(1) + (1)(2) & (1)(3) + (4)(1) + (1)(2) \\ (3)(1) + (1)(2) + (1)(1) & (3)(4) + (1)(1) + (1)(2) & (3)(3) + (1)(1) + (1)(2) \end{bmatrix}$$

$$= \begin{bmatrix} 10 & 10 & 9 \\ 6 & 15 & 12 \end{bmatrix}$$

Ex 6:

$$(2 \times 3)(3 \times 3)(3 \times 2) = (2 \times 3)(3 \times 2) = (2 \times 2):$$

$$\begin{bmatrix} 1 & 4 & 1 \\ 3 & 1 & 1 \end{bmatrix} \begin{bmatrix} 1 & 4 & 3 \\ 2 & 1 & 1 \\ 1 & 2 & 2 \end{bmatrix} \begin{bmatrix} 1 & 0 \\ 0 & 1 \\ 1 & 0 \end{bmatrix} = \begin{bmatrix} 10 & 10 & 9 \\ 6 & 15 & 12 \end{bmatrix} \begin{bmatrix} 1 & 0 \\ 0 & 1 \\ 1 & 0 \end{bmatrix} = \begin{bmatrix} 19 & 10 \\ 18 & 15 \end{bmatrix}$$

Idempotent matrix

$$AA = A \Rightarrow A^n = A$$

Ex 1:

$$A = \begin{bmatrix} 2 & -2 & -4 \\ -1 & 3 & 4 \\ 1 & -2 & -3 \end{bmatrix} \Rightarrow AA = \begin{bmatrix} 2 & -2 & -4 \\ -1 & 3 & 4 \\ 1 & -2 & -3 \end{bmatrix} \begin{bmatrix} 2 & -2 & -4 \\ -1 & 3 & 4 \\ 1 & -2 & -3 \end{bmatrix} = \begin{bmatrix} 2 & -2 & -4 \\ -1 & 3 & 4 \\ 1 & -2 & -3 \end{bmatrix}$$

$$\Rightarrow AAA = \begin{bmatrix} 2 & -2 & -4 \\ -1 & 3 & 4 \\ 1 & -2 & -3 \end{bmatrix} \begin{bmatrix} 2 & -2 & -4 \\ -1 & 3 & 4 \\ 1 & -2 & -3 \end{bmatrix} \begin{bmatrix} 2 & -2 & -4 \\ -1 & 3 & 4 \\ 1 & -2 & -3 \end{bmatrix} = \begin{bmatrix} 2 & -2 & -4 \\ -1 & 3 & 4 \\ 1 & -2 & -3 \end{bmatrix}$$

$$\Rightarrow A^n = \begin{bmatrix} 2 & -2 & -4 \\ -1 & 3 & 4 \\ 1 & -2 & -3 \end{bmatrix}^n = \begin{bmatrix} 2 & -2 & -4 \\ -1 & 3 & 4 \\ 1 & -2 & -3 \end{bmatrix} = A$$

Ex 2: (2X2) Determine if A is Idempotent without multiplication

$$A = \begin{pmatrix} a & b \\ c & d \end{pmatrix} \Rightarrow A^k = \begin{pmatrix} a^2 + bc & ab + bd \\ ca + cd & bc + d^2 \end{pmatrix}^k = \begin{pmatrix} a^2 + bc & ab + bd \\ ca + cd & bc + d^2 \end{pmatrix}$$

$$\begin{pmatrix} 4 & -1 \\ 12 & -3 \end{pmatrix}$$

$$a = a^2 + bc \quad \Rightarrow \quad 4 = 4^2 + (-1)(12) = 16 - 12 = 4$$

$$b = ab + bd \quad \Rightarrow \quad -1 = (4)(-1) + (-1)(-3) = -4 + 3 = -1$$

$$c = ca + cd \quad \Rightarrow \quad 12 = (12)(4) + (12)(-3) = 48 - 36 = 12$$

$$d = bc + d^2 \quad \Rightarrow \quad -3 = (-1)(12) + (-3)^2 = -12 + 9 = -3$$

$$\therefore \begin{pmatrix} 4 & -1 \\ 12 & -3 \end{pmatrix} \begin{pmatrix} 4 & -1 \\ 12 & -3 \end{pmatrix} = \begin{pmatrix} 4 & -1 \\ 12 & -3 \end{pmatrix} = \begin{pmatrix} 4 & -1 \\ 12 & -3 \end{pmatrix}^k, \text{Yes A is idempotent}$$

Rotation and Translate

Ex. 1

Give the 4×4 matrix that rotates points in $\mathbb{R}^3$ about the z-axis through an angle of $-30°$, and then translates by $\mathbf{p} = (5, -2, 1)$

Unit points in $\mathbb{R}^3$ and just $\boldsymbol{v} = \{\boldsymbol{e}_1, \boldsymbol{e}_2, \boldsymbol{e}_3\}$, note: $\boldsymbol{e}_n = (0, 0, \ldots 1, \ldots 0, 0)$

About the z-axis means to

Create a 3×3 rotation matrix for $-30°$ about z-axis

(1) We want to move a point on the xy-plane $30°$ towards $-y$-axis, which is $(\cos(-30°), \sin(-30°), 0) = \left(\frac{\sqrt{3}}{2}, -\frac{1}{2}, 0\right)$. Note: we are moving x in a positive direction, and y in a negative direction i.e. choose the angle wisely.

(2) Next we want to move a point in the xy-plane towards the positive x-axis (two positive coordinates) Look at the unit circle, coordinate $(0,1)$. We ant to move this $-30°$ the coordinate for this is $(\cos(60°), \sin(60°)) = \left(\frac{1}{2}, \frac{\sqrt{3}}{2}\right)$ just put this into 3×1 column vector $\left(\frac{1}{2}, \frac{\sqrt{3}}{2}, 0\right)$

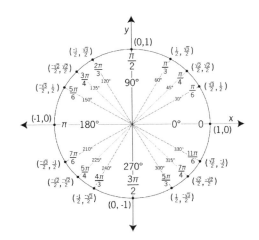

(3) Since we are going about the z-axis, the third coordinate $(0,0,1)$ does not move.

Finally, we get the following matrix A

$$A = \begin{bmatrix} \dfrac{\sqrt{3}}{2} & \dfrac{1}{2} & 0 \\ -\dfrac{1}{2} & \dfrac{\sqrt{3}}{2} & 0 \\ 0 & 0 & 1 \end{bmatrix} \Rightarrow \begin{bmatrix} \dfrac{\sqrt{3}}{2} & \dfrac{1}{2} & 0 & 0 \\ -\dfrac{1}{2} & \dfrac{\sqrt{3}}{2} & 0 & 0 \\ 0 & 0 & 1 & 0 \\ 0 & 0 & 0 & 1 \end{bmatrix}$$

Translated vector: Mapping $(x, y, z, 1) \rightarrow (x + 5, y - 2, z + 1, 1)$ gives the following matrix

$$\begin{bmatrix} x + 5 \\ y - 2 \\ z + 1 \\ 1 \end{bmatrix} = \begin{bmatrix} x + 0y + 0z + 5 \\ 0x - 0y + 0z - 2 \\ 0x + 0y + z + 1 \\ 0x + 0y + 0z + 1 \end{bmatrix} = \begin{pmatrix} 1 & 0 & 0 & 5 \\ 0 & 1 & 0 & -2 \\ 0 & 0 & 1 & 1 \\ 0 & 0 & 0 & 1 \end{pmatrix} \begin{pmatrix} x \\ y \\ z \\ 1 \end{pmatrix}$$

$$\therefore \begin{bmatrix} 1 & 0 & 0 & 5 \\ 0 & 1 & 0 & -2 \\ 0 & 0 & 1 & 1 \\ 0 & 0 & 0 & 1 \end{bmatrix} \begin{bmatrix} \dfrac{\sqrt{3}}{2} & \dfrac{1}{2} & 0 & 0 \\ -\dfrac{1}{2} & \dfrac{\sqrt{3}}{2} & 0 & 0 \\ 0 & 0 & 1 & 0 \\ 0 & 0 & 0 & 1 \end{bmatrix} = \begin{bmatrix} \dfrac{\sqrt{3}}{2} & \dfrac{1}{2} & 0 & 5 \\ -\dfrac{1}{2} & \dfrac{\sqrt{3}}{2} & 0 & -2 \\ 0 & 0 & 1 & 1 \\ 0 & 0 & 0 & 1 \end{bmatrix}$$

Ex. 2

Translate

Translate by $(-2, 3)$, and then scale the x-coordinate by 0.8 and the y-coordinate by 1.2.

Note: Whenever you translate a vector, add an additional dimension with element as #1 i.e.

$$\mathbb{R}^{n\times 1} \longmapsto \mathbb{R}^{(n+1)\times 1} \Rightarrow \begin{pmatrix} -2 \\ 3 \end{pmatrix} \to \begin{pmatrix} -2 \\ 3 \\ 1 \end{pmatrix}$$

Translate:

$$(x, y, 1) \to (x + 2, y + 3, 1)$$

Scale x-coordinate:

$$0.8(1, 0, 0) = (0.8, 0, 0)$$

Scale y-coordinate:

$$1.2(0, 1, 0) = (0, 1.2, 0)$$

Assemble the 3×3 matrix with the scaled positions:

$$\begin{bmatrix} 0.8 & 0 & 0 \\ 0 & 1.2 & 0 \\ 0 & 0 & 1 \end{bmatrix}$$

Assemble the 3×3 translate matrix

$$(x + 2, y + 3, 1) = \begin{bmatrix} x - 2 \\ y + 3 \\ 1 \end{bmatrix} = \begin{bmatrix} x + 0y - 2 \\ 0x + y + 3 \\ 0x + 0y + 1 \end{bmatrix} = \begin{pmatrix} 1 & 0 & -2 \\ 0 & 1 & 3 \\ 0 & 0 & 1 \end{pmatrix} \begin{pmatrix} x \\ y \\ 1 \end{pmatrix}$$

$$\therefore \begin{pmatrix} 0.8 & 0 & 0 \\ 0 & 1.2 & 0 \\ 0 & 0 & 1 \end{pmatrix} \begin{pmatrix} 1 & 0 & -2 \\ 0 & 1 & 3 \\ 0 & 0 & 1 \end{pmatrix} = \begin{pmatrix} 0.8 & 0 & -1.6 \\ 0 & 1.2 & 3.6 \\ 0 & 0 & 1 \end{pmatrix}$$

Rotate about a point (c, d)

Note:

D = dilate, R = rotation, T = translate. Scale $x \wedge y$ by α, rotate by θ, and translate (a, b)

$$D = \begin{bmatrix} \alpha & 0 & 0 \\ 0 & \alpha & 0 \\ 0 & 0 & 1 \end{bmatrix}, R = \begin{bmatrix} \cos\theta & -\sin\theta & 0 \\ \sin\theta & \cos\theta & 0 \\ 0 & 0 & 1 \end{bmatrix}, T = \begin{bmatrix} 1 & 0 & a \\ 0 & 1 & b \\ 0 & 0 & 1 \end{bmatrix}$$

$$\begin{bmatrix} 1 & 0 & c \\ 0 & 1 & d \\ 0 & 0 & 1 \end{bmatrix} \begin{bmatrix} \cos\theta & -\sin\theta & 0 \\ \sin\theta & \cos\theta & 0 \\ 0 & 0 & 1 \end{bmatrix} \begin{bmatrix} 1 & 0 & -c \\ 0 & 1 & -d \\ 0 & 0 & 1 \end{bmatrix}$$

Nilpotent matrix (eigenvalues are zero)

$$A^k_{nxn} = 0, \qquad k \le n$$

Ex 1:

$$A = \begin{bmatrix} 0 & 1 & 1 \\ 0 & 0 & 1 \\ 0 & 0 & 0 \end{bmatrix}$$

$$A^2 = \begin{bmatrix} 0 & 1 & 1 \\ 0 & 0 & 1 \\ 0 & 0 & 0 \end{bmatrix} \begin{bmatrix} 0 & 1 & 1 \\ 0 & 0 & 1 \\ 0 & 0 & 0 \end{bmatrix} = \begin{bmatrix} 0 & 0 & 1 \\ 0 & 0 & 0 \\ 0 & 0 & 0 \end{bmatrix}$$

$$A^3 = \begin{bmatrix} 0 & 1 & 1 \\ 0 & 0 & 1 \\ 0 & 0 & 0 \end{bmatrix} \begin{bmatrix} 0 & 1 & 1 \\ 0 & 0 & 1 \\ 0 & 0 & 0 \end{bmatrix} \begin{bmatrix} 0 & 1 & 1 \\ 0 & 0 & 1 \\ 0 & 0 & 0 \end{bmatrix} = \begin{bmatrix} 0 & 0 & 0 \\ 0 & 0 & 0 \\ 0 & 0 & 0 \end{bmatrix}$$

Ex 2:

Find k such that $A^k = \bar{0}$

$$\begin{bmatrix} 10 & -6 & 4 \\ 30 & -18 & 12 \\ 20 & -12 & 8 \end{bmatrix}\begin{bmatrix} 10 & -6 & 4 \\ 30 & -18 & 12 \\ 20 & -12 & 8 \end{bmatrix}$$

$$= \begin{bmatrix} [10 \; -6 \; 4]\begin{bmatrix} 10 \\ 30 \\ 20 \end{bmatrix} & [10 \; -6 \; 4]\begin{bmatrix} -6 \\ -18 \\ -12 \end{bmatrix} & [10 \; -6 \; 4]\begin{bmatrix} 4 \\ 12 \\ 8 \end{bmatrix} \\ [30 \; -18 \; 12]\begin{bmatrix} 10 \\ 30 \\ 20 \end{bmatrix} & [30 \; -18 \; 12]\begin{bmatrix} -6 \\ -18 \\ -12 \end{bmatrix} & [30 \; -18 \; 12]\begin{bmatrix} 4 \\ 12 \\ 8 \end{bmatrix} \\ [20 \; -12 \; 8]\begin{bmatrix} 10 \\ 30 \\ 20 \end{bmatrix} & [20 \; -12 \; 8]\begin{bmatrix} -6 \\ -18 \\ -12 \end{bmatrix} & [20 \; -12 \; 8]\begin{bmatrix} 4 \\ 12 \\ 8 \end{bmatrix} \end{bmatrix}$$

Note: $[a \quad b \quad c]\begin{bmatrix} d \\ e \\ f \end{bmatrix} = (a)(d) + (b)(e) + (c)(f)$

$$= \begin{bmatrix} 0 & 0 & 0 \\ 0 & 0 & 0 \\ 0 & 0 & 0 \end{bmatrix}$$

$$\therefore k = 2$$

Determinant rules

(1) $\det A^T = \det A$
(2) $\det A^{-1} = \frac{1}{\det A}$
(3) $\det AB = \det A \det B \Leftrightarrow A = nxn = B$
(4) $\det cA = c^n \det A \; for \; nxn$

$$\text{Given } \det A^{-1} = 5, \quad \det B^T = 6$$

Evaluate $\det(AB) + \det([5A]B^T), A = 4x4 = B$

$$\det(AB) + \det([5A]B^T) = \det A \det B + \det 5A \det B^T = \det A \det B + 5^4 \det A \det B$$

$$\because \det A^{-1} = \frac{1}{\det A} \therefore \det A^{-1} = 5 \Rightarrow \frac{1}{\det A} = 5 \Leftrightarrow \det A = \frac{1}{5}$$

155

$$= \frac{1}{5}(6) + 5^4 \left(\frac{1}{5}\right)(6) = \frac{6}{5} + 5^3 \cdot 6 = \frac{661}{30}$$

Proofs

Let A and P be square matrices, with P invertible. Show that $\det PAP^{-1} = \det A$.

Using determinant rule 2 i.e. $\det A^{-1} = \frac{1}{\det A}$, we find:

$$\det(PAP^{-1}) = \det P \det A \det P^{-1} = \frac{\det P \det A}{\det P} = \frac{\det P}{\det P} \det A = \det A$$

Find a formula for $\det(rA)$ when A is an $n \times n$ matrix.

Long version

$$A = LUD \Rightarrow \begin{bmatrix} a_{11} & \cdots & a_{1n} \\ \vdots & \ddots & \vdots \\ a_{n1} & \cdots & a_{nn} \end{bmatrix} = \begin{bmatrix} 1 & 0 & 0 \\ \vdots & 1 & 0 \\ l_{n1} & \cdots & 1 \end{bmatrix} \begin{bmatrix} 1 & \cdots & u_{1n} \\ 0 & 1 & \vdots \\ 0 & 0 & 1 \end{bmatrix} \begin{bmatrix} d_{11} & \cdots & 0 \\ \vdots & \ddots & \vdots \\ 0 & \cdots & d_{nn} \end{bmatrix}$$

$$\begin{bmatrix} 1 & 0 & 0 \\ \vdots & 1 & 0 \\ l_{n1} & \cdots & 1 \end{bmatrix} \begin{bmatrix} 1 & \cdots & u_{1n} \\ 0 & 1 & \vdots \\ 0 & 0 & 1 \end{bmatrix} r \begin{bmatrix} d_{11} & \cdots & 0 \\ \vdots & \ddots & \vdots \\ 0 & \cdots & d_{nn} \end{bmatrix} = \det\left(\begin{bmatrix} 1 & 0 & 0 \\ \vdots & 1 & 0 \\ l_{n1} & \cdots & 1 \end{bmatrix} \begin{bmatrix} 1 & \cdots & u_{1n} \\ 0 & 1 & \vdots \\ 0 & 0 & 1 \end{bmatrix} r \begin{bmatrix} d_{11} & \cdots & 0 \\ \vdots & \ddots & \vdots \\ 0 & \cdots & d_{nn} \end{bmatrix} \right)$$

$$\det\begin{bmatrix} 1 & 0 & 0 \\ \vdots & 1 & 0 \\ l_{n1} & \cdots & 1 \end{bmatrix} \det\begin{bmatrix} 1 & \cdots & u_{1n} \\ 0 & 1 & \vdots \\ 0 & 0 & 1 \end{bmatrix} \det\left(r \begin{bmatrix} d_{11} & \cdots & 0 \\ \vdots & \ddots & \vdots \\ 0 & \cdots & d_{nn} \end{bmatrix} \right) = (1)(1) \det\left(r \begin{bmatrix} d_{11} & \cdots & 0 \\ \vdots & \ddots & \vdots \\ 0 & \cdots & d_{nn} \end{bmatrix} \right)$$

$$= \det\begin{bmatrix} rd_{11} & \cdots & 0 \\ \vdots & \ddots & \vdots \\ 0 & \cdots & rd_{nn} \end{bmatrix} = rd_{11}rd_{22}\ldots rd_{nn} = r^n d_{11}d_{22}\ldots d_{nn} = r^n \det A$$

Short version

$$\det rA = \det(rLUD) = \det[(LU)(rD)] = \det(LU)\det(rD) = (1)(rd_1 rd_2 rd_3 \cdots rd_n)$$

$$= (1)r^n \det(D) = \det LU \, (r\det D) = r\det LU \det D = r\det LUD = r\det A$$

Determinate's of a (2x2) matrix

Various ways to check determinant

(2x2):

$$A = \begin{bmatrix} a & b \\ c & d \end{bmatrix} \Rightarrow \det(A) = |A| = \begin{vmatrix} a & b \\ c & d \end{vmatrix} = (a)(d) - (b)(c)$$

$$A = \begin{bmatrix} a & b \\ 0 & c \end{bmatrix} \Rightarrow \det(A) = |A| = \begin{vmatrix} a & b \\ 0 & c \end{vmatrix} = (a)(c)$$

$$A = \begin{bmatrix} a & 0 \\ 0 & b \end{bmatrix} \Rightarrow \det(A) = |A| = \begin{vmatrix} a & 0 \\ 0 & b \end{vmatrix} = (a)(b)$$

Formula:

$$\begin{vmatrix} 1 & -3 \\ 2 & 1 \end{vmatrix} = (1)(1) - 3(2) = 1 + 6 = 7$$

$$\begin{vmatrix} 1 & 2 \\ -1 & -2 \end{vmatrix} = (1)(-2) - (2)(-1) = -2 + 2 = 0$$

$$\begin{vmatrix} 1 & 3 \\ 0 & -3 \end{vmatrix} = (1)(-3) = -3$$

$$\begin{vmatrix} 1 & 0 \\ 0 & -5 \end{vmatrix} = (1)(-5) = -5$$

Row operation:

$$\begin{bmatrix} 1 & 3 \\ 4 & 5 \end{bmatrix} \sim \begin{bmatrix} 1 & 3 \\ 0 & -7 \end{bmatrix} \Rightarrow \begin{vmatrix} 1 & 3 \\ 4 & 5 \end{vmatrix} = (1)(-7) = -7$$

$$-4R1 + R2 = [-4 \quad -12] + [4 \quad 5] = [0 \quad -7] \Leftarrow R2$$

Note for future reference:

$$A = E_1 U \Rightarrow \begin{bmatrix} 1 & 3 \\ 4 & 5 \end{bmatrix} = \begin{bmatrix} 1 & 0 \\ 4 & 1 \end{bmatrix} \begin{bmatrix} 1 & 3 \\ 0 & -7 \end{bmatrix} \Rightarrow \det A = \det E_1 U = \det E_1 \det U = \begin{vmatrix} 1 & 0 \\ 4 & 1 \end{vmatrix} \begin{vmatrix} 1 & 3 \\ 0 & -7 \end{vmatrix}$$

$$= (1)(1)(1)(-7) = -7$$

Determinate of a (3x3) and higher matrices

Cofactor Expansion

Note:

$$\begin{vmatrix} a & b \\ c & d \end{vmatrix} = (a)(d) - (b)(c)$$

$$\begin{vmatrix} a & b & c \\ d & e & f \\ g & h & i \end{vmatrix} = +a\begin{vmatrix} e & f \\ h & i \end{vmatrix} - b\begin{vmatrix} d & f \\ g & i \end{vmatrix} + c\begin{vmatrix} d & e \\ g & h \end{vmatrix}$$

$$\begin{vmatrix} a & b & c & d \\ e & f & g & h \\ i & j & k & l \\ m & n & o & p \end{vmatrix} = +a\begin{vmatrix} f & g & h \\ j & k & l \\ n & o & p \end{vmatrix} - b\begin{vmatrix} e & g & h \\ i & k & l \\ m & 0 & p \end{vmatrix} + c\begin{vmatrix} e & f & h \\ i & j & l \\ m & n & p \end{vmatrix} - d\begin{vmatrix} e & f & g \\ i & j & k \\ m & n & o \end{vmatrix}$$

Cofactor expansion: (best for 3x3 and higher but row operations can be easier Note:

Pay attention to 0's

$$\begin{vmatrix} a & b & c \\ d & e & f \\ 0 & h & 0 \end{vmatrix} = +0\begin{vmatrix} b & c \\ e & f \end{vmatrix} - h\begin{vmatrix} a & c \\ d & f \end{vmatrix} + 0\begin{vmatrix} a & b \\ d & e \end{vmatrix} = -h\begin{vmatrix} a & c \\ d & f \end{vmatrix}$$

Example 1:

$$\begin{vmatrix} 1 & 2 & 2 \\ 2 & 1 & 1 \\ 1 & 3 & 4 \end{vmatrix} = +(1)\begin{vmatrix} 1 & 1 \\ 3 & 4 \end{vmatrix} - (2)\begin{vmatrix} 2 & 1 \\ 1 & 4 \end{vmatrix} + (2)\begin{vmatrix} 2 & 1 \\ 1 & 3 \end{vmatrix}$$

$$= +(1)[(1)(4) - (1)(3)] - (2)[(2)(4) - (1)(1)] + (2)[(2)(3) - (1)(1)] = -3$$

Example 2: (look for the zero's else it will be a pain!)

$$\begin{vmatrix} 1 & 3 & 3 & 1 \\ 3 & 2 & 1 & 1 \\ 0 & 0 & 0 & 4 \\ 1 & 2 & 3 & 0 \end{vmatrix} = +0\begin{vmatrix} 3 & 3 & 1 \\ 2 & 1 & 1 \\ 2 & 3 & 0 \end{vmatrix} - 0\begin{vmatrix} 1 & 3 & 1 \\ 3 & 1 & 1 \\ 1 & 3 & 0 \end{vmatrix} + 0\begin{vmatrix} 1 & 3 & 1 \\ 3 & 2 & 1 \\ 1 & 2 & 0 \end{vmatrix} - 4\begin{vmatrix} 1 & 3 & 3 \\ 3 & 2 & 1 \\ 1 & 2 & 3 \end{vmatrix}$$

$$= -4\begin{vmatrix} 1 & 3 & 3 \\ 3 & 2 & 1 \\ 1 & 2 & 3 \end{vmatrix} = (-4)(-8) = 32$$

Example 3:

$$\begin{vmatrix} 1 & 0 & 0 & 1 \\ 3 & 2 & 1 & 1 \\ 0 & 0 & 0 & 4 \\ 1 & 2 & 3 & 0 \end{vmatrix} = +0 \begin{vmatrix} 0 & 0 & 1 \\ 2 & 1 & 1 \\ 2 & 3 & 0 \end{vmatrix} - 0 \begin{vmatrix} 1 & 0 & 1 \\ 3 & 1 & 1 \\ 1 & 3 & 0 \end{vmatrix} + 0 \begin{vmatrix} 1 & 0 & 1 \\ 3 & 2 & 1 \\ 1 & 2 & 0 \end{vmatrix} - 4 \begin{vmatrix} 1 & 0 & 0 \\ 3 & 2 & 1 \\ 1 & 2 & 3 \end{vmatrix}$$

$$= -4 \begin{vmatrix} 1 & 0 & 0 \\ 3 & 2 & 1 \\ 1 & 2 & 3 \end{vmatrix} = -4 \left(+1 \begin{vmatrix} 2 & 1 \\ 2 & 3 \end{vmatrix} - 0 \begin{vmatrix} 3 & 1 \\ 1 & 3 \end{vmatrix} + 0 \begin{vmatrix} 3 & 2 \\ 1 & 2 \end{vmatrix} \right) = -4[(2)(3) - (1)(2)] = -4(4) = -16$$

Row Operations:

You must follow the exact element removal for this to work

$$\begin{bmatrix} * & * & * \\ 1st & * & * \\ 2nd & 3rd & * \end{bmatrix}, \quad \begin{bmatrix} * & * & * & * \\ 1st & * & * & * \\ 2nd & 4th & * & * \\ 3rd & 5th & 6th & * \end{bmatrix}$$

$$A = \begin{bmatrix} 1 & 2 & 2 \\ 2 & 1 & 1 \\ 1 & 3 & 4 \end{bmatrix} \Rightarrow \det A = -3$$

$$-2R1 + R2 = [-2 \quad -4 \quad -4] + [2 \quad 1 \quad 1] = [0 \quad -3 \quad -3] \Leftarrow R2$$

$$\begin{bmatrix} 1 & 2 & 2 \\ 2 & 1 & 1 \\ 1 & 3 & 4 \end{bmatrix} \sim \begin{bmatrix} 1 & 2 & 2 \\ 0 & -3 & -3 \\ 1 & 3 & 4 \end{bmatrix}$$

$$-R1 + R3 = [-1 \quad -2 \quad -2] + [1 \quad 3 \quad 4] = [0 \quad 1 \quad 2] \Leftarrow R3$$

$$\begin{bmatrix} 1 & 2 & 2 \\ 2 & 1 & 1 \\ 1 & 3 & 4 \end{bmatrix} \sim \begin{bmatrix} 1 & 2 & 2 \\ 0 & -3 & -3 \\ 1 & 3 & 4 \end{bmatrix} \sim \begin{bmatrix} 1 & 2 & 2 \\ 0 & -3 & -3 \\ 0 & 1 & 2 \end{bmatrix}$$

$$\frac{1}{3}R2 + R3 = [0 \quad -1 \quad -1] + [0 \quad 1 \quad 2] = [0 \quad 0 \quad 1] \Leftarrow R3$$

$$\therefore \begin{bmatrix} 1 & 2 & 2 \\ 2 & 1 & 1 \\ 1 & 3 & 4 \end{bmatrix} \sim \begin{bmatrix} 1 & 2 & 2 \\ 0 & -3 & -3 \\ 1 & 3 & 4 \end{bmatrix} \sim \begin{bmatrix} 1 & 2 & 2 \\ 0 & -3 & -3 \\ 0 & 1 & 2 \end{bmatrix} \sim \begin{bmatrix} 1 & 2 & 2 \\ 0 & -3 & -3 \\ 0 & 0 & 1 \end{bmatrix} \Rightarrow \det A = (1)(-3)(1) = -3$$

This works because we decomposed A using elementary matrices. You will probably touch on this later but here it is.

$$A = \begin{bmatrix} 1 & 2 & 2 \\ 2 & 1 & 1 \\ 1 & 3 & 4 \end{bmatrix} = \begin{bmatrix} 1 & 0 & 0 \\ 2 & 1 & 0 \\ 1 & 0 & 1 \end{bmatrix} \begin{bmatrix} 1 & 0 & 0 \\ 0 & 1 & 0 \\ 0 & -\frac{1}{3} & 1 \end{bmatrix} \begin{bmatrix} 1 & 2 & 2 \\ 0 & -3 & -3 \\ 0 & 0 & 1 \end{bmatrix} = \begin{bmatrix} 1 & 0 & 0 \\ 2 & 1 & 0 \\ 1 & -\frac{1}{3} & 1 \end{bmatrix} \begin{bmatrix} 1 & 2 & 2 \\ 0 & -3 & -3 \\ 0 & 0 & 1 \end{bmatrix}$$

$$= E_2 E_1 U = LU \Rightarrow \det LU = \det L \det U = (1)(-3) = -3$$

Vector Space, Subspace and Subset

A set is **vector space** if:	A set is a **subspace** if:
1. $u + v \in V$ 2. $u + v = v + u$ 3. $(u + v) + w = u + (v + w)$ 4. $u + 0 = u.$ 5. $u + (-u) = 0$ 6. $cu \in V.$ 7. $c(u + v) = cu + cv$ 8. $(c + d)u = cu + du$ 9. $c(du) = (cd)u$ 10. $1u = u$	a. The zero vector of V is in H. b. H is closed under vector addition. c. H is closed under scalar multiplication.

When showing the following sets are subspaces, the zero vectors is evaluating all constants at 0

Determine if the set is a subspace of $\mathbb{P}_n$

All polynomials of the form $p(t) = a + t^2,$ where $a \in \mathbb{R}$

1) $a = 0 \Rightarrow 0 + t^2 = t^2 \notin \mathbb{P}_3$ ∴ not a subspace

No

All polynomials in $\mathbb{P}_n$ such that $P(0) = 0$

(1)

$$P(0) = 0 \Rightarrow P(t) = a_1 t + a_2 t^2 + a_3 t^3 + \cdots + a_{n-1} t^{n-1} \therefore \{a_{n-1}\} = 0 \Rightarrow P(0) = 0$$

    Case 1: True

(2)

$$P_1 + P_2 = a_1 t + a_2 t^2 + a_3 t^3 + \cdots + a_{n-1} t^{n-1} + b_1 t + b_2 t^2 + b_3 t^3 + \cdots + b_{n-1} t^{n-1}$$

$$= (a + b)_1 t + (a + b)_2 t^2 + (a + b)_3 t^3 + \cdots + (a + b)_{n-1} t^{n-1} \Rightarrow (P_1 + P_2)(0) = 0$$

Case 2: True

(3)

$$cP = c(a_1 t + a_2 t^2 + a_3 t^3 + \cdots + a_{n-1} t^{n-1}) = ((ca)_1 t + (ca)_2 t^2 + (ca)_3 t^3 + \cdots + (ca)_{n-1} t^{n-1})$$
$$\Rightarrow cP(0) = 0$$

Case 3: True- Yes it is a subspace of $\mathbb{P}_n$

Cramer's rules

$$x_n = \frac{\det(A_n(\boldsymbol{b}))}{\det(A)}$$

The solution in a way you may already know is

Rref [{4,1,6},{3,2,7}]

$$\begin{bmatrix} 4 & 1 & | & 6 \\ 3 & 2 & | & 7 \end{bmatrix} \sim \begin{bmatrix} I_2 & | & 1 \\ & & 2 \end{bmatrix} \Rightarrow x = \begin{matrix} x_1 = 1 \\ x_2 = 2 \end{matrix}$$

Lets find this with "Cramer's Rule"

$$\begin{bmatrix} 4 & 1 & | & 6 \\ 3 & 2 & | & 7 \end{bmatrix} \Rightarrow A_1(\boldsymbol{b}) = \begin{bmatrix} 6 & 1 \\ 7 & 2 \end{bmatrix} \Rightarrow \det(A_1(\boldsymbol{b})) = (2)(6) - (1)(7) = 12 - 7 = 5$$

$$\therefore x_1 = \frac{\det(A_1(\boldsymbol{b}))}{\det(A)} = \frac{5}{5} = 1$$

$$\begin{bmatrix} 4 & 1 & | & 6 \\ 3 & 2 & | & 7 \end{bmatrix} \Rightarrow A_2(\boldsymbol{b}) = \begin{bmatrix} 4 & 6 \\ 3 & 7 \end{bmatrix} \Rightarrow \det(A_2(\boldsymbol{b})) = (4)(7) - (6)(3) = 10$$

$$\therefore x_2 = \frac{\det(A_2(\boldsymbol{b}))}{\det(A)} = \frac{10}{5} = 2$$

IMPORTANT:

Notice that the index of A is the location of $\boldsymbol{b}$ i.e. if you had a 4×4 $A_3(\boldsymbol{b}) = [\boldsymbol{v}_1 \quad \boldsymbol{v}_2 \quad \boldsymbol{b} \quad \boldsymbol{v}_3]$

Basis coordinate vector

Given a set $\mathcal{B}$, and vector x put $\mathcal{B}$ into a matrix equation $A\boldsymbol{u} = x \Rightarrow \boldsymbol{u} = [x]_{\mathcal{B}}$

Ex.1

$$b_1 = \begin{bmatrix} 1 \\ -3 \end{bmatrix}, b_2 = \begin{bmatrix} -3 \\ 5 \end{bmatrix}, x = \begin{bmatrix} -7 \\ 5 \end{bmatrix}$$

$$\begin{bmatrix} 1 & -3 \\ -3 & 5 \end{bmatrix} [x]_{\mathcal{B}} = \begin{bmatrix} -7 \\ 5 \end{bmatrix} \Rightarrow \begin{bmatrix} 1 & -3 & | & -7 \\ -3 & 5 & | & 5 \end{bmatrix} \sim \begin{bmatrix} 1 & 0 & | & 5 \\ 0 & 1 & | & 4 \end{bmatrix} \Rightarrow [x]_{\mathcal{B}} = (5,4)$$

$$\lor \because \det A \neq 0, [x]_{\mathcal{B}} = A^{-1}x = \frac{1}{[(1)(5) - (-3)(-3)]} \begin{bmatrix} 5 & 3 \\ 3 & 1 \end{bmatrix} \begin{bmatrix} -7 \\ 5 \end{bmatrix} = -\frac{1}{4} \begin{bmatrix} -20 \\ -16 \end{bmatrix} = \begin{bmatrix} 5 \\ 4 \end{bmatrix}$$

$$\therefore [x]_\mathcal{B} = \begin{bmatrix} 5 \\ 4 \end{bmatrix}$$

Ex. 2

$$b_1 = \begin{bmatrix} -3 \\ 1 \\ -4 \end{bmatrix}, b_2 = \begin{bmatrix} 7 \\ 5 \\ -6 \end{bmatrix}, x = \begin{bmatrix} 11 \\ 0 \\ 7 \end{bmatrix}$$

$$[x]_\mathcal{B} = \begin{bmatrix} c_1 \\ c_2 \\ \vdots \\ c_n \end{bmatrix} \Leftrightarrow \mathcal{B} = \{b_1, b_2, \dots, b_n\} \Rightarrow b_1 c_1 + b_2 c_2 + \cdots + b_n c_n = \boldsymbol{x}$$

$$\begin{bmatrix} -3 \\ 1 \\ -4 \end{bmatrix} c_1 + \begin{bmatrix} 7 \\ 5 \\ -6 \end{bmatrix} c_2 = \begin{bmatrix} 11 \\ 0 \\ 7 \end{bmatrix} \Rightarrow \begin{bmatrix} -3 & 7 & | & 11 \\ 1 & 5 & | & 0 \\ -4 & -6 & | & 7 \end{bmatrix} \sim \begin{bmatrix} 1 & 0 & | & -\frac{5}{2} \\ 0 & 1 & | & \frac{1}{2} \\ 0 & 0 & | & \frac{2}{0} \end{bmatrix}$$

$$\therefore [x]_\mathcal{B} = \frac{1}{2}\begin{pmatrix} -5 \\ 2 \end{pmatrix}$$

Adjugate of a matrix

$$A^{-1} = \frac{\text{ajd}(A)}{\det(A)}$$

$$A = \begin{bmatrix} a & b \\ c & d \end{bmatrix} \quad \Rightarrow \quad \text{adj}(A_{2\times 2}) = \begin{bmatrix} +d & -b \\ -c & +a \end{bmatrix}$$

$$A = \begin{bmatrix} a & b & c \\ d & e & f \\ g & h & i \end{bmatrix} \quad \Rightarrow \quad \text{adj}(A_{3\times 3}) = \begin{bmatrix} +\begin{vmatrix} e & f \\ h & i \end{vmatrix} & -\begin{vmatrix} d & f \\ g & i \end{vmatrix} & +\begin{vmatrix} d & e \\ g & h \end{vmatrix} \\ -\begin{vmatrix} b & c \\ h & i \end{vmatrix} & +\begin{vmatrix} a & c \\ g & i \end{vmatrix} & -\begin{vmatrix} a & b \\ g & h \end{vmatrix} \\ +\begin{vmatrix} b & c \\ e & f \end{vmatrix} & -\begin{vmatrix} a & c \\ d & f \end{vmatrix} & +\begin{vmatrix} a & b \\ d & e \end{vmatrix} \end{bmatrix}^T$$

$$A = \begin{bmatrix} a & b & c & d \\ e & f & g & h \\ i & j & k & l \\ m & n & o & p \end{bmatrix} \quad \Rightarrow \quad \text{adj}(A_{4\times 4})$$

$$= \begin{bmatrix} +\begin{vmatrix} f & g & h \\ j & k & l \\ n & o & p \end{vmatrix} & -\begin{vmatrix} e & g & h \\ i & k & l \\ m & o & p \end{vmatrix} & +\begin{vmatrix} e & f & h \\ i & j & l \\ m & n & p \end{vmatrix} & -\begin{vmatrix} e & f & g \\ i & j & k \\ m & n & o \end{vmatrix} \\ -\begin{vmatrix} b & c & d \\ j & k & l \\ n & o & p \end{vmatrix} & +\begin{vmatrix} a & c & d \\ i & k & l \\ m & o & p \end{vmatrix} & -\begin{vmatrix} a & b & d \\ i & j & l \\ m & n & p \end{vmatrix} & +\begin{vmatrix} a & b & c \\ i & j & k \\ m & n & o \end{vmatrix} \\ +\begin{vmatrix} b & c & d \\ f & g & h \\ n & o & p \end{vmatrix} & -\begin{vmatrix} a & c & d \\ e & g & h \\ m & o & p \end{vmatrix} & +\begin{vmatrix} a & b & d \\ i & j & l \\ m & n & p \end{vmatrix} & -\begin{vmatrix} a & b & c \\ i & j & k \\ m & n & o \end{vmatrix} \\ -\begin{vmatrix} b & c & d \\ f & g & h \\ j & k & l \end{vmatrix} & +\begin{vmatrix} a & c & d \\ e & g & h \\ i & k & l \end{vmatrix} & -\begin{vmatrix} a & b & d \\ e & f & h \\ e & j & l \end{vmatrix} & +\begin{vmatrix} a & b & c \\ e & f & g \\ i & j & k \end{vmatrix} \end{bmatrix}^T$$

Compute the Adjugate

$$A = \begin{bmatrix} 1 & 1 & 3 \\ -2 & 2 & 1 \\ 0 & 1 & 1 \end{bmatrix}$$

$$B = \begin{bmatrix} a & b & c \\ d & e & f \\ g & h & i \end{bmatrix} \Rightarrow \text{adj}(B) = \begin{bmatrix} +\begin{vmatrix} e & f \\ h & i \end{vmatrix} & -\begin{vmatrix} d & f \\ g & i \end{vmatrix} & +\begin{vmatrix} d & e \\ g & h \end{vmatrix} \\ -\begin{vmatrix} b & c \\ h & i \end{vmatrix} & +\begin{vmatrix} a & c \\ g & i \end{vmatrix} & -\begin{vmatrix} a & b \\ g & h \end{vmatrix} \\ +\begin{vmatrix} b & c \\ e & f \end{vmatrix} & -\begin{vmatrix} a & c \\ d & f \end{vmatrix} & +\begin{vmatrix} a & b \\ d & e \end{vmatrix} \end{bmatrix}^T$$

$$\text{adj}(A) = \begin{bmatrix} +\begin{vmatrix} 2 & 1 \\ 1 & 1 \end{vmatrix} & -\begin{vmatrix} -2 & 1 \\ 0 & 1 \end{vmatrix} & +\begin{vmatrix} -2 & 2 \\ 0 & 1 \end{vmatrix} \\ -\begin{vmatrix} 1 & 3 \\ 1 & 1 \end{vmatrix} & +\begin{vmatrix} 1 & 3 \\ 0 & 1 \end{vmatrix} & -\begin{vmatrix} 1 & 1 \\ 0 & 1 \end{vmatrix} \\ +\begin{vmatrix} 1 & 3 \\ 2 & 1 \end{vmatrix} & -\begin{vmatrix} 1 & 3 \\ -2 & 1 \end{vmatrix} & +\begin{vmatrix} 1 & 1 \\ -2 & 2 \end{vmatrix} \end{bmatrix}^T$$

$$= \begin{bmatrix} +[(2)(1)-(1)(1)] & -[(-2)(1)-(1)(0)] & +[(-2)(1)-(2)(0)] \\ -[(1)(1)-(3)(1)] & +[(1)(1)-(3)(0)] & -[(1)(1)-(1)(0)] \\ +[(1)(1)-(2)(3)] & -[(1)(1)-(3)(-2)] & +[(1)(2)-(1)(-2)] \end{bmatrix}^T$$

$$= \begin{bmatrix} 1 & 2 & -2 \\ 2 & 1 & -1 \\ -5 & -7 & 4 \end{bmatrix}^T = \begin{bmatrix} 1 & 2 & -5 \\ 2 & 1 & -7 \\ -2 & -1 & 4 \end{bmatrix}$$

Inverse of a 2x2 Matrix

Inverse of (2×2):

Option 1)

$$[A|I] \sim [I|A^{-1}]$$

$$\begin{bmatrix} -3 & 2 & | & 1 & 0 \\ 1 & 3 & | & 0 & 1 \end{bmatrix} \sim \begin{bmatrix} 1 & 0 & | & -\dfrac{3}{11} & \dfrac{2}{11} \\ 0 & 1 & | & \dfrac{1}{11} & \dfrac{3}{11} \end{bmatrix}$$

Option 2)

$$A = \begin{bmatrix} a & b \\ c & d \end{bmatrix} \Rightarrow A^{-1} = \frac{\text{adj}(A)}{\det(A)} = \frac{1}{ad-bc}\begin{bmatrix} d & -b \\ -c & a \end{bmatrix} \wedge Ax = b \Rightarrow x = A^{-1}b \Leftrightarrow \det A \neq 0$$

$$A = \begin{bmatrix} -3 & 2 \\ 1 & 3 \end{bmatrix} \Rightarrow A^{-1} = \frac{1}{(-3)(3)-(2)(1)}\begin{bmatrix} 3 & -2 \\ -1 & -3 \end{bmatrix} = -\frac{1}{11}\begin{bmatrix} 3 & -2 \\ -1 & -3 \end{bmatrix} = \frac{1}{11}\begin{bmatrix} -3 & 2 \\ 1 & 3 \end{bmatrix}$$

Solve a system of equations with an inverse

Theorem:

$$Ax = b \quad \Rightarrow \quad A^{-1}Ax = A^{-1}b \quad \Rightarrow \quad Ix = A^{-1}b \quad \Rightarrow \quad x = A^{-1}b \quad \Leftrightarrow \quad \det(A) \neq 0$$

(Note: $\vec{x} = x = (x_1, x_2, \dots, x_n)$)

$$\begin{bmatrix} -3 & 2 \\ 1 & 3 \end{bmatrix}x = \begin{bmatrix} 2 \\ 1 \end{bmatrix} \quad \Rightarrow \quad x = -\frac{1}{11}\begin{bmatrix} 3 & -2 \\ -1 & -3 \end{bmatrix}\begin{bmatrix} 2 \\ 1 \end{bmatrix} = -\frac{1}{11}\begin{bmatrix} [3 & -2]\begin{bmatrix} 2 \\ 1 \end{bmatrix} \\ [-1 & -3]\begin{bmatrix} 2 \\ 1 \end{bmatrix} \end{bmatrix}$$

$$= -\frac{1}{11}\begin{bmatrix} (3)(2)+(-2)(1) \\ (-1)(2)+(-3)(1) \end{bmatrix}$$

$$= -\frac{1}{11}\begin{bmatrix} 6-2 \\ -2-3 \end{bmatrix} = -\frac{1}{11}\begin{bmatrix} 4 \\ -5 \end{bmatrix} = \begin{bmatrix} -\frac{4}{11} \\ \frac{5}{11} \end{bmatrix}$$

Similarly you could solve with rref i.e.

$$\begin{bmatrix} -3 & 2 \\ 1 & 3 \end{bmatrix}x = \begin{bmatrix} 2 \\ 1 \end{bmatrix} \quad \Rightarrow \quad \left[\begin{array}{cc|c} -3 & 2 & 2 \\ 1 & 3 & 1 \end{array}\right] \sim \left[\begin{array}{cc|c} 1 & 0 & -\frac{4}{11} \\ 0 & 1 & \frac{5}{11} \end{array}\right]$$

Inverse of 3x3

$$A\mathbf{x} = b \quad \Rightarrow \quad A^{-1}A\mathbf{x} = A^{-1}b \quad \Rightarrow \quad I\mathbf{x} = A^{-1}b \quad \Rightarrow \quad \mathbf{x} = A^{-1}b \quad \Leftrightarrow \quad \det(A) \neq 0$$

Option 1)

$$[A|I] \quad \sim \quad [I|A^{-1}]$$

$$A = \begin{bmatrix} 1 & 1 & 2 \\ 1 & 2 & 1 \\ 2 & 1 & 1 \end{bmatrix} \text{ (symmetric matrix)}$$

$$\begin{bmatrix} 1 & 1 & 2 & | & 1 & 0 & 0 \\ 1 & 2 & 1 & | & 0 & 1 & 0 \\ 2 & 1 & 1 & | & 0 & 0 & 1 \end{bmatrix} \sim \begin{bmatrix} 1 & 0 & 0 & | & -\frac{1}{4} & -\frac{1}{4} & \frac{3}{4} \\ 0 & 1 & 0 & | & -\frac{1}{4} & \frac{3}{4} & -\frac{1}{4} \\ 0 & 0 & 1 & | & \frac{3}{4} & -\frac{1}{4} & -\frac{1}{4} \end{bmatrix} \Rightarrow A^{-1} = -\frac{1}{4}\begin{bmatrix} 1 & 1 & -3 \\ 1 & -3 & 1 \\ -3 & 1 & 1 \end{bmatrix}$$

Option 2)

$$A^{-1} = \frac{\text{adj}(A)}{\det(A)}$$

$$A = \begin{bmatrix} 1 & 1 & 2 \\ 1 & 2 & 1 \\ 2 & 1 & 1 \end{bmatrix} \Rightarrow \det A = -4 \quad \wedge \quad \text{adj}(A) = \begin{bmatrix} +\begin{vmatrix} 2 & 1 \\ 1 & 1 \end{vmatrix} & -\begin{vmatrix} 1 & 1 \\ 2 & 1 \end{vmatrix} & +\begin{vmatrix} 1 & 2 \\ 2 & 1 \end{vmatrix} \\ -\begin{vmatrix} 1 & 2 \\ 1 & 1 \end{vmatrix} & +\begin{vmatrix} 1 & 2 \\ 2 & 1 \end{vmatrix} & -\begin{vmatrix} 1 & 1 \\ 2 & 1 \end{vmatrix} \\ +\begin{vmatrix} 1 & 2 \\ 2 & 1 \end{vmatrix} & -\begin{vmatrix} 1 & 2 \\ 1 & 1 \end{vmatrix} & +\begin{vmatrix} 1 & 1 \\ 1 & 2 \end{vmatrix} \end{bmatrix}$$

$$= \begin{bmatrix} +[(2)(1)-(1)(1)] & -[(1)(1)-(1)(2)] & +[(1)(1)-(2)(2)] \\ -[(1)(1)-(1)(2)] & +[(1)(1)-(2)(2)] & -[(1)(1)-(1)(2)] \\ +[(1)(1)-(2)(2)] & -[(1)(1)-(1)(2)] & +[(1)(2)-(1)(1)] \end{bmatrix}$$

$$= \begin{bmatrix} 1 & 1 & -3 \\ 1 & -3 & 1 \\ -3 & 1 & 1 \end{bmatrix} \text{ (also symmetric)}$$

$$\therefore A^{-1} = \frac{\text{adj}(A)}{\det A} = -\frac{1}{4}\begin{bmatrix} 1 & 1 & -3 \\ 1 & -3 & 1 \\ -3 & 1 & 1 \end{bmatrix} \text{ (also symmetric)}$$

Trace

$$tr(A) = \sum \lambda_n$$

$$\det(A - I\lambda) = 0$$

Ex 1:

$$A = \begin{bmatrix} 1 & 2 & 2 & 2 \\ 0 & 2 & 2 & 2 \\ 0 & 0 & 1 & 1 \\ 0 & 0 & 0 & -1 \end{bmatrix} \Rightarrow tr(A) = 1 + 2 + 1 - 1 = 3$$

Ex 2:

$$A = \begin{bmatrix} 1 & 2 & 2 \\ 2 & 2 & 1 \\ 1 & 2 & 2 \end{bmatrix} \Rightarrow \det(A - I\lambda) = \begin{vmatrix} 1 - \lambda & 2 & 2 \\ 2 & 2 - \lambda & 1 \\ 1 & 2 & 2 - \lambda \end{vmatrix} = 0$$

$$\Rightarrow (1 - \lambda)\begin{vmatrix} 2 - \lambda & 1 \\ 2 & 2 - \lambda \end{vmatrix} - (2)\begin{vmatrix} 2 & 1 \\ 1 & 2 - \lambda \end{vmatrix} + (2)\begin{vmatrix} 2 & 2 - \lambda \\ 1 & 2 \end{vmatrix} = 0$$

$$\Rightarrow (1 - \lambda)[(2 - \lambda)(2 - \lambda) - (2)(1)] - (2)[(2)(2 - \lambda) - (1)(1)] + (2)[(2)(2) - (1)(2 - \lambda)]$$

$$= (5 - \lambda)\lambda^2 = 0 \quad \Rightarrow \quad \lambda = \{0,5\}$$

$$\therefore tr(A) = 0 + 5 = 5$$

Ex 3:

Given $tr(A) = 5 \wedge \det(A) = 6$, find A

$$A = \begin{bmatrix} a & 1 \\ 0 & d \end{bmatrix}$$

$$\det(A) = ad = 6$$

$$tr(A) = a + d = 5$$

$$\therefore d = 5 - a \Rightarrow a(5 - a) = 6 \Rightarrow 5a - a^2 = 6 \Rightarrow a^2 - 5a + 6 = (a - 2)(a - 3) = 0$$

$$\Leftrightarrow a = 2 \vee a = 3 \Rightarrow d = 2 \vee d = 3$$

$$\therefore (a, d) = (2,3) \vee (a, d) = (3,2)$$

$$\Rightarrow A = \begin{bmatrix} 2 & 1 \\ 0 & 3 \end{bmatrix} \vee \begin{bmatrix} 3 & 1 \\ 0 & 2 \end{bmatrix}$$

Cholesky Decomposition

$$A = LDU = LDL^T = LD^{\frac{1}{2}}D^{\frac{1}{2}}L^T = \left(LD^{\frac{1}{2}}\right)\left(D^{\frac{1}{2}}L^T\right) = K^*K$$

$$A = \begin{bmatrix} 9 & 0 & -27 & 18 \\ 0 & 9 & -9 & -27 \\ -27 & -9 & 99 & -27 \\ 18 & -27 & -27 & 121 \end{bmatrix}$$

Use elementary matrices to find L (watch lesson on Elementary Matrices and or LDU decomposition)

$$L = \begin{bmatrix} 1 & 0 & 0 & 0 \\ 0 & 1 & 0 & 0 \\ -9 & -3 & 1 & 0 \\ 6 & -9 & 0 & 1 \end{bmatrix} \wedge U = L^T = \begin{bmatrix} 1 & 0 & -9 & 6 \\ 0 & 1 & -3 & -9 \\ 0 & 0 & 1 & 0 \\ 0 & 0 & 0 & 1 \end{bmatrix}$$

$$D = \begin{bmatrix} 9 & 0 & 0 & 0 \\ 0 & 9 & 0 & 0 \\ 0 & 0 & 9 & 0 \\ 0 & 0 & 0 & 4 \end{bmatrix} \Rightarrow D^{\frac{1}{2}} = \begin{bmatrix} 3 & 0 & 0 & 0 \\ 0 & 3 & 0 & 0 \\ 0 & 0 & 3 & 0 \\ 0 & 0 & 0 & 2 \end{bmatrix}$$

$$\therefore LD^{\frac{1}{2}}D^{\frac{1}{2}}L^T = \left(\begin{bmatrix} 1 & 0 & 0 & 0 \\ 0 & 1 & 0 & 0 \\ -9 & -3 & 1 & 0 \\ 6 & -9 & 0 & 1 \end{bmatrix}\begin{bmatrix} 3 & 0 & 0 & 0 \\ 0 & 3 & 0 & 0 \\ 0 & 0 & 3 & 0 \\ 0 & 0 & 0 & 2 \end{bmatrix}\right)\left(\begin{bmatrix} 3 & 0 & 0 & 0 \\ 0 & 3 & 0 & 0 \\ 0 & 0 & 3 & 0 \\ 0 & 0 & 0 & 2 \end{bmatrix}\begin{bmatrix} 1 & 0 & -9 & 6 \\ 0 & 1 & -3 & -9 \\ 0 & 0 & 1 & 0 \\ 0 & 0 & 0 & 1 \end{bmatrix}\right)$$

$$= \begin{bmatrix} 3 & 0 & 0 & 0 \\ 0 & 3 & 0 & 0 \\ -9 & -3 & 3 & 0 \\ 6 & -9 & 0 & 2 \end{bmatrix}\begin{bmatrix} 3 & 0 & -9 & 6 \\ 0 & 3 & -3 & -9 \\ 0 & 0 & 3 & 0 \\ 0 & 0 & 0 & 2 \end{bmatrix} = K^*K$$

Eigenvalues

$$A = \begin{bmatrix} 1 & 2 & 2 \\ 2 & 1 & 1 \\ 0 & 0 & 1 \end{bmatrix} \quad \Rightarrow \quad \det(A - I\lambda) = \begin{vmatrix} 1-\lambda & 2 & 2 \\ 2 & 1-\lambda & 1 \\ 0 & 0 & 1-\lambda \end{vmatrix}$$

$$\begin{vmatrix} 1-\lambda & 2 & 2 \\ 2 & 1-\lambda & 1 \\ 0 & 0 & 1-\lambda \end{vmatrix} = 0 \cdot \begin{vmatrix} 2 & 2 \\ 1-\lambda & 1 \end{vmatrix} - 0 \cdot \begin{vmatrix} 1-\lambda & 2 \\ 2 & 1 \end{vmatrix} + (1-\lambda)\begin{vmatrix} 1-\lambda & 2 \\ 2 & 1-\lambda \end{vmatrix}$$

$$\therefore (1-\lambda)\begin{vmatrix} 1-\lambda & 2 \\ 2 & 1-\lambda \end{vmatrix} = (1-\lambda)[(1-\lambda)^2 - 4] = (1-\lambda)(-3 - 2\lambda + \lambda^2)$$
$$= (1-\lambda)(\lambda + 1)(\lambda - 3)$$

Characteristic Polynomial: $p(\lambda) = (1-\lambda)(\lambda+1)(\lambda-3) \Rightarrow p(\lambda) = 0 \Leftrightarrow \lambda = \{-1, 1, 3\}$

$$eigenvalues(A) = \{-1, 1, 3\}$$

Eigenvectors

Part II - Easiest way to find Eigen Vectors

$$A = \begin{bmatrix} 1 & 2 & 2 \\ 2 & 1 & 1 \\ 0 & 0 & 1 \end{bmatrix} \quad \Rightarrow \quad \det(A - I\lambda) = \begin{vmatrix} 1-\lambda & 2 & 2 \\ 2 & 1-\lambda & 1 \\ 0 & 0 & 1-\lambda \end{vmatrix} = 0 \quad \Rightarrow \quad \lambda = \{-1, 1, 3\}$$

$$\lambda_1 \Rightarrow \begin{bmatrix} 1-(-1) & 2 & 2 \\ 2 & 1-(-1) & 1 \\ 0 & 0 & 1-(-1) \end{bmatrix} = \begin{bmatrix} 2 & 2 & 2 \\ 2 & 2 & 1 \\ 0 & 0 & 2 \end{bmatrix} \sim \begin{bmatrix} 1 & 1 & 0 \\ 0 & 0 & 1 \\ 0 & 0 & 0 \end{bmatrix} \Rightarrow x = s_1 \begin{pmatrix} -1 \\ 1 \\ 0 \end{pmatrix} \Rightarrow v_1 = \begin{pmatrix} -1 \\ 1 \\ 0 \end{pmatrix}$$

$$\lambda_2 \Rightarrow \begin{bmatrix} 1-1 & 2 & 2 \\ 2 & 1-1 & 1 \\ 0 & 0 & 1-1 \end{bmatrix} = \begin{bmatrix} 0 & 2 & 2 \\ 2 & 0 & 1 \\ 0 & 0 & 0 \end{bmatrix} \sim \begin{bmatrix} 1 & 0 & \frac{1}{2} \\ 0 & 1 & 1 \\ 0 & 0 & 0 \end{bmatrix} \Rightarrow x = s_2 \begin{pmatrix} -\frac{1}{2} \\ -1 \\ 1 \end{pmatrix} \Rightarrow v_2 = \begin{pmatrix} -1 \\ -2 \\ 2 \end{pmatrix}$$

$$\lambda_3 \Rightarrow \begin{bmatrix} 1-3 & 2 & 2 \\ 2 & 1-3 & 1 \\ 0 & 0 & 1-3 \end{bmatrix} = \begin{bmatrix} -2 & 2 & 2 \\ 2 & -2 & 1 \\ 0 & 0 & -2 \end{bmatrix} \sim \begin{bmatrix} 1 & -1 & 0 \\ 0 & 0 & 1 \\ 0 & 0 & 0 \end{bmatrix} \Rightarrow x = s_3 \begin{pmatrix} 1 \\ 1 \\ 0 \end{pmatrix} \Rightarrow v_3 = \begin{pmatrix} 1 \\ 1 \\ 0 \end{pmatrix}$$

Note: s is a free variable i.e. $s_1 = 1, s_2 = 2, s_3 = 1$

$$\therefore \Lambda = \left\{ \begin{pmatrix} -1 \\ 1 \\ 0 \end{pmatrix}, \begin{pmatrix} -1 \\ -2 \\ 2 \end{pmatrix}, \begin{pmatrix} 1 \\ 1 \\ 0 \end{pmatrix} \right\}$$

Diagonlize a Matrix

Part III - Diagonlize $A = [\{1,2,2\}, \{2,1,1\}, \{0,0,1\}]$, **note** $\det(A) \neq 0 \therefore A = SDS^{-1}$

$$A = \begin{bmatrix} 1 & 2 & 2 \\ 2 & 1 & 1 \\ 0 & 0 & 1 \end{bmatrix} \Rightarrow \det(A - I\lambda) = \begin{vmatrix} 1-\lambda & 2 & 2 \\ 2 & 1-\lambda & 1 \\ 0 & 0 & 1-\lambda \end{vmatrix} = 0 \Rightarrow \lambda = \{-1, 1, 3\}$$

$$\{v_1, v_2, v_3\} = \left\{ \begin{pmatrix} -1 \\ 1 \\ 0 \end{pmatrix}, \begin{pmatrix} -1 \\ -2 \\ 2 \end{pmatrix}, \begin{pmatrix} 1 \\ 1 \\ 0 \end{pmatrix} \right\}$$

$$A = SDS^{-1} = [v_1 \ v_2 \ v_3][\lambda_1 e_1 \ \lambda_2 e_2 \ \lambda_3 e_3][v_1 \ v_2 \ v_3]^{-1}$$

Note: $e_n = (0, 0, \cdots, 1, \cdots, 0)$

$$\therefore A = SDS^{-1} = \begin{bmatrix} -1 & -1 & 1 \\ 1 & -2 & 1 \\ 0 & 2 & 0 \end{bmatrix} \begin{bmatrix} -1 & 0 & 0 \\ 0 & 1 & 0 \\ 0 & 0 & 3 \end{bmatrix} \begin{bmatrix} -1 & -1 & 1 \\ 1 & -2 & 1 \\ 0 & 2 & 0 \end{bmatrix}^{-1}$$

$$= \begin{bmatrix} -1 & -1 & 1 \\ 1 & -2 & 1 \\ 0 & 2 & 0 \end{bmatrix} \begin{bmatrix} -1 & 0 & 0 \\ 0 & 1 & 0 \\ 0 & 0 & 3 \end{bmatrix} \begin{bmatrix} -\dfrac{1}{2} & \dfrac{1}{2} & \dfrac{1}{4} \\ 0 & 0 & \dfrac{1}{2} \\ \dfrac{1}{2} & \dfrac{1}{2} & \dfrac{3}{4} \end{bmatrix}$$

Singular Value Decomposition

$$A = U\Sigma V^T, \qquad A = \begin{bmatrix} 1 & 1 \\ 0 & 1 \\ -1 & 1 \end{bmatrix}$$

Identify the unknowns

$$V^T = eigenvectors(A^T A)^T = \begin{bmatrix} v_1 \\ v_2 \end{bmatrix}$$

$$U = \begin{bmatrix} \dfrac{1}{\sigma_1} A v_1 & \dfrac{1}{\sigma_2} A v_2 & \dfrac{NS(A^T)}{|NS(A^T)|} \end{bmatrix}, \qquad \Sigma = \begin{bmatrix} \sigma_1 & 0 \\ 0 & \sigma_2 \\ 0 & 0 \end{bmatrix} \quad \Leftrightarrow \quad \sigma_n = \sqrt{\lambda_n}$$

$$\therefore A = \begin{bmatrix} \dfrac{1}{\sigma_1} A v_1 & \dfrac{1}{\sigma_2} A v_2 & \dfrac{NS(A^T)}{|NS(A^T)|} \end{bmatrix} \begin{bmatrix} \sigma_1 & 0 \\ 0 & \sigma_2 \\ 0 & 0 \end{bmatrix} [v_1 \quad v_2]^T$$

Find all values

$$A = \begin{bmatrix} 1 & 1 \\ 0 & 1 \\ -1 & 1 \end{bmatrix} \Rightarrow A^T A = \begin{bmatrix} 2 & 0 \\ 0 & 3 \end{bmatrix} \Rightarrow \{\lambda_1, \lambda_2\} = \{3,2\} \wedge \{v_1, v_2\} = \left\{ \binom{0}{1}, \binom{1}{0} \right\}$$

$$\therefore V^T = \begin{bmatrix} 0 & 1 \\ 1 & 0 \end{bmatrix}$$

$$U = \begin{bmatrix} \dfrac{1}{\sqrt{3}} \begin{bmatrix} 1 & 1 \\ 0 & 1 \\ -1 & 1 \end{bmatrix} \begin{bmatrix} 0 \\ 1 \end{bmatrix} & \dfrac{1}{\sqrt{2}} \begin{bmatrix} 1 & 1 \\ 0 & 1 \\ -1 & 1 \end{bmatrix} \begin{bmatrix} 1 \\ 0 \end{bmatrix} & \dfrac{NS(A^T)}{|NS(A^T)|} \end{bmatrix}$$

$$NS(A^T) \Rightarrow A^T x = 0 \Rightarrow \begin{bmatrix} 1 & 1 & 1 & | & 0 \\ 1 & 0 & -1 & | & 0 \end{bmatrix} \sim \begin{bmatrix} 1 & 0 & -1 & | & 0 \\ 0 & 1 & 2 & | & 0 \end{bmatrix} \Rightarrow x = x_3 \begin{pmatrix} 1 \\ -2 \\ 1 \end{pmatrix}, x_3 = free = 1 \therefore u_3$$

$$= \begin{pmatrix} 1 \\ -2 \\ 1 \end{pmatrix}$$

$$|u_3| = \sqrt{1 + 4 + 1} = \sqrt{6}$$

$$\Rightarrow U = \begin{bmatrix} \dfrac{1}{\sqrt{3}} & \dfrac{1}{\sqrt{2}} & \dfrac{1}{\sqrt{6}} \\ \dfrac{1}{\sqrt{3}} & 0 & -\dfrac{2}{\sqrt{6}} \\ \dfrac{1}{\sqrt{3}} & -\dfrac{1}{\sqrt{2}} & \dfrac{1}{\sqrt{6}} \end{bmatrix}, \quad \therefore A = \begin{bmatrix} \dfrac{1}{\sqrt{3}} & \dfrac{1}{\sqrt{2}} & \dfrac{1}{\sqrt{6}} \\ \dfrac{1}{\sqrt{3}} & 0 & -\dfrac{2}{\sqrt{6}} \\ \dfrac{1}{\sqrt{3}} & -\dfrac{1}{\sqrt{2}} & \dfrac{1}{\sqrt{6}} \end{bmatrix} \begin{bmatrix} \sqrt{3} & 0 \\ 0 & \sqrt{2} \\ 0 & 0 \end{bmatrix} \begin{bmatrix} 0 & 1 \\ 1 & 0 \end{bmatrix} = \begin{bmatrix} 1 & 1 \\ 0 & 1 \\ -1 & 1 \end{bmatrix}$$

System of differential equations

Note: $[SDS^{-1}]^k = SD^kS^{-1}$ (easy to prove, try it out with k=1,2,3,4... hint $SS^{-1} = I$)

$$\frac{dX}{dt} = AX \Rightarrow dX = XAdt \Rightarrow \frac{1}{X}dx = Adt \Rightarrow \ln|X| = At + C_1 \Rightarrow X = e^{C_1 + At} = e^{C_1}e^{At} = Ce^{At}$$

$$\therefore X = Ce^{At} \Rightarrow X = C\sum_{k=0}^{\infty} \frac{A^k t^k}{k!} = C\sum_{k=0}^{\infty} \frac{SD^kS^{-1}t^k}{k!} = CS\sum_{k=0}^{\infty} \frac{D^k t^k}{k!}S^{-1}$$

$$\begin{matrix} x_1' = 3x_1 + x_2 - x_3 \\ x_2' = x_1 + 3x_2 - x_3 \\ x_3' = 3x_1 + 3x_2 - x_3 \end{matrix} \Rightarrow X' = \begin{pmatrix} 3 & 1 & -1 \\ 1 & 3 & -1 \\ 3 & 3 & -1 \end{pmatrix} X \Rightarrow X = C\sum_{k=0}^{\infty} \begin{pmatrix} 3 & 1 & -1 \\ 1 & 3 & -1 \\ 3 & 3 & -1 \end{pmatrix}^k \frac{t^k}{k!}$$

Diagonlize A, $A = \begin{pmatrix} 3 & 1 & -1 \\ 1 & 3 & -1 \\ 3 & 3 & -1 \end{pmatrix} \Rightarrow A = \begin{pmatrix} 1 & 1 & -1 \\ 1 & 0 & 1 \\ 3 & 1 & 0 \end{pmatrix} \begin{pmatrix} 1 & 0 & 0 \\ 0 & 2 & 0 \\ 0 & 0 & 2 \end{pmatrix} \begin{pmatrix} -1 & -1 & 1 \\ 3 & 3 & -2 \\ 1 & 2 & -1 \end{pmatrix}$

$$\therefore C\sum_{k=0}^{\infty} \left[\begin{pmatrix} 1 & 1 & -1 \\ 1 & 0 & 1 \\ 3 & 1 & 0 \end{pmatrix} \begin{pmatrix} 1 & 0 & 0 \\ 0 & 2 & 0 \\ 0 & 0 & 2 \end{pmatrix} \begin{pmatrix} -1 & -1 & 1 \\ 3 & 3 & -2 \\ 1 & 2 & -1 \end{pmatrix} \right]^k \frac{t^k}{k!}$$

$$= C\begin{pmatrix} 1 & 1 & -1 \\ 1 & 0 & 1 \\ 3 & 1 & 0 \end{pmatrix} \sum_{k=0}^{\infty} \left[\begin{pmatrix} 1 & 0 & 0 \\ 0 & 2 & 0 \\ 0 & 0 & 2 \end{pmatrix} \right]^k \frac{t^k}{k!} \begin{pmatrix} -1 & -1 & 1 \\ 3 & 3 & -2 \\ 1 & 2 & -1 \end{pmatrix}$$

$$= C\begin{pmatrix} 1 & 1 & -1 \\ 1 & 0 & 1 \\ 3 & 1 & 0 \end{pmatrix} \begin{pmatrix} \displaystyle\sum_{k=0}^{\infty} \dfrac{1^k t^k}{k!} & 0 & 0 \\ 0 & \displaystyle\sum_{k=0}^{\infty} \dfrac{2^k t^k}{k!} & 0 \\ 0 & 0 & \displaystyle\sum_{k=0}^{\infty} \dfrac{2^k t^k}{k!} \end{pmatrix} \begin{pmatrix} -1 & -1 & 1 \\ 3 & 3 & -2 \\ 1 & 2 & -1 \end{pmatrix}$$

$$= (c_1 \quad c_2 \quad c_3) \begin{pmatrix} 1 & 1 & -1 \\ 1 & 0 & 1 \\ 3 & 1 & 0 \end{pmatrix} \begin{pmatrix} e & 0 & 0 \\ 0 & e^2 & 0 \\ 0 & 0 & e^2 \end{pmatrix} \begin{pmatrix} -1 & -1 & 1 \\ 3 & 3 & -2 \\ 1 & 2 & -1 \end{pmatrix}$$

Or use a formula (easiest with three eigenvectors)

$$X = c_1 v_1 e^{\lambda_1} + c_2 v_2 e^{\lambda_2} + c_3 v_3 e^{\lambda_3} = c_1 \begin{pmatrix} 1 \\ 1 \\ 3 \end{pmatrix} e + c_2 \begin{pmatrix} 1 \\ 0 \\ 1 \end{pmatrix} e^2 + c_3 \begin{pmatrix} -1 \\ 1 \\ 0 \end{pmatrix} e^2$$

Linear Programming: Simplex Method

Solve the linear programming problem by the simplex method.

Maximize $P = 5x + 4y$ subject to $3x + 5y \leq 145$ and $4x + y \leq 104$ and $x \geq 0$ and $y \geq 0$

Simplex Tableau: (note: $P = 5x + 4y \Rightarrow P - 5x - 4y = 0$)

x	y	u	v	P	Constant
3	5	1	0	0	145
4	1	0	1	0	104
-5	-4	0	0	1	0

1st Since $-4 > -5$ the second column is the pivot column

2nd Perform $\frac{1}{5}R1 \wedge -\frac{1}{4}R3$ to make column 2 have 1's

x	y	u	v	P	Constant
$\frac{3}{5}$	1	$\frac{1}{5}$	0	0	29
$\frac{4}{5}$	1	0	1	0	104
$\frac{5}{4}$	1	0	0	$\frac{1}{4}$	0

3rd We want column two to be a unit column i.e. $\{0,1,0\}$ perform $R2 - R1 \wedge R2 - R3$

x	y	u	v	P	Constant
$\frac{17}{5}$	0	$-\frac{1}{5}$	1	0	75
4	1	0	1	0	104
$\frac{11}{4}$	0	0	1	$-\frac{1}{4}$	104

4th Repeat for column 1 $\{1,0,0\}$ $-\frac{20}{17}R1 + R2 \wedge -\frac{5}{17}\left(\frac{11}{4}\right)R1 + R3$

x	y	u	v	P	Constant
$\frac{17}{5}$	0	$-\frac{1}{5}$	1	0	75
0	1	$\frac{4}{17}$	$-\frac{3}{17}$	0	$\frac{268}{17}$

0	0	$\dfrac{11}{68}$	$\dfrac{13}{68}$	$-\dfrac{1}{4}$	$-\dfrac{2947}{68}$

5th $\dfrac{5}{17}R1 \wedge -4R3$

x	y	u	v	P	Constant
1	0	$-\dfrac{1}{17}$	1	0	$\dfrac{375}{17}$
0	1	$\dfrac{4}{17}$	$-\dfrac{3}{17}$	0	$\dfrac{268}{17}$
0	0	$-\dfrac{11}{17}$	$-\dfrac{13}{17}$	1	$\dfrac{2947}{17}$

Maximize $P = 5x + 4y$ subject to $3x + 5y \leq 145$ and $4x + y \leq 104$ and $x \geq 0$ and $y \geq 0$

$$\max\{P\} = \frac{2947}{17} \Leftrightarrow (x,y) = \frac{1}{17}(375, 268)$$

DIFFERENTIAL EQUATIONS

Intro to the first-order differential equation

$y' = x \quad \Rightarrow \quad \dfrac{dy}{dx} = x$

Type:

First-order-nonhomogeneous linear differential equation

Solution Method:

Separable variable

Answer:

Explicit-general solution

$dy = x\,dx$

$\Rightarrow \quad \displaystyle\int dy = \int x\,dxy$

$\Rightarrow \quad y + c_1 = \dfrac{1}{2}x^2 + c_2$

$\Rightarrow \quad y = \dfrac{1}{2}x^2 + c_2 - c_1, \qquad$ note: $c_2 - c_1 = c_3 = C$

$\therefore \quad y = \dfrac{1}{2}x^2 + C$

174

Homogeneous A differential equation that has a function of which <u>does contain</u> the variable that is being differentiated.	$$y^{(n)} + \cdots y^n + \cdots = 0$$ Example: $$y^{(5)} - y'' + \frac{y'}{y}x^2 - \cos(xy) = 0$$
Nonhomogeneous A differential equation that has a function of which <u>does not contain</u> the variable that is being differentiated.	$$f_{m+1}y^{(n)} + \cdots f_m(x)y^n + \cdots = g(x)$$ Example: $$y^{(5)} - y'' + \frac{y'}{y}x^2 - \cos(2x) = 0$$
Linear A differential equation that contains only derivatives in the numerator state, has the highest power of the variable being differentiated is 1, and the differentiated variable is not being operated on.	Example: $$y^{(n)} + y^{(n-1)} + \cdots y = 0$$ $$a_n(x)y^{(n)} + a_{n-1}(x)y^{(n-1)} + \cdots = 0$$
Non-linear A differential equation where the differentiated variable is also being operated on by functions.	Example: $$y'' + \frac{y'}{y}x^2 - \cos(2x) = 0, \qquad \frac{1}{y} = y^{-1}$$ $$y^{(5)} - y'' + y'x^2 - \cos(xy) = 0$$ $$yy' = x$$

Note: Make sure to understand how the following terms relate to a DE i.e. the type of DE will tell you what method to use in order to solve the DE

Type: Order – Linearity – Homogeneity

Problem:
- Initial-Value Problem (IVP) has a *Particular Solution*
- NON-IVP has a *General Solution* (Constant C in solution)
- Explicit Solution: $y = f(x)$
- Implicit solution: $y^n \cdots = f(x, \dots)$

The order of a differential equation is dependent upon the highest derivative e.g. $y''' + y'' = 0$ is a third-order differential equation.

Note: Do not confuse y^n with $y^{(n)}$
- $y^{(n)}$ is the nth derivative
- y^n is the nth power

$$\text{e.g. } y^4 = y \cdot y \cdot y \cdot y \text{ where } y^{(4)} = \frac{d}{dx}\left(\frac{d}{dx}\left(\frac{d}{dx}\left(\frac{d}{dx}y\right)\right)\right)$$

Order of derivative notation: $Y, y, y', y'', y''', y^{(4)}, \dots y^{(n)}$

Respect to time: $\dot{y}, \ddot{y}, \dddot{y} \equiv y'(t), y''(t), y'''(t) \equiv \frac{dy}{dt}, \frac{d^2y}{dt^2}, \frac{d^3y}{dt^3}$

Lets look at a couple examples of equations that are linear and nonlinear.

$y^5 + xy'' - \frac{d^6y}{dx^6} = \sin(xy)$, Sixth-Order-Nonlinear and homogeneous

$xy'' - \frac{d^6y}{dx^6} = \sin(x)$, Sixth-Order-Linear and nonhomogeneous

$y'' + y' + yx = 0$, Second-Order-Linear and homogeneous

$y'' + yy' = \ln x$, Second-Order-Nonlinear and nonhomogeneous Note: Although the power of y is 1 in this case, it is dependent upon y' making it nonlinear.

$y''' + y^2 + xe^y = 0$, Third-Order-Nonlinear and homogeneous

1st Order Solution Methods

Separable Variable
Scenario

The separable variable equation is pretty much just an average integration problem you may have encountered in calculus. The idea is that you have a first-order DE and it is in the form of a function of x, y, and $f(x, y)$ can be found in a DE e.g. $f(x, y)y' = p(x)$, which can be separated into the form $g(y)dy = h(x)dx$. The separable variable could also be viewed as $y' = f_1(y)f_2(x)$

Ex. 1 (Explicit vs. Implicit)

Given $f(x, y) = xy$ and $p(x) = x^2$

Solve $f(x, y)y' = p(x)$

Type:

First-Order-Nonlinear-Nonhomogeneous-ODE

ODE- *Ordinary Differential Equation*
PDE- *Partial Differential Equations*

Solution Method: Separable Variable

$f(x, y)y' = p(x)$

$\Rightarrow \quad xyy' = x^2$

$\Rightarrow \quad xy\frac{dy}{dx} = x^2$

$\Rightarrow \quad ydy = xdx$

$\Rightarrow \quad \int ydy = \int xdx$

Answer: Implicit-General Solution

$$\Rightarrow \quad \frac{y^2}{2} + c_1 = \frac{x^2}{2} + c_2$$

$$\Rightarrow \quad y^2 + c_3 = x^2 + c_4$$

$$\Rightarrow \quad y^2 = x^2 + c_4 - c_3 = x^2 + c_5$$

$$\therefore \quad y^2 = x^2 + C$$

Ex. 2 (Separable Variable)

Solve the DE
$$xy' - x = 2$$

Type: first-order-linear nonhomogeneous differential equation

Solution: Separable Variable

Answer: Explicit-General Solution

$$x\frac{dy}{dx} = 2 + x$$

$$\Rightarrow \quad \frac{dy}{dx} = \frac{2+x}{x}$$

$$\Rightarrow \quad dy = \frac{2+x}{x} dx$$

$$\Rightarrow \quad \int dy = \int \frac{2+x}{x} dx$$

$$\Rightarrow \quad y + c_1 = 2\ln|x| + x + c_2$$

$$\therefore \quad y = 2\ln|x| + x + C$$

Ex. 3 *(IVP Problem)

Give the implicit solution to the IVP: $-yx^{-1} = x'(y)$; $y(-3) = 4$

$$-\frac{y}{x} = \frac{dx}{dy} \quad \Rightarrow \quad y\,dy = x\,dx \quad \Rightarrow \quad \int y\,dy = -\int x\,dx \quad \Rightarrow \quad \frac{1}{2}y^2 = -\frac{1}{2}x^2 + c_2 - c_1$$

$$\Rightarrow \quad y^2 + x^2 = 2(c_2 + c_1) = C$$

Solving implicitly

$$y = \pm\sqrt{C - x^2}$$

Lets solve this implicitly first $(-3)^2 + (5)^2 = 25 = C$ so $x^2 + y^2 = 5^2$ a circle centered at the origin with radius 5.

Now lets take a look at this explicitly

$$-3 = \begin{cases} -\sqrt{C - (4)^2} \\ +\sqrt{C - (5)^2} \end{cases}$$

But wait! Because $\sqrt{u} \geq 0 \; \forall_u \in R - 3 =$

1st Order Linear Non-homogeneous i.e. y'+P(x)y=Q(x)
Process

Given a first order linear non-homogeneous differential equation of the form $y' + P(x)y = Q(x)$ the solution is:

$$y = \frac{1}{I(x)}\left[\int I(x)Q(x)\,dx + C\right], \qquad I(x) = e^{\int p(x)dx}$$

Ex. 1

$$\frac{dy}{dx} + \frac{9}{x}y = \frac{1}{x^8}$$

$$P(x) = \frac{9}{x}, \qquad Q(x) = \frac{1}{x^8}, \qquad I(x) = e^{\int \frac{9}{x}dx} = e^{9\ln|x|} = e^{\int \ln|x^9|} = x^9$$

$$\Rightarrow \quad y = \frac{1}{x^9}\left[\int x^9 \cdot \frac{1}{x^8}\,dx + c_1\right] = \frac{1}{x^9}\left[\int x\,dx + c_1\right] = \frac{1}{x^9}\left[\frac{1}{2}x^2 + c_1\right] = \frac{1}{x^9}\left[\frac{x^2 + 2\cdot c_1}{2}\right]$$

$$= \frac{x^2 + C}{2x^9}$$

Ex. 2

$$y \cdot \sin(x)\,dy - y^2 \cdot \csc(x)\,dx = y \cdot \csc(x)\,dx$$

There are many forms DE's can take on and many solutions to them, some are easier than others so the only true way to understand when to use what is to expose your self to many situations.

$$y^{-1}\csc(x)\frac{1}{dx}(y \cdot \sin(x)\,dy - y^2 \cdot \csc(x)\,dx = y \cdot \csc(x)\,dx) \quad \Rightarrow \quad \frac{dy}{dx} - \csc^2(x)\,y = \csc^2(x)$$

$$\therefore \quad P(x) = -\csc^2(x), \qquad Q(x) = \sec(x), \qquad I(x) = e^{\int -\csc^2(x)dx} = e^{\cot(x)}$$

$$y = \frac{1}{e^{\cot(x)}}\left[\int e^{\cot(x)} \cdot \csc^2(x)\,dx + C\right] = e^{-\cot(x)}\left[-e^{\cot(x)} + C\right] = -1 + Ce^{-\cot(x)}$$

$$\therefore \quad y(x) = Ce^{-\cot(x)} - 1$$

Exact Differential Equation

The exact equation is not very common and stems from partial derivatives. The solution is generally very simple.

Situation

$$f_x(x,y)dx + f_y(x,y)dy = 0 \quad \Leftrightarrow \quad \frac{\partial}{\partial y}f_x = \frac{\partial}{\partial x}f_y$$

This implies that there is a common function $h(x,y)$ in each individual antiderivative

Ex. 1

$$(x^2 - y^2)dx + (y^2 - 2xy)dy = 0$$

$$f_x = x^2 - y^2 \quad \Rightarrow \quad \frac{\partial}{\partial y}f_x = -2y$$

$$f_y = y^2 - 2xy \quad \Rightarrow \quad \frac{\partial}{\partial x}f_y = -2y$$

$$\therefore \quad \frac{\partial}{\partial y}f_x = -2y = \frac{\partial}{\partial x}f_y$$

So this is an exact equation

All you have to do is integrate and find the common term and recall from several variable calculus that we are integrating a multiple variable function that the constant added is a function of the variable not being integrated i.e.

$$\int (x^2 - y^2)\,dx = 0 \quad \Rightarrow \quad \frac{1}{3}x^3 - xy^2 + k(y) = c_1$$

$$\int (y^2 - 2xy)\,dy = 0 \quad \Rightarrow \quad \frac{1}{3}y^3 - xy^2 + l(x) = c_2$$

From this we can easily identify $k(y)$ and $l(x)$ or it may just be easy to see the similarity i.e. think about taking partial derivatives of $f(x,y) = \frac{1}{3}x^3 - xy^2 + \frac{1}{3}y^3$

$$k(y) = \frac{1}{3}y^3, \qquad l(x) = \frac{1}{3}x^3, \qquad \text{common term} = -xy^2$$

$$\therefore \quad f(x,y) = \frac{1}{3}x^3 - xy^2 + \frac{1}{3}y^3 = C$$

There are other approaches to this; in fact you could solve this in on straight shot by just integrating the whole equation and identifying the common term but check with your teacher how much detail they would prefer.

Note: This problem is not likely to show up on exams (maybe a quiz) because it is such a rare case and is really very simple to solve. Your exams will most likely have all second order or higher differential equations.

General, Particular and Superposition Solutions

For differential equations of higher order than 1, there will be multiple solutions i.e. $y_1, y_2, \ldots, y_n$ where each individual y and all the y's together are solutions to the DE.

General Solution

The general solution contains a constant e.g. $y = x + Ce^{\sin(x)}$

Particular Solution

The particular solution contains no constants, usually due to an initial value or as part of a non-homogeneous solution.

Superposition Solution

For DE's with multiple solutions, the sum of the solutions is also a solution i.e. $y = c_1 y_1 + c_2 y_2 + \cdots + c_n y_n$ and in a non-homogeneous situation the solution will be the sum of the solution to the homogenous part of the equation and the non-homogenous part generally noted as $y = y_c + y_p$.

The general solution is generally noted as y_c and the particular y_p giving the solution to be $y = y_c + y_p$

$$y = (c_1 y_{c,1} + c_2 y_{c,2} + \cdots + c_n y_{c,n}) + (y_{p,1} + y_{p,2} + \cdots + y_{p,n})$$

Linear Homogenous with Constant Coefficients
Scenario

$$a_1 y^{(n)} + \cdots + a_2 y^{(n-k)} + \cdots + a_m y = 0$$

Auxiliary equation

Substitute $y = e^{rt}$ into the equation, eliminate e^{rt} and solve for r

$$a_1 r^n + \cdots + a_2 r^{(n-k)} + \cdots + a_m = 0$$

Solution(s)

If r has a pair of solutions

$$y_c = c_1 e^{r_1 t} + c_2 e^{r_2 t}$$

If r has n repeating solutions

$$y_c = c_1 e^{rt} + c_2 t e^{rt} + c_3 t^2 e^{rt} + \cdots + c_n t^{n-1} e^{rt}$$

If r has a pair of complex solutions

$$r = \alpha \pm i\beta, \qquad y = e^{\alpha t} \cos(\beta t) + e^{\alpha t} \sin(\beta t)$$

Generally Speaking

$$ay'' + by + cy = 0, \qquad y = e^{mx}, \qquad y' = me^{mx}, \qquad y'' = m^2 e^{mx}$$

$$\Rightarrow \quad a[m^2 e^{mx}] + b[me^{mx}] + c[e^{mx}] = e^{mx}[am^2 + bm + c] = 0$$

Identify $e^{mx} > 0$ so it has no purpose for our solution leaving $am^2 + bm + c = 0$, which is the auxiliary equation and the quadratic equation may be used to solve it.

$$am^2 + bm + c = 0, \qquad m = \frac{-b \pm \sqrt{b^2 - 4ac}}{2a}$$

Two-real $b^2 - 4ac > 0$

$$y = c_1 e^{m_1 x} + c_2 e^{m_2 x}$$

Repeated $b^2 - 4ac = 0$

$$y = c_1 e^{mx} + c_2 x e^{mx}$$

Complex i.e. $b^2 - 4ac < 0 \quad \Rightarrow \quad x = \alpha \pm i\beta$

$$y = e^{\alpha x}[c_1 \cos(\beta x) + c_2 \sin(\beta x)]$$

Ex. 1

$$3y'' + 4y' + 5y = 0$$

Extract auxiliary equation i.e. $3r^2 + 4r + 5 = 0$, solve for r

$$r = \frac{-4 \pm \sqrt{16 - 4 \cdot 3 \cdot 5}}{2 \cdot 3} = -\frac{4}{6} \pm \frac{\sqrt{-44}}{6} = -\frac{2}{3} \pm i\frac{2}{6}\sqrt{11} = -\frac{2}{3} \pm i\frac{1}{3}\sqrt{11}$$

$$\alpha = -\frac{2}{3}, \qquad \beta = \frac{\sqrt{11}}{3}$$

$$\therefore \quad y = e^{\left(-\frac{2}{3}\right)t}\left[c_1 \cos\left(\frac{\sqrt{11}}{3}t\right) + c_2 \sin\left(\frac{\sqrt{11}}{3}t\right)\right]$$

The other two are easy to solve with the given formulas. What we are really interested in now is how to use the given formulas for higher order DE's.

Ex. 2

$$3y''' + 4y' = 0$$

The auxiliary equation is $3r^3 + 0 \cdot r^2 + 4r + 0 = 3r^3 + 4r = 0$

$$3r^3 + 4r = 0 \quad \Rightarrow \quad r(3r^2 + 4) = 0 \quad \Rightarrow \quad r = 0 \quad \& \quad r = 0 \pm i\frac{2}{\sqrt{3}}$$

We now have 3 solutions i.e. $y = c_1 y_1 + c_2 y_2 + c_3 y_3$

The complex scenario should be pretty obvious just plug it into the formula

$$c_1 y_1 + c_2 y_2 = e^{0 \cdot t}\left[c_1 \cos\left(\frac{2}{\sqrt{3}}t\right) + c_2 \sin\left(\frac{2}{\sqrt{3}}t\right)\right] = c_1 \cos\left(\frac{2}{\sqrt{3}}t\right) + c_2 \sin\left(\frac{2}{\sqrt{3}}t\right)$$

What about the solution 0? 0 is repeated once hence

$$c_3 y_3 = c_3 e^{0 \cdot t} = c_3(1) = c_3$$

$$\therefore \quad y = c_1 \cos\left(\frac{2}{\sqrt{3}}t\right) + c_2 \sin\left(\frac{2}{\sqrt{3}}t\right) + c_3$$

Ex. 3

$$y''' + 8y = 0$$

$$x^3 + a^3 = (x + a)(x^2 - ax + a^2)$$

$$r^3 + 8 = 0 \quad \Rightarrow \quad (r + 2)(r^2 - 2r + 4) = 0 \quad \Rightarrow \quad r = \{-2, 1 \pm i\sqrt{3}\}$$

$$y_{1,2} = e^t\left[c_1 \cos(\sqrt{3}t) + c_2 \sin(\sqrt{3}t)\right], \qquad y_3 = c_3 e^{-2t}$$

$$\therefore \quad y = e^t\left[c_1 \cos(\sqrt{3}t) + c_2 \sin(\sqrt{3}t)\right] + c_3 e^{-2t}$$

Ex. 4

$$y^{(4)} + 8y''' = 0 \quad \Rightarrow \quad r^4 + 8r^3 = r^3(r + 8) = 0 \quad \Rightarrow \quad r^3 = 0, \quad r = -8$$

Zero is repeated three times here

$$y_{1,2,3} = c_1 e^{0 \cdot x} + c_2 x e^{0 \cdot x} + c_3 x^2 e^{0 \cdot x} = c_1 + c_2 x + c_3 x^2, \qquad y_4 = c_4 e^{-8x}$$

$$\therefore \quad y = c_1 + c_2 x + c_3 x^2 + c_4 e^{-8x}$$

Ex. 5 IVP y(0)=1, y'(0)=2, y"(0)=3, y'"(0)=4

Using the solution from example 4

$$y_c = c_1 + c_2 x + c_3 x^2 + c_4 e^{-8x}$$

$$y' = c_2 + 2c_3 x - 8c_4 e^{-8x}, \qquad y'' = 2c_3 + 64c_4 e^{-8x}, \qquad y''' = -512 c_4 e^{-8x}$$

$$y(0) = 1 \quad \Rightarrow \quad 1 = c_1 + c_2 \cdot 0 + c_3 \cdot 0 + c_4 e^0 = c_1 + c_4$$

$$y'(0) = 2 \quad \Rightarrow \quad 2 = c_2 + 2c_3 \cdot 0 - 8c_4 e^0 = c_2 - 8c_4$$

$$y''(0) = 3 \quad \Rightarrow \quad 3 = 2c_3 + 64c_4 e^0 = 2c_3 + 64c_4$$

$$y'''(0) = 4 \quad \Rightarrow \quad 4 = -512 c_4 e^0 = -512 c_4$$

Solve the system

$$c_1 + c_4 = 1, \qquad c_2 - 8c_4 = 2, \qquad 2c_3 + 64c_4 = 3, \qquad -512 c_4 = 4$$

$$c_1 = \frac{129}{128}, \qquad c_2 = \frac{31}{16}, \qquad c_3 = \frac{7}{4}, \qquad c_4 = -\frac{1}{128}$$

$$\therefore \quad y_p = \frac{129}{128} + \frac{31}{16} x + \frac{7}{4} x^2 - \frac{1}{128} e^{-8x}$$

Reduction of Order
Process

Given a second order linear homogeneous DE of the form $y'' + P(x)y' + Q(x) = 0$ accompanied with $y_1(x)$

Solution

Since the first solution is given, you must find the second solution, which is:

$$y_2(x) = y_1(x) \int \frac{e^{-\int P(x)dx}}{[y_1(x)]^2} dx, \qquad \therefore \ y = c_1 y_1 + c_2 \left(y_1(x) \int \frac{e^{-\int P(x)dx}}{[y_1(x)]^2} dx \right)$$

Ex. 1

$$x^2y'' + 2xy' - 6y = 0, \qquad y_1 = x^2$$

Find $P(x)$

$$\frac{1}{x^2}[x^2y'' + 2xy' - 6y = 0] \quad \Rightarrow \quad y'' + \frac{2}{x}y' - \frac{6}{x^2}y = 0 \quad \Rightarrow \quad P(x) = \frac{2}{x}$$

$$\therefore \quad y_2 = x^2 \int \frac{e^{-\int \frac{2}{x}dx}}{(x^2)^2}dx = x^2 \int \frac{e^{-2\ln|x|}}{x^4}dx = x^2 \int \frac{e^{\ln|x^{-2}|}}{x^4}dx = x^2 \int \frac{x^{-2}}{x^4}dx = x^2 \int x^{-6}\,dx$$

$$= x^2\left[\frac{1}{-5}x^{-5}\right] = -\frac{1}{5}x^{-3} \quad \Rightarrow \quad y_2 = \frac{1}{x^3}$$

The constant can be ignored because a constant times a constant is a constant

$$\therefore \quad y = c_1 x^2 + \frac{c_2}{x^3}$$

At this point it should become obvious that $c_1 + c_2 + \cdots + c_n = C$, this is also true for numbers i.e. $c_1 + 5 + e + \ln(10) + e^{c_3} + 6c_2 = C$. In other words: a constant with a constant is a constant.

Substitution
General Situation

The method of substation works well with DE's that look similar to an exact equation i.e.

$$(x^2 + 4xy)dx + (y^2 - 4x^2)dy = 0$$

We can check for an exact and see that $\partial_y f_x = 4x \neq -8x = \partial_x f_y$ so we know we cannot use that method because they are not equal.

Substitution Solution Method

Set $y = v(x) \cdot x$ and take the derivative i.e. $y' = v(x) + x \cdot v'(x)$ and solve for dy.

$$\frac{dy}{dx} = v + x \cdot \frac{dv}{dx} \quad \Rightarrow \quad dx\left[\frac{dy}{dx} = v + x \cdot \frac{dv}{dx}\right] \quad \Rightarrow \quad dy = vdx + xdv$$

If you use this method and it gets really sloppy, it probably is not the best choice so try something else; lets see how this DE plays out.

Substitute y and dy and simplify i.e.

$$\left(x^2 + 4x(vx)\right)dx + \left((vx)^2 - 4x^2\right)(vdx + xdv) = 0$$

$$\Rightarrow \quad x^2 dx + 4x^2 v dx + x^2 v^3 dx + x^3 v^2 dv - 4x^2 v dx - 4x^3 dv = 0$$

$$\Rightarrow \quad x^2 dx + x^2 v^3 dx + 4x^2 v dx - 4x^2 v dx + x^3 v^2 dv - 4x^3 dv = 0$$

$$\Rightarrow \quad \frac{1}{x^2}(x^2 dx + x^2 v^3 dx + x^3 v^2 dv - 4x^3 dv = 0)$$

$$\Rightarrow \quad dx + v^3 dx + x v^2 dv - 4x dv = 0$$

$$\Rightarrow \quad (1 + v^3)dx + x(v^2 - 4)dv = 0 \quad \Rightarrow \quad x(v^2 - 4)dv = -(1 + v^3)dx$$

$$\Rightarrow \quad \frac{v^2 - 4}{1 + v^3}dv = -\frac{1}{x}dx$$

Now integrate the separable variable differential equation.

$$\int \left[\frac{v^2}{1 + v^3} - \frac{4}{1 + v^3} \right] dv = -\int \frac{1}{x}dx$$

At this point, it is just a really tedious calculus problem. $\left(v = \frac{y}{x} \right)$ Two of the integrals are simple i.e.

$$\frac{1}{3}\ln|1 + v^3| - 4\int \frac{1}{1 + v^3}dv = -\ln|x| + C \quad \Rightarrow \quad \frac{1}{3}\ln\left|1 + \left(\frac{y}{x}\right)^3\right| - 4\int \frac{1}{1 + v^3}dv = -\ln|x| + C$$

We just need to integrate $\frac{1}{1+v^3}$. This is a very complicated integral to do by hand. I used Wolfram|Alpha to complete this.

$$\therefore \frac{1}{1 + v^3} = \frac{1}{6}\left(-\ln(v^2 - v + 1) + 2\ln(v + 1) + 2\sqrt{3}\tan^{-1}\left(\frac{2v - 1}{\sqrt{3}}\right) \right)$$

$$\Rightarrow \quad \frac{1}{3}\ln\left|1 + \left(\frac{y}{x}\right)^3\right| - 4\frac{1}{6}\left(-\ln(v^2 - v + 1) + 2\ln(v + 1) + 2\sqrt{3}\tan^{-1}\left(\frac{2v - 1}{\sqrt{3}}\right) \right) = -\ln|x| + C$$

$$\Rightarrow \quad \frac{1}{3}\ln\left|1 + \left(\frac{y}{x}\right)^3\right| - 4\frac{1}{6}\left(-\ln\left(\left(\frac{y}{x}\right)^2 - \frac{y}{x} + 1\right) + 2\ln\left(\frac{y}{x} + 1\right) + 2\sqrt{3}\tan^{-1}\left(\frac{2\left(\frac{y}{x}\right) - 1}{\sqrt{3}}\right) \right)$$
$$= -\ln|x| + C$$

This was a very loaded situation; it is highly unlikely to see something like this in an undergraduate DE course.

When to use this method? If you have a situation with a first-order differential equation that is not linear and the exact equation method does not work or is two complicated and vice versa.

Integrating Factors

When you have the "exact equation" looking situation but it is not an exact equation i.e.

$$Mdx + Ndy = 0 \quad \& \quad \frac{\partial M}{\partial y} \neq \frac{\partial N}{\partial x}$$

Then you can multiply the whole equation by $\mu(x)$ or $\mu(y)$ and it will then become an exact equation.

$$\mu(x) = e^{\int \frac{M_y - N_x}{N} dx}, \qquad \mu(y) = e^{\int \frac{N_x - M_y}{M} dy}$$

Ex. 1

$$(xy)dx + (2x^2 + 3y^2 - 20)dy = 0$$

$$M = xy, \qquad N = 2x^2 + 3y^2 - 20$$

$$\frac{\partial M}{\partial y} = x \neq 4x = \frac{\partial N}{\partial x}, \qquad \frac{M_y - N_x}{N} = \frac{-3x}{2x^2 + 3y^2 - 20}, \qquad \frac{N_x - M_y}{M} = \frac{3x}{xy} = \frac{3}{y}$$

We are looking for the one that has a single variable and also easiest to integrate.

$$\therefore \quad \mu(y) = e^{\int \frac{3}{y} dy} = e^{3 \ln|y|} = e^{\ln|y^3|} = y^3$$

Now multiply the original equation by y^3

$$y^3 \cdot [(xy)dx + (2x^2 + 3y^2 - 20)dy = 0] \quad \Rightarrow \quad (xy^4)dx + (2x^2y^3 + 3y^5 - 20y^3)dy = 0$$

$$\therefore \quad \frac{\partial}{\partial y}(xy^4) = 4xy^{4-1} = 4xy^3 \quad \Rightarrow \quad 4xy^3 = 2(2xy^3) = \frac{\partial}{\partial x}(2x^2y^3 + 3y^5 - 20y^3) \quad \Leftrightarrow \quad \frac{\partial M}{\partial y}$$

$$= \frac{\partial N}{\partial x}$$

Thus, it is an exact equation now. Integrate all the way through and identify the equivalent term i.e.

$$\int (xy^4)\, dx = c_1 \quad \Rightarrow \quad \left(\frac{1}{2}x^2y^4 + g(y)\right) = c_1$$

$$\int (2x^2y^3 + 3y^5 - 20y^3)\, dy = c_2 \quad \Rightarrow \quad \left(\frac{1}{2}x^2y^4 + \frac{1}{2}y^6 - 5y^4 + h(x)\right) = c_1$$

Setting these two equations equal (there are many ways to find this by the way, this is just one method, see exact equations) finding $g(y)$ and $h(x)$

$$\left(\frac{1}{2}x^2y^4 + \left(\frac{1}{2}y^6 - 5y^4\right) + h(x)\right) = \left(\frac{1}{2}x^2y^4 + g(y) + 0\right)$$

$$\Rightarrow \quad \frac{1}{2}x^2y^4 = \frac{1}{2}x^2y^4 = f(x,y), \qquad g(y) = \left(\frac{1}{2}y^6 - 5y^4\right), \qquad h(x) = 0, \qquad c_1 + c_2 = C$$

$$f(x,y) + g(y) + h(x) = C \quad \therefore \quad \frac{1}{2}x^2y^4 + \frac{1}{2}y^6 - 5y^4 = C$$

SECOND ORDER DIFFERENTIAL EQUATIONS

Linear Homogenous with Constant Coefficients
Scenario

$$a_1 y^{(n)} + \cdots + a_2 y^{(n-k)} + \cdots + a_m y = 0$$

Auxiliary equation

Substitute $y = e^{rt}$ into the equation, eliminate e^{rt} and solve for r

$$a_1 r^n + \cdots + a_2 r^{(n-k)} + \cdots + a_m = 0$$

Solution(s)

If r has a pair of solutions

$$y_c = c_1 e^{r_1 t} + c_2 e^{r_2 t}$$

If r has n repeating solutions

$$y_c = c_1 e^{rt} + c_2 t e^{rt} + c_3 t^2 e^{rt} + \cdots + c_n t^{n-1} e^{rt}$$

If r has a pair of complex solutions

$$r = \alpha \pm i\beta, \qquad y = e^{\alpha t} c_1 \cos(\beta t) + e^{\alpha t} c_2 \sin(\beta t)$$

Generally Speaking

$$ay'' + by + cy = 0, \qquad y = e^{mx}, \qquad y' = me^{mx}, \qquad y'' = m^2 e^{mx}$$

$$\Rightarrow \quad a[m^2 e^{mx}] + b[me^{mx}] + c[e^{mx}] = e^{mx}[am^2 + bm + c] = 0$$

Identify $e^{mx} > 0$ so it has no purpose for our solution leaving $am^2 + bm + c = 0$, which is the auxiliary equation and the quadratic equation may be used to solve it.

$$am^2 + bm + c = 0, \qquad m = \frac{-b \pm \sqrt{b^2 - 4ac}}{2a}$$

Two-real $b^2 - 4ac > 0$

$$y = c_1 e^{m_1 x} + c_2 e^{m_2 x}$$

Repeated $b^2 - 4ac = 0$

$$y = c_1 e^{mx} + c_2 x e^{mx}$$

Complex i.e. $b^2 - 4ac < 0 \quad \Rightarrow \quad x = \alpha \pm i\beta$

$$y = e^{\alpha x}[c_1 \cos(\beta x) + c_2 \sin(\beta x)]$$

Ex. 1

$$3y'' + 4y' + 5y = 0$$

Extract auxiliary equation i.e. $3r^2 + 4r + 5 = 0$, solve for r

$$r = \frac{-4 \pm \sqrt{16 - 4 \cdot 3 \cdot 5}}{2 \cdot 3} = -\frac{4}{6} \pm \frac{\sqrt{-44}}{6} = -\frac{2}{3} \pm i\frac{2}{6}\sqrt{11} = -\frac{2}{3} \pm i\frac{1}{3}\sqrt{11}$$

$$\alpha = -\frac{2}{3}, \qquad \beta = \frac{\sqrt{11}}{3}$$

$$\therefore \quad y = e^{\left(-\frac{2}{3}\right)t}\left[c_1 \cos\left(\frac{\sqrt{11}}{3}t\right) + c_2 \sin\left(\frac{\sqrt{11}}{3}t\right)\right]$$

The other two are easy to solve with the given formulas. What we are really interested in now is how to use the given formulas for higher order DE's.

Ex. 2

$$3y''' + 4y' = 0$$

The auxiliary equation is $3r^3 + 0 \cdot r^2 + 4r + 0 = 3r^3 + 4r = 0$

$$3r^3 + 4r = 0 \quad \Rightarrow \quad r(3r^2 + 4) = 0 \quad \Rightarrow \quad r = 0 \quad \& \quad r = 0 \pm i\frac{2}{\sqrt{3}}$$

We now have 3 solutions i.e. $y = c_1 y_1 + c_2 y_2 + c_3 y_3$

The complex scenario should be pretty obvious just plug it into the formula

$$c_1 y_1 + c_2 y_2 = e^{0 \cdot t}\left[c_1 \cos\left(\frac{2}{\sqrt{3}}t\right) + c_2 \sin\left(\frac{2}{\sqrt{3}}t\right)\right] = c_1 \cos\left(\frac{2}{\sqrt{3}}t\right) + c_2 \sin\left(\frac{2}{\sqrt{3}}t\right)$$

What about the solution 0? 0 is repeated once hence

$$c_3 y_3 = c_3 e^{0 \cdot t} = c_3(1) = c_3$$

$$\therefore \quad y = c_1 \cos\left(\frac{2}{\sqrt{3}}t\right) + c_2 \sin\left(\frac{2}{\sqrt{3}}t\right) + c_3$$

Ex. 3

$$y''' + 8y = 0$$

$$x^3 + a^3 = (x + a)(x^2 - ax + a^2)$$

$$r^3 + 8 = 0 \quad \Rightarrow \quad (r + 2)(r^2 - 2r + 4) = 0 \quad \Rightarrow \quad r = \{-2, 1 \pm i\sqrt{3}\}$$

$$y_{1,2} = e^t[c_1 \cos(\sqrt{3}t) + c_2 \sin(\sqrt{3}t)], \qquad y_3 = c_3 e^{-2t}$$

$$\therefore \quad y = e^t[c_1 \cos(\sqrt{3}t) + c_2 \sin(\sqrt{3}t)] + c_3 e^{-2t}$$

Ex. 4

$$y^{(4)} + 8y''' = 0 \quad \Rightarrow \quad r^4 + 8r^3 = r^3(r + 8) = 0 \quad \Rightarrow \quad r^3 = 0, \qquad r = -8$$

Zero is repeated three times here

$$y_{1,2,3} = c_1 e^{0 \cdot x} + c_2 x e^{0 \cdot x} + c_3 x^2 e^{0 \cdot x} = c_1 + c_2 x + c_3 x^2, \qquad y_4 = c_4 e^{-8x}$$

$$\therefore \quad y = c_1 + c_2 x + c_3 x^2 + c_4 e^{-8x}$$

Ex. 5 IVP y(0)=1, y'(0)=2, y"(0)=3, y'''(0)=4

Using the solution from example 4

$$y_c = c_1 + c_2 x + c_3 x^2 + c_4 e^{-8x}$$

$$y' = c_2 + 2c_3 x - 8c_4 e^{-8x}, \qquad y'' = 2c_3 + 64c_4 e^{-8x}, \qquad y''' = -512c_4 e^{-8x}$$

$$y(0) = 1 \quad \Rightarrow \quad 1 = c_1 + c_2 \cdot 0 + c_3 \cdot 0 + c_4 e^0 = c_1 + c_4$$

$$y'(0) = 2 \quad \Rightarrow \quad 2 = c_2 + 2c_3 \cdot 0 - 8c_4 e^0 = c_2 - 8c_4$$

$$y''(0) = 3 \quad \Rightarrow \quad 3 = 2c_3 + 64c_4 e^0 = 2c_3 + 64c_4$$

$$y'''(0) = 4 \quad \Rightarrow \quad 4 = -512c_4 e^0 = -512c_4$$

Solve the system

$$c_1 + c_4 = 1, \qquad c_2 - 8c_4 = 2, \qquad 2c_3 + 64c_4 = 3, \qquad -512c_4 = 4$$

$$c_1 = \frac{129}{128}, \qquad c_2 = \frac{31}{16}, \qquad c_3 = \frac{7}{4}, \qquad c_4 = -\frac{1}{128}$$

$$\therefore \quad y_p = \frac{129}{128} + \frac{31}{16}x + \frac{7}{4}x^2 - \frac{1}{128}e^{-8x}$$

Reduction of Order

Process

Given a second order linear homogeneous DE of the form $y'' + P(x)y' + Q(x) = 0$ accompanied with $y_1(x)$

Solution

Since the first solution is given, you must find the second solution, which is:

$$y_2(x) = y_1(x) \int \frac{e^{-\int P(x)dx}}{[y_1(x)]^2} dx, \qquad \therefore y = c_1 y_1 + c_2 \left(y_1(x) \int \frac{e^{-\int P(x)dx}}{[y_1(x)]^2} dx \right)$$

Ex. 1

$$x^2 y'' + 2xy' - 6y = 0, \qquad y_1 = x^2$$

Find $P(x)$

$$\frac{1}{x^2}[x^2 y'' + 2xy' - 6y = 0] \quad \Rightarrow \quad y'' + \frac{2}{x}y' - \frac{6}{x^2}y = 0 \quad \Rightarrow \quad P(x) = \frac{2}{x}$$

$$\therefore \quad y_2 = x^2 \int \frac{e^{-\int \frac{2}{x}dx}}{(x^2)^2}dx = x^2 \int \frac{e^{-2\ln|x|}}{x^4}dx = x^2 \int \frac{e^{\ln|x^{-2}|}}{x^4}dx = x^2 \int \frac{x^{-2}}{x^4}dx = x^2 \int x^{-6}\,dx$$

$$= x^2 \left[\frac{1}{-5}x^{-5}\right] = -\frac{1}{5}x^{-3} \quad \Rightarrow \quad y_2 = \frac{1}{x^3}$$

The constant can be ignored because a constant times a constant is a constant

$$\therefore \quad y = c_1 x^2 + \frac{c_2}{x^3}$$

At this point it should become obvious that $c_1 + c_2 + \cdots + c_n = C$, this is also true for numbers i.e. $c_1 + 5 + e + \ln(10) + e^{c_3} + 6c_2 = C$. In other words: a constant with a constant is a constant.

Substitution
General Situation

The method of substation works well with DE's that look similar to an exact equation i.e.

$$(x^2 + 4xy)dx + (y^2 - 4x^2)dy = 0$$

We can check for an exact and see that $\partial_y f_x = 4x \neq -8x = \partial_x f_y$ so we know we cannot use that method because they are not equal.

Substitution Solution Method

Set $y = v(x) \cdot x$ and take the derivative i.e. $y' = v(x) + x \cdot v'(x)$ and solve for dy.

$$\frac{dy}{dx} = v + x \cdot \frac{dv}{dx} \quad \Rightarrow \quad dx\left[\frac{dy}{dx} = v + x \cdot \frac{dv}{dx}\right] \quad \Rightarrow \quad dy = vdx + xdv$$

If you use this method and it gets really sloppy, it probably is not the best choice so try something else; lets see how this DE plays out.

Substitute y and dy and simplify i.e.

$$\left(x^2 + 4x(vx)\right)dx + \left((vx)^2 - 4x^2\right)(vdx + xdv) = 0$$

$$\Rightarrow \quad x^2 dx + 4x^2 vdx + x^2 v^3 dx + x^3 v^2 dv - 4x^2 vdx - 4x^3 dv = 0$$

$$\Rightarrow \quad x^2 dx + x^2 v^3 dx + 4x^2 vdx - 4x^2 vdx + x^3 v^2 dv - 4x^3 dv = 0$$

$$\Rightarrow \quad \frac{1}{x^2}(x^2 dx + x^2 v^3 dx + x^3 v^2 dv - 4x^3 dv = 0)$$

$$\Rightarrow \quad dx + v^3 dx + xv^2 dv - 4xdv = 0$$

$$\Rightarrow \quad (1 + v^3)dx + x(v^2 - 4)dv = 0 \quad \Rightarrow \quad x(v^2 - 4)dv = -(1 + v^3)dx$$

$$\Rightarrow \quad \frac{v^2 - 4}{1 + v^3} dv = -\frac{1}{x} dx$$

Now integrate the separable variable differential equation.

$$\int \left[\frac{v^2}{1 + v^3} - \frac{4}{1 + v^3} \right] dv = -\int \frac{1}{x} dx$$

At this point, it is just a really tedious calculus problem. $\left(v = \frac{y}{x} \right)$ Two of the integrals are simple i.e.

$$\frac{1}{3} \ln|1 + v^3| - 4 \int \frac{1}{1 + v^3} dv = -\ln|x| + C \quad \Rightarrow \quad \frac{1}{3} \ln \left| 1 + \left(\frac{y}{x} \right)^3 \right| - 4 \int \frac{1}{1 + v^3} dv = -\ln|x| + C$$

We just need to integrate $\frac{1}{1+v^3}$. This is a very complicated integral to do by hand. I used Wolfram|Alpha to complete this.

$$\therefore \frac{1}{1 + v^3} = \frac{1}{6} \left(-\ln(v^2 - v + 1) + 2\ln(v + 1) + 2\sqrt{3} \tan^{-1} \left(\frac{2v - 1}{\sqrt{3}} \right) \right)$$

$$\Rightarrow \quad \frac{1}{3} \ln \left| 1 + \left(\frac{y}{x} \right)^3 \right| - 4 \frac{1}{6} \left(-\ln(v^2 - v + 1) + 2\ln(v + 1) + 2\sqrt{3} \tan^{-1} \left(\frac{2v - 1}{\sqrt{3}} \right) \right) = -\ln|x| + C$$

$$\Rightarrow \quad \frac{1}{3} \ln \left| 1 + \left(\frac{y}{x} \right)^3 \right| - 4 \frac{1}{6} \left(-\ln \left(\left(\frac{y}{x} \right)^2 - \frac{y}{x} + 1 \right) + 2\ln \left(\frac{y}{x} + 1 \right) + 2\sqrt{3} \tan^{-1} \left(\frac{2 \left(\frac{y}{x} \right) - 1}{\sqrt{3}} \right) \right)$$
$$= -\ln|x| + C$$

This was a very loaded situation; it is highly unlikely to see something like this in an undergraduate DE course.

When to use this method? If you have a situation with a first-order differential equation that is not linear and the exact equation method does not work or is two complicated and vice versa.

Bessel's Equation of Order v

Form

$$x^2 y'' + xy' + (x^2 - v^2)y = 0$$

Solution to First Kind Bessel ($v = $ fraction)

$$y = c_1 J_v(x) + c_2 J_{-v}(x)$$

$$J_v(x) = \sum_{n=0}^{\infty} \frac{(-1)^n}{n!\,\Gamma(1+v+n)} \left(\frac{x}{2}\right)^{2n+v}, \qquad J_{-v}(x) = \sum_{n=0}^{\infty} \frac{(-1)^n}{n!\,\Gamma(1-v+n)} \left(\frac{x}{2}\right)^{2n-v}$$

$$16x^2y'' + 16xy' + (16x^2 - 1)y = 0$$

$$\Rightarrow \quad x^2y'' + xy' + \left(x^2 - \left(\frac{1}{4}\right)^2\right)y = 0$$

$$v = \frac{1}{4}$$

Solution to Second Kind Bessel ($v =$ integer)

$$y = c_1 J_v(x) + c_2 Y_v(x), \qquad Y_v(x) = \frac{\cos(v\pi)\,J_v(x) - c_2 J_{-v}(x)}{\sin(v\pi)}$$

$$16x^2y'' + 16xy' + (16x^2 - 1)y = 0$$

$$\Rightarrow \quad x^2y'' + xy' + (x^2 - 9)y = 0$$

$$v = 3$$

Solution to Third Kind Bessel ($\alpha x = t$)

$$x^2y'' + xy' + (\alpha^2 x^2 - v^2)y = 0 \quad \Rightarrow \quad x^2y'' + xy' + (t^2 - v^2)y = 0$$

Solution

$$y = c_1 J_v(t) + c_2 Y_v(t) = c_1 J_v(\alpha x) + c_2 Y_v(\alpha x)$$

$$16x^2y'' + 16xy' + (16x^2 - 1)y = 0$$

$$\alpha = 4$$

Variation of parameters

$$y'' + 4y' = 3\sin x$$

1st solve homogenous using constant coefficients

$$y'' + 4y' = 0 \quad \Rightarrow \quad y_h = c_1 e^{-4x} + c_2$$

2nd Solve the particular solution using variations of parameters

Identify $y_1, y_2, g(x)$

$$y_1 = e^{-4x}, \qquad y_2 = 1, \qquad g(x) = 3\sin(x)$$

Compute Wronskian

$$W(x) = \begin{vmatrix} y_1 & y_2 \\ y_1' & y_2' \end{vmatrix} \Rightarrow \begin{vmatrix} e^{-4x} & 1 \\ -4e^{-4x} & 0 \end{vmatrix} = (e^{-4x})(0) - (1)(-4e^{-4x}) = 4e^{-4x}$$

$$y_p = u_1 y_1 + u_2 y_2$$

$$u_1 = -\int \frac{y_1 g}{W}\, dx = -\int \frac{e^{-4x}\, 3\sin(x)}{4e^{-4x}}\, dx = \frac{3}{4}\int -\sin(x)\, dx = \frac{3}{4}\cos(x)$$

$$u_2 = \int \frac{y_2 g}{W}\, dx = \int \frac{3\sin(x)}{4e^{-4x}}\, dx = \frac{3}{4}\int e^{4x}\sin(x)\, dx = -\frac{3}{68}e^{4x}(4\sin(x) + \cos(x))$$

$$\therefore y = y_h + y_p$$
$$\Rightarrow$$
$$y = c_1 e^{-4x} + c_2 + \frac{3}{4}\cos(x)\, e^{-4x} - \frac{3}{68}e^{4x}(4\sin(x) + \cos(x))$$

Method of undetermined coefficients

$$y'' + 2y' + 5y = xe^{-x}$$

$$y = y_c + y_p$$

i)

$$r^2 + 2r + 5 = 0 \quad \Leftrightarrow \quad r = -1 \pm 2i \quad \Rightarrow \quad y_c = e^{-x}[c_1\cos(2x) + c_2\sin(2x)]$$

ii)

$$y_p = Axe^{-x}, y' = Ae^{-x} - Axe^{-x}, y'' = -Ae^{-x} - [Ae^{-x} - Axe^{-x}] = -2Ae^{-x} + Axe^{-x}$$

$$y'' + 2y' + 5y = xe^{-x}$$

$$\Rightarrow [Axe^{-x} - 2Ae^{-x}] + 2[Ae^{-x} - Axe^{-x}] + 5[Axe^{-x},] = xe^{-x}$$

$$\Rightarrow \quad Ax - 2A + 2A - 2Ax + 5Ax = x$$

$$\Rightarrow \quad 4Ax = x \Rightarrow A = \frac{1}{4}$$

$$\therefore y = e^{-x}[c_1 \cos(2x) + c_2 \sin(2x)] + \frac{x}{4}e^{-x}$$

Second Solution for Reduction of Order

Find the **general solution** of

From $y = y_h + y_p$ the h implies the homogeneous solution also the general solution, the p implies the particular solution. This problem will not be easy to find the particular solution, hence it states "find the general solution".

$$(x^2 - 1)y'' - 2xy' + 2y = x^2 + 1$$

We need to make a guess on the solution for y_1. Since the coefficients are polynomials, we should also choose a polynomial to be y_1. Start with the easiest option i.e. $y_1 = x$. Why did we choose this? Well, $y = x \Rightarrow y' = 1 \Rightarrow y'' = 0 \therefore (x^2 - 1)(0) - 2x(1) + 2(x) = -2x + 2x = 0$. We chose it because it zeroes the homogeneous solution.

Formula:

$$y'' + P(x)y' + Q(x)y = 0, \quad y_1 = y_1(x), \quad y_2 = vy_1, \quad v = \int \frac{1}{(y_1)^2} e^{-\int P(x)dx} dx$$

$$\frac{1}{x^2 - 1}[(x^2 - 1)y'' - 2xy' + 2y = x^2 + 1] \Rightarrow y'' + \left(-\frac{2x}{x^2 - 1}\right)y' + \left(\frac{2}{x^2 - 1}\right)y = \frac{x^2 + 1}{x^2 - 1}$$

$$\therefore P(x) = -\frac{2x}{x^2 - 1} \Rightarrow v = \int \frac{1}{(x)^2} e^{-\int \left(-\frac{2x}{x^2 - 1}\right)dx} dx = \int \frac{1}{x^2} e^{\int \frac{\frac{d}{dx}(x^2 - 1)}{x^2 - 1} dx} dx = \int \frac{1}{x^2} e^{\ln|x^2 - 1|} dx$$

$$\int \frac{1}{x^2}(x^2 - 1) dx = \int 1 - x^{-2} dx = x + \frac{1}{x}$$

$$\therefore y_h = c_1 x + x\left(x + \frac{1}{x}\right)c_2 = c_1 x + (x^2 + 1)c_2$$

Solve for the particular using undetermined coefficients

(If you try $Ax^2 + Bx + C$ it won't work so move up the polynomial)

$$y_p = Ax^3 + Bx^2 + Cx + D \quad \Rightarrow \quad y_p' = 3Ax^2 + 2Bx + C \quad \Rightarrow \quad y_p'' = 6Ax + 2B$$

$$(x^2 - 1)y'' - 2xy' + 2y = x^2 + 1$$

$$\Rightarrow \quad (x^2 - 1)(6Ax + 2B) - 2x(3Ax^2 + 2Bx + C) + 2(Ax^3 + Bx^2 + Cx + D) = x^2 + 1$$

$$\Rightarrow 2Ax^3 - 6Ax - 2B + 2D = (0)x^3 + (1)x^2 + (0)x + (1)x^0$$

$$\Rightarrow no \ solution \ again \dots$$

Try variation of parameters

$$W = \begin{vmatrix} x & x^2 + 1 \\ 1 & 2x \end{vmatrix} = 2x^2 - (x^2 + 1) = x^2 - 1$$

$$u_1 = \int \frac{y_2 g}{W} dx = \int \frac{(x^2 + 1)^2}{x^2 - 1} dx$$

$$u_2 = \int \frac{y_1 g}{W} dx = \int \frac{x(x^2 + 1)}{x^2 - 1} dx$$

Unit Circle

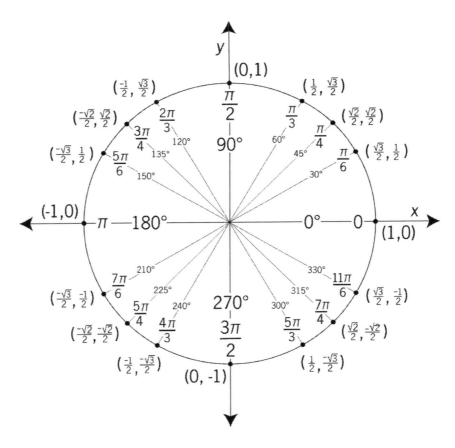

49041336R00109

Made in the USA
Lexington, KY
20 August 2019